Dramatic Apparitions and Theatrical Ghosts

Related titles available from Methuen Drama

Anxious Masculinity in the Drama of Arthur Miller and Beyond: Salesmen,
Sluggers, and Big Daddies,
Claire Gleitman
978-1-3502-7111-1

Greek Tragedy and the Digital,
Edited by George Rodosthenous and Angeliki Poulou
978-1-3501-8585-2

Staging Technology: Medium, Machinery, and Modern Drama,
Craig N. Owens
978-1-3501-6857-2

Staging the End of the World: Theatre in a Time of Climate Crisis,
Brian Kulick
978-1-3503-0995-1

Theatres of Contagion: Transmitting Early Modern to
Contemporary Performance,
Edited by Fintan Walsh
978-1-3500-8598-5

Tragedy since 9/11: Reading a World out of Joint,
Jennifer Wallace
978-1-3500-3562-1

Tragicomedy,
Brean Hammond
978-1-3501-4430-9

Dramatic Apparitions and Theatrical Ghosts

The Staging of Illusion across Time and Cultures

Edited by Ann C. Hall and Alan Nadel

methuen | drama

LONDON • NEW YORK • OXFORD • NEW DELHI • SYDNEY

METHUEN DRAMA
Bloomsbury Publishing Plc
50 Bedford Square, London, WC1B 3DP, UK
1385 Broadway, New York, NY 10018, USA
29 Earlsfort Terrace, Dublin 2, Ireland

BLOOMSBURY, METHUEN DRAMA and the Methuen Drama logo are
trademarks of Bloomsbury Publishing Plc

First published in Great Britain 2023

Cover design by Ben Anslow
Cover image: Dry ice smoke clouds fog floor texture.
(© Victor / AdobeStock)

A catalogue record for this book is available from the British Library.

A catalog record for this book is available from the Library of Congress.

ISBN: HB: 978-1-3503-7169-9
       ePDF: 978-1-3503-7171-2
       eBook: 978-1-3503-7170-5

Typeset by RefineCatch Limited, Bungay, Suffolk

To find out more about our authors and books visit www.bloomsbury.com
and sign up for our newsletters.

To
Sarah Hall Nelson and Zachary Hall Nelson
Josephine Amy Nadel, not yet three and already inspired to perform
and
To our specters on and off the stage.

Contents

Illustrations

Contributors

Ben Furnish teaches in the liberal arts program at the Kansas City Art Institute, USA, and he is editor of BkMk Press. He is the author of *Nostalgia in Jewish-American Theater and Film, 1979-2004*. He holds a PhD in theatre and film studies from the University of Kansas.

Ann C. Hall is a Professor in the Department of Comparative Humanities at the University of Louisville, USA. She is the author of *A Kind of Alaska: Women in the Plays of Eugene O'Neill, Harold Pinter, and Sam Shepard*, and *Phantom Variations: The Adaptations of Gaston Leroux's Phantom of the Opera, 1925 to the Present*. She has edited and co-edited a number of anthologies on women, drama, and media. She is currently the President of the International Harold Pinter Society and editor of *The Harold Pinter Review*. She has recently become the Drama editor for the *Routledge Encyclopedia of Modernism*.

Beth A. Kattelman is a Professor and Curator of The Ohio State University's Lawrence and Lee Theatre Research Institute, USA. She holds a doctorate in theatre from Ohio State and a Master of Library and Information Science from Kent State. Kattelman's research focuses on stage and film horror entertainments and the technology of special effects. Her work has been published in numerous anthologies and journals, including *Theatre Journal*, *Puppetry International*, *The Journal of Popular Culture* and *Theatre Survey*. She is co-editor with Magdalena Hodalska of *Frightful Witnessing: The Rhetoric and (Re)Presentation of Fear, Horror and Terror*, and in 2022 she published "The Sound of Evil: How the Sound Design of *Hereditary* Manifests the Unseen and Triggers Fear" in the journal *Horror Studies*.

Jennifer Larson teaches literature, film, and writing in the Department of English and Comparative Literature at the University of North Carolina at Chapel Hill, USA. She is the author of *Understanding Nikky Finney* (forthcoming), *Understanding Walter Mosley*, and *Understanding Susan Lori-Parks*, as well as the co-editor of *The Sentimental Mode: Essays in Literature, Film and Television* and the assistant editor of *Reading Contemporary African American Drama: Fragments of History, Fragments of Self*. Her work has appeared in *Women's Studies* and *The South Carolina Review*, as well as several essay collections.

Amy Muse is Professor of English at the University of St. Thomas in St. Paul, Minnesota, USA. Author of *The Drama and Theater of Sarah Ruhl*, she has also published essays on Ruhl in *The Journal of Dramatic Theory and Criticism*, *Text & Presentation*, *The Theater of Paula Vogel: Practice, Pedagogy, and Influences*, and the *Routledge Anthology of Women's Theater Theory and Dramatic Criticism*. She serves on the board of the Comparative Drama Conference and is editor of *Text & Presentation*.

Alan Nadel, William T. Bryan Chair in American Literature and Culture at the University of Kentucky, USA, is the author of six books on post-WWII American literature, including: *Invisible Criticism: Ralph Ellison and the American Canon*, *Containment Culture*, *Demographic Angst: Cultural Narratives and American Films of the 1950s*, and *The Theater of August Wilson*. He has also edited two volumes of essays on August Wilson, *May All Your Fences Have Gates* and *August Wilson: Completing the 20th-Century Cycle*. His essays have appeared in over 25 edited collections and 35 different academic journals, including: *Theater*, *American Drama*, *American Quarterly*, *Narrative*, *boundary II*, and *Contemporary Literature*. He has won prizes for the best essay in *Modern Fiction Studies* and in *PMLA*. His poetry has appeared in *Paris Review*, *Partisan Review*, *Georgia Review*, *New England Review*, *Sewanee Review*, and elsewhere.

Margaret O'Donnell Noodin is Professor of English and Associate Dean of the Humanities at the University of Wisconsin–Milwaukee, USA. She is the author of *Bawaajimo: A Dialect of Dreams in Anishinaabe Language and Literature* and two collections of poetry in Anishinaabemowin and English, *Weweni* and *What the Chickadee Knows*. To hear her work, visit www.ojibwe. net.

Craig N. Owens, PhD, is Professor of English and dean of The John Dee Bright College at Drake University where he has taught courses on modern and contemporary drama, playwriting, Irish literature, and critical theory. He is the author of *Staging Technology: Medium, Machinery, and Modern Drama* (Methuen 2021), co-editor, with Stephen Schneider, of *The Shaken and the Stirred: The Year's Work in Cocktail Culture* (Indiana University Press 2020), and editor of *Pinter Et Cetera* (Cambridge Scholars 2009). His essays on Bernard Shaw, Harold Pinter, and Samuel Beckett have appeared in *Modern Drama*, *Shaw*, *The Journal of the M/MLA*, and *The Harold Pinter Review*. His work in popular music, film, and television includes essays on *Six Feet Under*, James Bond novels and films, *The Big Lebowski*, and Lady Gaga. His play Open House won the 2013 Tallgrass Theatre Playwright's Workshop award.

Andrew Rabin is a professor in the Department of English at the University of Louisville, USA. His research focuses on the law and literature of early medieval England. His books include *Crime and Punishment in Anglo-Saxon*

England (2020), *Wulfstan: Old English Legal Writings* (2020), *The Disputatio Puerorum: A Ninth-Century Monastic Instructional Text* (2017), and *The Political Writings of Archbishop Wulfstan of York* (2015). In addition, he has edited multiple essay collections on early English law and published articles in such journals as *Modern Philology, Studies in Philology,* the *Journal of English and Germanic Philology, Neuphilologische Mitteilungen,* and (because he occasionally likes to publish in venues that don't have "philology" in the title) *Speculum.* Rabin is a fellow of the Royal Historical Society.

Judith Roof recently retired as Professor of English and William Shakespeare Chair in English at Rice University, USA. She has published books and essays on narrative theory, studies in sexuality, Hollywood cinema, DNA, hoaxes, comedy, and on the work of such authors as Beckett, Pinter, Duras, Woolf, and Percival Everett.

Christopher Salamone is a Lecturer in English at the University of Oxford (Mansfield College), UK. His research interests include how and why early modern printers and authors associated the figure of the ghost with various facets of literary production; and the textual afterlife of Shakespearean fragments. The latter is the subject of his first monograph, *Shakespeare and the Eighteenth Century Miscellany* (2023), as well as an article in *Eighteenth Century Life* exploring the fragmentation of Shakespeare's works across eighteenth-century poetic miscellanies.

John Timpane has taught English at Rutgers University and Lafayette College, USA; his published work includes essays on comic theory, Shakespeare, August Wilson, Ntozake Shange, and Tennessee Williams. He was also the Commentary Page Editor (1997–2008) and later the Books Editor and Theater Critic (2008–2019) for *The Philadelphia Inquirer.* Among his books are (with Nancy H. Packer) *Writing Worth Reading* (1994) and (with Roland Reisley) *Usonia, N.Y.: Building a Community with Frank Lloyd Wright* (2000).

Kevin J. Wetmore, Jr. is Professor and Chair of Theatre Arts at Loyola Marymount University, USA. He is the author or co-author of ten books, including *Modern Asian Theater and Performance, 1900-2000* and *Back from the Dead,* as well as the editor of over a dozen books including *Revenge Drama in Renaissance Europe and Japanese Theater, The Methuen Anthology of Modern Asian Drama,* and *Staging Irish Dramas in Japanese Theater: Studies in Comparative Theatrical Performance.* He is also the author of dozens of articles about Japanese theatre, horror culture, Shakespeare, and other topics, and has contributed to numerous encyclopedias about Asian theatre.

Preface

The Revenant, the Phoenix, Lazarus, Dracula: Civilizations over countless ages, in global locales, have been occupied with the dead, whose population increasingly outnumbers the living. Given this extreme ratio between the extant and the lost, ghost stories understandably proliferate human existence, and this book's production is one more.

It was a project that emerged at an academic conference several years ago from a conception formulated by Dr. Johanna Frank of the University of Windsor, to whom we are gratefully indebted. Her prospectus had been diligently constructed, the contributors carefully selected, and the abstracts duly assembled. For sundry reasons, however, the project, like many dreams and visions, died in the dark footlights of a show that never opened or, perhaps more aptly, failed to materialize at a séance that never found its medium. The more we talked about ghosts in drama, however, the more we felt summoned to the project's resurrection.

But just as every drama is a form of ghost story—extensive scholarship attests to this—every resurrection is a form of creation. Does the risen Phoenix duplicate exactly the creature of its earlier demise, or must its ashes necessarily tint the new wings? Uncertain at the outset of our discussion, we decided to sift those ashes further at the annual Comparative Drama Conference, an always stimulating assemblage of experts, carefully organized in recent years by Bill Boles. After the conference, in an airport restaurant in Orlando, we spent hours scribbling on scraps of paper the names of plays containing ghosts, and all the traditions that invoked them, while we waited out countless flight delays. Thanks to the time afforded us by Frontier Airlines, our list proliferated like a stereotypical Zombie Apocalypse, such that we might, at that point, have titled this book on ghosts *Night of the Living Dead*.

But our list was much larger than coherent, more generic than systematic. Clearly, if we included chapters covering every play containing a ghost or a character haunted by memories, figures, or fears, if we surveyed every culture that dramatized the ghostly, we would not be proposing a collection but outlining an encyclopedia. More importantly, winnowing the rubric forced us to decide what we meant by a theatrical ghost. Although not one ghost appears on stage in *A Long Day's Journey into Night*, barely a syllable in the play fails to evoke a specter—of Catholicism or Irishness, of addiction or parsimony, of failed ambition or indulged degeneracy, of pop melodrama or Shakespeare. And, in the aftermath of Freud, how do we differentiate the absence of an actual ghost in O'Neill from *Death of a Salesman*'s Expressionist presentation of a haunting memory or a lost ancestor? Although in twenty-first-century Western culture—pace New Agers—it may seem oxymoronic to be literal-minded about ghosts, we nevertheless decided to limit ourselves to "real" ghosts, lest, like Hamlet, we stab blindly through a curtain rather than knowingly adhere to the mandate of the kingdom's guiding spirit. We thought this limitation was important not only because it helpfully constrained the size of our enterprise, but also because it provided a more incisive heuristic with which to gauge and mediate dimensions of dramatic illusion.

If one quality of theatrical performance is the way it seduces us into the credibility of the unreal, ghosts on stage remind us of the deceptive seduction we are undergoing. "What's Hecuba to him, or he to Hecuba that he should weep for her?" Hamlet ponders, aghast at an actor's "monstrous" usurpation of reality, wherein "this player here, but in a fiction, in a dream of passion, could force his soul so to his own conceit." Hamlet's outrage owes in part to his own failure to assume his mandated role, and in equal part to his awareness that the source of that mandate is a ghost. If it is monstrous that an audience take a player's agony as real, is it not doubly so that Hamlet might similarly misapprehend the ghost; as he makes clear, "the spirit I have seen may be the devil." Hamlet thus cues the audience to the same quandary: If the ghost they have seen foregrounds the danger of Hamlet's succumbing to illusion, does not Hamlet, himself, foreground the same thing for the audience? "Real" ghosts in drama may serve an array of functions, but, we felt, they give those functions a uniquely meta-critical aura, one we decided that merited attention.

In addition, we felt that the way we delimited the collection would allow our reading audience to contextualize their roles as parts of historically and culturally specific theatrical audiences by contemplating what it might mean, for instance, to see a ghost on stage at a time and place when differentiating a demon from the Holy Ghost had profound implications for the dispossession of the audience's souls. We were reminded of an acquaintance, a British Renaissance scholar, who reported, on returning from a year teaching in Japan, that his students there could not understand Hamlet: "Your ancestor is murdered. His ghost instructs you to take revenge. Since the charge is unambiguous, what could cause a dilemma? They couldn't see why Hamlet was waiting." So too the exposure of radical differences provides opportunities to identify sites of transcultural values. Those same Japanese students got Macbeth completely: "Ruthless ambition was something they had no trouble grasping."

Thus, while Ibsen, the author of *Ghosts*, joined O'Neill and Miller, among many others, in falling outside the conceptual margins we set, their replacement by discussions of ancient Greek, medieval English, Native American, and No drama allowed this collection to offer some sense of the variety of spectral meanings that can haunt dramatic performances. While "some sense" differs, we know, from "comprehensive knowledge," space constraints made impossible a collection dedicated to the range of possibilities we had originally imagined. Within the space we had and the commensurate space we could allow each chapter, therefore, we were delighted by the collection's scope. Some of our contributors came from the original prospectus, and others were solicited to fill gaps or, in some cases, on shorter notice to replace contributions that, as it turned out, could not serve the ends of the book as we finally conceived it. We are grateful to all our contributors— exemplary professionals in every way—each of whose illuminating chapters made the book richer. We are also grateful to three smart, enthusiastic readers whose suggestions for polishing and organizing the collection gave the final version a sharpness we otherwise might not have achieved. From outset to conclusion our editor, Mark Dudgeon, helped us foreground a governing rationale that solidified the collection's through-line, and his assistant, Ella Wilson, expeditiously shepherded the book's production, a task that would have been impossible were it not for the swift, meticulous, and completely outstanding efforts of University of Kentucky graduate research assistant, Emily Naser-Hall. Thanks, too, to W. Stephen Gilbert for his careful and conscientious indexing.

Finally, we want to thank our spouses, Geoffrey Nelson and Sharon Kopyc, who have for decades shared with us our visits to the theatre, accompanied the aftermath of these haunting visitations, and supported our gathering the dramatic spirits that reside between these covers.

Ann C. Hall
University of Louisville
Alan Nadel
University of Kentucky

Summoning the Illusion within the Illusion: An Introduction

Ann C. Hall and Alan Nadel

The Theatrical / Absurd / Uncanny

This is a fact of drama, perhaps its most universal: the stage is a ghostly place, inhabited by otherworldly creatures who act as though they were alive, who suffer the pangs and foibles of strange specters, and who invite us to do the same.

These staged creatures move and speak possessed by knowledge of times and spaces unknown to us, evoked by the passions of and feelings for persons who are not alive, who were never alive, but nonetheless are brought to life though an uncanny rendition of agents and mediums: actors and authors in touch with the ticks and temperaments, the blatant motives and secret agonies of the undead. If, in fiction and fable, the concept of the "ghost" invokes a conceptual space at the overlapping margins of inimical states—life and death, past and present, substantial and intangible, eternal and quotidian, spiritual and profane—nothing implicates the ghostly more than live drama. In its requisite liminalities, after all, all theatre of all kinds is the theatre of the absurd, every play a passion play.

When Hamlet, perhaps drama's most dramatic dramaturg, tries in vain to distinguish the motive and cue for passion evoked by play-acting from that exacted by a ghostly encounter, he finds himself unavoidably drawn toward the seductive and threatening connections between the ghostly actor and the haunted spectator. Asking about the leader of the theatrical troupe, "What's Hecuba to him or he to Hecuba that he should weep for her?" Hamlet finds himself unable to separate the demonic pleasure of tragedy from the tragic fear of the uncanny: "The spirit I have seen / May be the devil, and the devil hath power / T'assume a pleasing shape." If Hamlet's dilemma is complicated rather than resolved when he decides, ironically, that drama itself ("The play's the thing . . .") will differentiate spectral experience from theatrical illusion, his decision is grounded in the confusion endemic to the concept of ghosts and what they dramatize, to the shared dualities that unite theatre with ghosts. As Alice Rayner explains:

> Theatre is not simply a second world. Rather, like the linguistic tropes of metaphor and metonymy, theatrical doubling invokes two dissimilar elements and finds the points of overlap, such that the double negative, 'not not' and the dualism 'is and is not' do not so much present an ontological truth as they indicate the limits of dualistic thought. Any point at which dualistic, oppositional thought is invoked but then breaks down might be said to be theatrical.[1]

For this reason, Rayner and Marvin Carlson, the authors of the two most cogent theoretical examinations of theatre as a haunted phenomenon, ground many insights in the doubling that characterizes performance. For Carlson, therefore, ghosting is a form of remembering, demonstrating how theatre, as a cultural activity, is "deeply involved with memory and haunted by repetition."[2] In some cultures, he points out, "there is scarcely an element of the theatrical experience . . . that audiences cannot immediately recognize as having witnessed before."[3]

The eerie experience implicit in this doubling has been associated with the Freudian "uncanny." Freud's examination of the troubling inference of the familiar-made-unfamiliar, which produces an estrangement from the self in the form of a recollection, has helped explain the kinship between theatrical repetition and haunting.[4] Rayner thus believes that "all theatre insists on the reality of ghosts."[5] In a similar vein, Carlson uses the term "ghosting" to identify "one of the characteristic features of theatre."[6] Ghosting, for Carlson, signifies the presentation "of the identical thing [the audience] has encountered before, although now in a somewhat different context. . . . Thus a recognition . . . of identity becomes part of the reception process, with results that can complicate this process considerably."[7]

This returns us to theatre's dualistic historical moment, that is, both the moment of the theatrical performance and the moment that is performed on stage. The ghost is also the indominable instantiation of a previously fragile, that is mortal, version of the same entity, a version no longer subject to the frights it can cause, the frailty of the human condition, for is not human existence conditioned upon the *corpus* of a corpse subject to the slings and arrows of outrageous fortune? Any life lacking the threat of instant termination would, obviously, be inhuman. In this respect, the ghost does not duplicate but rather undoes the living creature, the historical subject, the *corpus delicti*. The ghost, in other words, confronts human existence not by means of replication but of reversal, thereby questioning, if not the existence of an afterlife, then the need for one. Ghosts thus challenge the boundary between temporal and eternal, the intimations of Heaven and its opposite, upon which so much Western theology is based. They satirize the fabled portal to the Hereafter with an alternate column in the bookmaker's book on Pascal's wager. But if immortality is the product of death, rather than of avoiding it, then to live forever by dying may be the premise of theatre. If, as Rayner claims, theatre is "a fundamentally human space where we humans encounter not only the dead who have gone before but also the images of our own mortality,"[8] that is why the triumph over not remembering brings theatre to life.

For drama is also a form of remembering that emerges from the visceral experience the live audience shares with the live performer, something that Rayner touches upon in her chapter on going to the theatre, thus fulfilling an appointment delimited by the designated confluence of disparate, and in some ways, irreconcilable temporalities:[9] "By going to the theatre at a certain time, I enter a space in which a repetition is planned but still open to accident."[10]

But only a few theatrical roles are ghosts, a distinction not unrelated to the kind of accident upon which Rayner focuses. For Rayner, "the ghost is not so much an element of theatre as it is an inhabitant of all its elements."[11] Similarly, Carlson, extrapolating from Ibsen's famous quote, states that "just as one might say every play might be called *Ghosts*, so, with equal justification, one might argue, that every play is a memory play,"[12] such that he views all theatre as "deeply involved with memory and haunted by repetition."[13] Working off of Carlson and Rayner, Mary Luckhurst and Emilie Morin, in their recent collection *Theatre and Ghosts*, "make the case for the particular advantages of putting spectrality and theatre studies in dialogue and we stress the illuminating ways in which plays and performances can be newly analyzed and understood through a focus on tropes of the ghostly and representations of haunting."[14] All these scholars help illuminate the pervasive tropic import of the ghostly, the representational role of the live actor, which imposes an inherent limitation on consideration of the role or function, specifically, of theatrical ghosts.

When we first conceived this collection, we construed the ghost and the act of haunting as broadly as possible, only to discover that in so doing we were allowing—in fact requiring—the object of our study, our *raison d'être*, to dissolve into a specter, haunting our pages but never materializing. If ghosts constitute the quintessence of theatre, a point made convincingly by Carlson and Rayner, why not place them center stage? If we don't believe in ghosts (at least within the parameters of the stage) or if we are afraid of them, then how can we confront how the dramatic is produced and what it produces? Is exorcized theatre possible? And even if it is possible and/or desirable—one could make the case that Brecht might think so—doesn't exorcism require the presence of a ghost?

The Ghost

The reason for exploring ghosts in drama, therefore, is that if theatre is haunted, if ghosting is everywhere, even in the Naturalism of Zola, Gorki, the Kitchen Sink drama of John Osborne, or the well-made plays of Terrance Rattigan, then the role of ghost would have no particular significance. The attention given King Hamlet accrues only to his symbolic status or the complexity of Shakespeare's creation. Not invalid points, but also insufficient for the spectrum of implications evoked by the designation: ghost.

First of all, if theatre is a haunted and haunting phenomenon, ghosts immediately introduce explicit or implicit elements of metacommentary. Making visible crucial elements of the dramatic, they help reveal vital dynamics of theatre and of theatricality. In this context, as illusions of illusions, they foreground many dramatic themes common to a wide variety of periods and cultures. When Kevin Wetmore points out, for example, that ghosts in Japanese theatre come back "to make things right, and to enforce justice before they finally leave this plane," he is identifying as well an aspect of ancient Greek drama, found also in English drama, from the Early Modern period to Noël Coward's *Blithe Spirit*. In contemporary Irish drama, as well as contemporary African American drama, as Craig Owens and Jennifer Larson make clear, ghosts are often agents of revenge. More generally, throughout sundry cultures and historical periods, ghosts manifest the impetus of the past to affect the present, or perhaps, the desire of audiences across times and culture to believe they do.

The Universal and the Historical (Ghost)

This is not to say, however, that these elements are universal or a-historical. Despite some noteworthy themes evoked by our broad study, why ghosts appear in drama, how they are represented on stage, and what functions they serve reflect telling signs of their time and culture. Although one must not deny that powerful dramatic figures can invoke meanings and effects transcending the imaginative parameters of their initial performance, it is equally narrow-minded to divorce them from the effects they had on the audiences for whom they were created. Those audiences lived in cultures informed by ideological beliefs and temporal conditions that framed the reception of the staged drama and dramatized ghosts haunting all imaginative performance. The study of ghosts and their dramatic staging, therefore, is the study of what haunts sundry times and cultures. At the same time, because the ghost-onstage is always already metatheatrical, it helps unpack the theatricality that characterized those times and places. They reveal what must be disguised as well as the techniques—verbal, physical, and technical—for effecting drama's illusions and allusions. The reception of theatrical effects "reflect ideological preoccupations with the nature of reality, sensory perception, and rational thought," Beth Kattelman importantly explains. These effects "not only reveal the social values of their time, but they also provide potent insights into attitudes toward advances in science, improved manufacturing techniques, and a preoccupation with ideas about the veracity of the senses."

About Ancient Greek drama, John Timpane points out, "Athens was a city-state arising from an ancient warrior culture focused on kinship, tribal ties, and honor, the supreme value, governed by immemorial rules and expectations. In this urbanized warrior culture, everything was an agon." Because for the Athenians, "ghosts are made of anxiety," he explains, they reminded the Athenian populace "of the things we least wish to be reminded of, chief among them death and its transformations." Similarly, because of death's omnipresence in the Medieval European world, the boundaries between life and death rendered death less a termination than a transition, one resonant with the resurrection of Christ. In that world, Andrew Rabin makes clear, ghosts were part of the culture's negotiating "relics of saints" in relation to "the walking corpses of the damned." Thus, to view the first documented dramatic performance in England "solely as liturgical ritual is to overlook the complex web of belief, social norm, and cultural practice that shaped its composition and reception." The ghostly presence in that play therefore requires imagining a world marked by the impossibility of divorcing the supernatural from the spiritual because, in the world of Medieval Europe, treating ghosts (or the ghostly) as imaginative was sacrilegious.

The Protestant Reformation, however, threw many social norms and cultural practices into contention. In light of what Christopher Salamone notes was the implicitly anti-Catholic attitude of the Early Modern English stage, the ghostly, instead of manifesting the truth of the Eucharist, foregrounded its demonic duplicity.[15] Scenes of haunting were "inflected by a mixture of popular folklore and recent intertheatrical conventions, as well as a complex range of contextual, theological disputes over the authenticity and ontological status of ghostly presence." The Early Modern controversy over ghosts, Salamone explains, entailed "finding scriptural and classical precedents for the idea that ghosts may, for example, be counterfeits undertaken by diabolic (or living Catholic) entities, or by hallucinatory shadows, conjured by an over-actively melancholic imagination."

With the closing of the theatres for a generation and the dawning of the enlightenment, ghosts on stage disappeared. While ghosts haunted James Boswell, few playwrights cast specters on stage. Samuel Foote, whose canon of work included many satires and whose career included avoiding prosecution from the Lord Chamberlain and others, wrote one of the only dramas with a ghost. In *The Orators* (1762) a ghost is a defendant in a trial. The case serves as a metaphor for ghosts in drama at this time—it is dismissed for lack of a ghostly jury. Of course, there were ghosts in the usual Shakespearean productions of the time, but Benjamin Breen suggests that ghosts were just too illogical for this "age of reason." The popularization and promulgation of scientific devices such as the telescope, and even the discovery of alcoholic "spirits," solved supernatural problems with the scientific method.

The technological inventions of the nineteenth century, however, had the reverse effect. With the telegraph and other developments, theatres and psychics concluded that if we could communicate across the miles, we could certainly communicate across the boundary between life and death. Kattelman's work on "Pepper's Ghost" documents the reemergence of the theatrical ghost, thanks to new technology.

Ben Furnish's chapter returns to the fissure between the spiritual and the religious in Paddy Chayefsky's 1960 play, *The Tenth Man*. If the presumed audience treats the exorcized ghost as a figurative convention, Furnish makes clear that *The Tenth Man* forces its audience to consider the implications of tacitly accepting an existence devoid of faith. The play "remains haunted by the implication that dybbuks might be real and exorcisms efficacious, not just for the subject possessed by a ghost but for the community performing rituals bereft of their rites, and the audience for whom that community is surrogate." *The Tenth Man* thus draws on traditions that unified ghettoized communities over centuries of Jewish diaspora, predating the Early Modern period. Drawn from a major work of the Yiddish theatre, *The Dybbuk*, written in 1920, *The Tenth Man* adapted, as *The Dybbuk* had before it, the agency of tradition to weave spiritual love and transcendent faith into a drama that both resisted and accepted the onslaught of assimilation. Ghosts in this tradition thus represent the spiritual in a world that has largely drained rituals of their spiritual content.

At the other extreme, Japanese dramatic conventions—dating to centuries when ghost figures were scant in Western drama—rely on the certainty of ghosts. Even a ghost that visits in a dream, therefore, is regarded as real. This facilitates dramatizing ghosts in several genres, each, as Kevin Wetmore explains, with discrete characteristics: "Nō ghosts are sad and regretful; kabuki and bunraku ghosts are vengeful, angry and violent; kyōgen ghosts, as parodies of nō ghosts, reduce the tragic apparitions of nō to their ludicrous extreme."

If all these forms of Japanese drama empower ghosts, in much Native American drama, ghosts act less as agents than as guides in a world where the temporal points of "past," "present," and "future" lack chronological authority, so that, as Margaret Noodin notes, they "revisit or previsit disparate points in time and place, in effect disrupting time as it informs dominant narratives." In this way, the ghosts enable dialogues between circumstances and cultures that, when disciplined under the temporal order of Western rationalism, cannot interact. In so doing, these Native American ghosts reveal how Western rationalism freezes the past, making the spirits of the ancestors fixtures in a history produced in the present. In contradistinction to that fixity, contemporary Native American drama, using ghosts as "active guides to overlapping times and places," attempts to guide us to sites of fluidity that make recognition and resolution possible.

If in contemporary Native American drama, ghosts help guide the audience to the reconciliation of historical division, in the contemporary drama of Sarah Ruhl, they enact reconciliations more personal than historical. Ruhl's ghosts, Amy Muse explains, engage characters in the "stubborn hope of [the] grieving," so that it may become possible to reassure the dead as well as to be reassured by them. This dynamic places Ruhl's dramas in the generic tradition of the séance, which also creates highly orchestrated occasions for the dead to speak. Thus, as Muse points out about Ruhl's play *For Peter Pan on Her 70th Birthday*, "in theatre you also never really die."

Because Ruhl's plays, therefore, reflect the last two centuries' trend to regard ghosts as secular and personal, her work may also suggests the séance as implicit paradigm for the use of ghosts in modern drama. Contemporaneous to the rise of Darwinism, the Fox sisters staged séances so convincing as to initiate a craze of spiritualism that effectively moved the primary realm of ghosts from the theological to the supernatural. By ignoring the need for an informing cosmology, the séance turned the ghostly presence into pure theatre. At a time when contrived melodrama was the dominant theatrical mode, this form of theatre pointed the way toward a natural and psychological realism, because the séance ceremony, despite its theatricality, denied fabrication. The ghostly encounter entailed believing only that the performance was real.

Imbricating the spiritual and the theatrical, the séance thus epitomized in some ways the notions of theatricality foundational to drama. These include staging, performativity, and a negotiated skepticism toward worldly and otherworldly alike. Because the séance entails skepticism ("give me a sign that it is really you"), it forms the liminal margin without which dramatic performance loses its centrality; performers in plays are tasked with providing constant signs that "it is really us." In the tension between this relentless display of proof and its relentless disavowal resides the ghostliness of the theatrical medium, making ghosts, simultaneously, quintessential drama and metatheatrical devices. This self-consciousness, nevertheless, has a substantial tradition. As early as the Early Modern period, Salamone notes, ghosts served as "metatheatrical threshold devices, which playfully disrupt the illusion of fictional presence with speakers who are neither entirely 'here,' in the audience's reality, or 'there,' in the fictional stage-world." The metatheatrical aspects of the ghostly are even more prominent in plays where faith or the "real" experiences of individual characters are not the presumed sites of audience identification.

This potential of the séance is exploited in *Blithe Spirit.* Representing the play's séance(s) as both intentional hoax and unintentional medium, the play satirizes romantic nostalgia for old loves, who retain their allure so long as entanglements are not actually renewed. It does so by using the séance to literalize both the relationship's end and its resurrection. If Noël Coward is ridiculing how spouses invariably realize moments when, figuratively, they want to kill one another, his process reveals the imaginative nature of theatrical dieges because, as Judith Roof points out, in *Blithe Spirit* the ghostly figure "operates as the fulcrum of two simultaneous, layered, linked, but ultimately different diegeses: the pragmatic mundanity of the séance as a species of hoax and the realized imaginary of its success."

Blithe Spirit thus exposes the metatheatrical aspects of ghosts in drama. It "explores the capacity of theatre both to define its spatio-temporal locus and to enlarge this staged diegesis beyond the stage," Roof explains, such that when "history and memory become the suddenly visible and audible reserve for an ongoing onstage drama . . . theatre literally emerges from an imaginary called into place by a 'medium,' in this case theatre itself."

When exposed as a means for ridicule, that metatheatricality, so valuable in understanding drama's efficacy, can also become the object of that ridicule, as in plays by such playwrights as Sam Shepard and David Mamet, who wrote plays in which ghosts, Ann Hall notes, "dramatize the uneasy relationship between fiction and reality and the difficulty of interpretation under such conditions." The status of the ghostly, thematized by Mamet's *The Shawl*, in reflecting a contemporary skepticism about spiritualism independent of its religious implications, replaces the séance's medium with the medium of theatre itself. It does so, Hall explains, by representing "the uncanny that makes theatre necessary and possible by luring the audience into an otherworld that mysteriously makes possible a 'cleansing awe.'"

In Irish drama, the metatheatrical effects come not from converting spiritual skepticism into theatrical awe, but by substituting for that awe in plays where, Craig Owens notes, "characters returned from the dead fail to haunt properly," so that the past "returns to catalyze comic misinterpretations by reconfiguring otherwise indecipherable meanings and unknowable truths." This phenomenon uses metatheatrics to articulate historically specific cultural narratives of Irish marginalization and inaction.

In the work of August Wilson and Suzan-Lori Parks, the metatheatrical invocation of ghosts also serves historically specific ends. For these African American playwrights, the tension between "possession" as spiritual inhabitation and "possession" as forced servitude informs ghostly visitation. As Parks explains, "The definition of possession cancels itself out. The relationship between possessor and possessed is, like ownership is, multidirectional."[16] Parks's dramatic enterprise, therefore, as Jennifer Larson makes clear, comprises "a quest to discover who haunts whom and why," and her Pulitzer Prize-winning play *Topdog/Underdog* "posits that productively communing with ghosts and their hauntings can foster healing, create opportunities for agency, and/or lead to a more inclusive understanding of history—both personal and communal."

August Wilson's *Gem of the Ocean* similarly employs the ameliorative power of ghosts. Wilson inverts, Alan Nadel explains, "the procedure of the séance, wherein the living call forth ghosts. Instead of summoning ghosts into the material world, Barlow [a character seeking redemption] must ask the ghosts to admit him to their city, thereby acknowledging the reality of their jurisdiction." That jurisdiction, in the city built under the Atlantic Ocean from the bones of those lost in the Middle Passage, comparably assaults the notion of possession by reminding us that "possession" was the rubric that enabled capitalists to convert human beings into property.

If property resides at the heart of ghostly possession, then ghosts not only seek to possess properties but, in so doing, they manifest properties. Nor are these two usages of "property" a facile pun, for the properties of ghosts cannot be disarticulated from the properties they claim. And both forms of property are as varied as the theatrical imagination. Ghosts can be anxiety-producing reminders, or active claimants. They can reflect the omnipresence of death in a given time or place, or they can help the audience resist that omnipresence. They can make demands on the living, or they can be subject to the demands of the living.

They can affirm specific theological cosmologies or undermine them. In the Native American drama Noodin discusses, moreover, "indigenous and

Christian traditions may be reconciled, as two very different spirits share their need to be remembered." At the same time, Hall reminds us, while "Shepard's and Mamet's ghosts serve to bridge the audience/stage divide, the playwrights represent their ghosts differently. Shepard's ghost functions in some ways like the return of the repressed," but they do not generate the artistic energy that Mamet's do. Ghosts can underscore the temporal limitations of theatre, or they can openly defy them. As Roof insightfully notes about *Blithe Spirit*, "the onstage clash between the reappearance of an offstage past and the onstage present, between the dead and the living, extends theatrical space/time to the dilation of 'Always.'"

But the theatrical disruption of time also instantiates its historical disruption. Time continues to be "out of joint" for African Americans, for example, because, according to Nadel, "the specter of slavery remains enthroned as the revenant father of capitalism: the fallen King Hamlet, always seeking revenge for the loss of his realm." In these circumstances, whether in regard to the fictional history of Elsinore or the actual history of the slave trade, drama has the capacity, through its command of time, to haunt present conditions with the presence of past disruptions. This is why, once Hamlet recognizes that time is out of joint, the play becomes "the thing" that will capture the conscience of the King (King Claudius? King Hamlet? Both?). The play *within* the play will make the King play *out* the effects of the act that haunts him, effects that will cause him to betray his own act. Hamlet's instructions to the actors, therefore, are intended to ensure that they act more credibly than his uncle. For theatre—like its paradigmatic site, the séance—no matter how convincing, can never completely escape the séance's informing question, "How can I be sure it is really you?" Ghosts in drama thus foreground theatre's symbiotic relationship between myth and veracity: myth is the ghost of veracity, attempting to impose veracity on those living in the present, such that they are inhabited by the myth of "truth," that is, haunted by an authority capable of transcending facts.

For this reason, Salamone asks us to consider, what of the offstage spectator? "[I]n what ways might the character's contestation and questioning of spectral presence apply to the early modern audience?" For the Medieval audience, ghosts are bodies that rise, not souls, while for the Early Modern audience, moral didacticism, as Salamone claims, "requires rather than negates a virtuous mode of spectatorship, one aware of the effort and identity of the tragedian effecting an act of similitude in which an audience imaginatively collaborates."

In Japanese drama, on the other hand, Wetmore shows how discrete audiences each mandate a different function for the ghost.

Both nō and kyōgen are aimed at an audience from the ruling and warrior classes, for whom death in battle is a real possibility, but nō spirits are internalized—invoked memories that seek to be released of their attachments—while kyōgen ghosts are mock-nō ghosts, trivializing and satirizing what nō takes seriously. Kabuki and bunraku, on the other hand, offer violent, externalized ghosts, aimed outward, at the people who have harmed them. They seek vengeance and justice.

Spirits and their Summoning

Remembering that Western drama emerged out of Dionysian vegetation rites helps us connect theatre's embodied spirits to the vestiges of the spiritual. (Hence the phrase "spirits" unites the entities invoked in ancient performances with the elixirs that empowered those performances and the community intoxicated by the fruits of the performances.) Every drama, moreover, is haunted by the belief system of its audience and the conditions of its production, no matter how estranged any specific play may be from the conventional wisdom and informing dogma of its time and place. Thus ghosts, in the way they are represented on stage, the concepts their staging represents, and the conditions of agency they dramatically negotiate provide copious avenues for understanding and producing all drama.

Given, therefore, that ghostliness is endemic both historically and ontologically to the conventions of drama and the condition of theatre, staged entities marked as ghosts should accrue significant attention, but the opposite is true. The centrality of ghosts in the concept of drama seems directly proportional to its marginality in theatre scholarship. To help address that apparent gap in contemporary scholarship, this volume collects chapters examining the various ways ghosts are represented on the page and on the stage, and the wide spectrum of themes and beliefs their creations have represented in literary and performance history, in sundry eras and cultures, such that spectral readings of plays and playwrights may summon interpretations that bring new life to the dead.

Given that no single volume, of course could provide a comprehensive analysis of the numerous presentations of ghosts in in the world's treasury of theatrical production, the sampling here more accurately suggests some interpretive matrices that, by allowing insights into specific works, may provide useful heuristics for understanding some dimensions of some dramatic works and of the cultures that produced them. Although such a collection admits no natural structure, we have chosen, somewhat arbitrarily, to organize the collection chronologically, moving from Ancient Greece to contemporary America, in light of which we have placed Beth Kattelman's between the discussion of Early Modern drama and the chapter on the mid-century British play, *Blithe Spirit*, because, as we noted, the eighteenth century was a neo-classical period more focused on perfecting recycled forms than introducing innovative perspectives. The Romantic Revolution, which followed or, arguably, replaced eighteenth-century rationalism, was fueled by poetry rather than drama, and thus privileged closet dramas (which necessarily blurred the distinction between figurative and literal ghosts) and Gothic fiction (which did the same). With the developments in stage technology that proliferated on the Victorian stage, as Kattelman explains, varieties of ghostly experience become more widely integral to dramatic production.

This organization will necessarily highlight historical differences over cross-cultural connections, but because we firmly believe each of the chapters can stand alone as solid critical analysis, we hope the reader will be able to recognize how the themes and topics throughout haunt the thinking from chapter to chapter.

Notes

1　Alice Rayner, *Ghosts: Death's Double and the Phenomena of Theatre* (Minneapolis: University of Minnesota Press, 2006), xii.

2　Marvin Carlson, *The Haunted Stage: The Theatre as Memory Machine* (Ann Arbor: University of Michigan Press, 2003), 11.

3　Ibid.

4　See Rayner, x.

5　Ibid., xii.

6　Carlson, 6–7.

7　Ibid., 7.

8　Rayner, xii–xiii.

9　Rayner, 1–32.

10　Ibid., 29.

11　Ibid., xv.

12　Carlson, 2.

13　Ibid., 11.

14　Mary Luckhurst and Emilie Morin, eds., *Theatre and Ghosts: Materiality, Performance, and Modernity* (London: Palgrave Macmillan, 2014), 2.

15　This is one of the implications, in Book I of *The Faerie Queene*, of Spenser's naming the Pope's avatar Duessa.

16　Suzan-Lori Parks, "Possession," in *The America Play and Other Works* (New York: Theatre Communications Group, 1995), 3.

Works Cited

Carlson, Marvin. *The Haunted Stage: The Theatre as Memory Machine.* Ann
    Arbor: University of Michigan Press, 2003.
Luckhurst, Mary and Emilie Morin, eds. *Theatre and Ghosts: Materiality,
    Performance, and Modernity.* London: Palgrave Macmillan, 2014.
Parks, Suzan-Lori. "Possession," in *The America Play and Other Works.* New York:
    Theatre Communications Group, 1995.
Rayner, Alice. *Ghosts: Death's Double and the Phenomena of Theatre.*
    Minneapolis: University of Minnesota Press, 2006.

1

Made of Anxiety: Two (or Three) Ghosts in Aeschylus

John Timpane

European drama begins with a ghost story.

The oldest drama we have is that of *Persians* by Aeschylus. It features the ghost of the Persian king Darius, father to Xerxes, whose army has recently suffered terrible reversals. *Persians*, part of a trilogy that took first prize at the Dionysia Festival in Athens in 472 BCE,[1] is based heavily on the facts of recent history, especially the battle of Salamis in 480 BCE, not quite eight years before.[2] Salamis brought heavy defeat to the invaders, savaging the Persian navy and killing thousands of soldiers. A second Greek victory followed at Plataea in 479 BCE, effectively ending the Persian thrust into the Greek peninsula. The "present" of *Persians* happens between those two battles; Plataea is prophesied by the ghost of Darius.

Fourteen years later, the ghost of Clytemnestra, slain queen of Argos,[3] appears in *The Eumenides* (first recorded performance 458 BCE), last play in the trilogy known as the *Oresteia*. That trilogy portrays what Fiona McHardy has called "the most worked subject in extant tragedy," the murder of Clytemnestra by her son, Orestes.[4] First in the trilogy is *Agamemnon*, named after the king who returns home from the Trojan War, only to be murdered by Clytemnestra, continuing an ancient series of family murders. In the second play, *The Libation Bearers*, Orestes, spurred on by the god Apollo, kills her and flees the persecution of the Furies, goddesses tasked with punishing matricides. And in *The Eumenides*, the ghost of Clytemnestra appears, challenging gods and human beings alike to contend with the heritage of revenge.

A third ghost does not appear but is very potent: that of Agamemnon in *The Libation Bearers*. Of all three ghosts, his is the least "present," a trace sensed in indirect reports. Daughter Electra and son Orestes agonize over what to say to their father's spirit and how to say it; Clytemnestra, the king's murderer, cannot hope to gain the ghost's favor or allay its (supposed) cry for justice. The viscerally present absence of Agamemnon's ghost extends into

The Eumenides, where Orestes says he is confident of his father's protection. That confidence is vindicated.

Ghosts are made of anxiety. They are constant reminders of the things we least wish to be reminded of, chief among them death and its transformations.[5] The ghosts of Aeschylus enlist anxieties over fate, vengeance, gender relations, the wild, destabilizing potential of anger and violence, and even the instability of democracy itself. Worries are present whenever a ghost and its absences are around; ghosts embody them or speak them, as if the worries themselves were throwing their voices. If a ghost makes contact, it is a sure sign of unfinished business.

Ghost Culture

Greek culture, a kluge of local and regional traditions, pantheons, myths, beliefs, and practices, made plenty of room for ghosts. Earthly life was shot through with the presence and interventions of spiritual entities, including gods, spirits, and principals (sometimes treated as personal, sometimes not) of fate and chaos. Extreme psychological or neurological states were understood as the actions of *daimones* or *theoi*—gods or spirits that intervened in the actions of the *psyche*.[6] While human will and choice stood large in the Greek understanding of ethics and character, so did *moira* (one's personal "portion" or fate), *ate* (a principle of disorder), and *anangke* ("the inevitable" or destiny). Greek culture embraced this paradox: human beings are wholly responsible for what they do, yet their choices and acts fit within the uncontrollable aims of fate.

Athens was a city-state arising from an ancient warrior culture focused on kinship, tribal ties, and honor, the supreme value, governed by immemorial rules and expectations. In this urbanized warrior culture, everything was an agon, from war to the plays of Aeschylus to the judicial system to the dialogues of Plato. Besides the catastrophes of war between Persians and Greeks, *Persians* evokes the generational tension between the honorable, successful soldier-king Darius and his disgraceful, failed son, Xerxes. In the *Oresteia*, the ghost of Clytemnestra sets off agons involving male and female domains, the struggle between aristocratic and democratic ethics, and much else. The ghosts of Aeschylus are the vessels of those agons, their voices the voices of those debates.

An atavistic animism saw divinity in all things, to be honored, worshipped, and sometimes placated. Tragedy in Aeschylus is punctuated with animist ritual as human beings address earth, sea, and nature, plead for forgiveness or protection, or promise revenge. Thus Atossa (widow of Darius) and the Chorus in *Persians*, and Clytemnestra, Orestes, and Electra in *The Libation Bearers* prepare elaborate rituals addressing or summoning ghosts. Those rituals begin with libations to the Earth, which may help ghosts hear prayers or journey from the underworld. In *Persians*, the lists of war dead portray the natural world helping to desecrate Persian corpses.

What Ghosts Were

A ghost was the spirit of a once-living person now consigned to the underworld. It was what remained of that person and what returned, recalling Jacques Derrida's notion of the "revenant" that "begins by coming back."[7] Ghosts could be summoned to the living world. They might be sent by third parties such as gods or other spirits, or they could come on their own for their own reasons. A visit by a ghost is difficult, solemn, and awkward; much importance attaches to its fugitive nature. The ghost of Darius is anxious to appear and go, leery of being upbraided back in the underworld for staying too long. The ghost of Clytemnestra and its scathing agenda are gone after only a few, long-resonating lines. The ghost of Agamemnon never comes at all.

Ghosts might also come in dreams. Anxiety dreams, to be sure, were familiar to the Greeks. Such dreams begin both *Persians* and *The Libation Bearers*, prompting Atossa and queen Clytemnestra respectively to contact or mollify the ghosts of their husbands. Dreams in general, however, were often seen as not internal events but rather visitations passively beheld by the dreamer, who did not so much "have" the dream as "see" it.[8] A verb often used for what a ghost did in dreams was *phoitan*, meaning "visit." The ghost of Clytemnestra visits the Furies in a dream, and that of Agamemnon may be implicit in the nightmare of Clytemnestra in *The Libation Bearers*. The ghost is a visiting stranger from elsewhere.

Ghosts are usually ignorant of what happens in the living world although a few, such as the ghost of Clytemnestra, have partial knowledge. Ghosts care. They are intensely concerned with personal and family honor, prestige, reputation, possessions, kin, friends, and matters of pollution and revenge. Between the underworld and the living world, aims and desires may diverge or clash. Understanding and communication are forbidding; the divide is bridged only reluctantly and with greatest effort. Translation is an issue. What ghosts say in dreams or earthly visits may require priests or seers to interpret.

Calling up the Ghost

Darius, icon of the racial and cultural other, was an awe-inspiring and ominous figure, renowned for might, riches, administrative acumen, and military strategy. Yet the ghost of Darius speaks in the voice of the Greek world, taking a Greek view of recent history and the sufferings to come, brimming with Greek horror at his son's *hamartia* (his massive, tragic error in judgment), *hubris* (prideful defiance of the gods), insults against Zeus and Poseidon, and *nemesis* (the future retributions his son has earned).

Most of *Persians* is devoted to Atossa and the Chorus of elders fearing the bad, learning the worst, and deciding to raise the ghost. After her nightmare, the elders advise her to make libations "to the Earth and the dead."[9] and to ask the ghost's blessings—not yet, however, to summon it. Perhaps the dream may not be ominous after all.

A Messenger then arrives from Salamis. "Since I was there and did not merely hear it at second hand," he says with almost journalistic precision, "I can tell you exactly what kind of catastrophe happened."[10] Then follows the Messenger's account of Salamis, the no less disastrous carnage at Psyttaleia, and the Persian forces' chaotic retreat. The Messenger lists famous warriors slain, violent absences. The natural world joins forces, as islands, beaches, sea, and sky combine to desecrate the corpses:[11] "Artembares, commander of ten thousand cavalry, now is being smashed against Silenia's savage shore ... Lilaios and Arsames, and a third, Argestes, defeated, crash against the hard land."[12]

Why is the Ghost Desired?

Nobody really wants to call up a ghost. Several reasons are floated: comfort, advice, prophecy, blessings to keep away further evil. Sheer anxiety, though, is the main driver. After the Messenger's litany of calamities, "everything is full of terror."[13] Atossa thus assembles "propitiatory libations for my son's father"[14]—milk from a ritually pure cow,[15] honey, wine, olives, and flowers—to appease both the earth and the dead.[16] She asks the Chorus to sing a ritual hymn to "summon the divine spirit of Darius."[17] The Chorus approves: perhaps the ghost will know of a "remedy to our distress."[18] Hardly convincing: what "remedy" could there possibly be?

And whom do the living want when they want the ghost of Darius? The choric hymn is an act of constructing the ghost, putting together a figment made of memory, nostalgia for better times, visions of greatness, and the dead king's reputation for intelligence and good fortune. The ritual bids to control the shape of the apparition, to create a custom spirit; otherwise, there's no telling what you'll get. The hymning Chorus showers the wished-for ghost with praise, calling Darius "divine" and "beloved," "Susa-born god of the Persians."[19] The Darius they want is the Darius they remember, the fate-blessed warrior-king, Darius at the peak. That is how the Chorus begs the ghost to appear, in the full regalia of authority: "raise your saffron-dyed slipper, show the bangles of your kingly headdress."[20] They define the ghost in terms of a man who is gone: they want a specter of absence.

Ghosts stand somewhere among here and there, then and now; they blur absence and presence. As Andrew Buse and Peter Stott write, "A ghost cannot properly be said to belong to the past."[21] Not, I would add, if it is standing on stage, speaking to you. Besides, "a ghost is clearly not the same thing as the person who shares its proper name."[22] Darius is not on-stage; the ghost of Darius is. The presence of the latter marks the absence of the former. Thus the Chorus seeks the comfort of the ruler's robes, slippers, and tiara. When a ghost appears on-stage, it feels like both a return and a debut, as Buse and Stott note: a return because the ghost recalls the person, a debut because the ghost itself is "here" for the first time. Grief renders the ghost a violent absence, a loss.

Aeschylus precedes the appearance of the ghost with a poetic touch that defines its proper realm. The Chorus ends its ritual hymn with questions about why the calamity happened: "Why did our land lose all the triremes, ships, ships that once were, ships that are no more?" That's at best a meager paw at a translation. The Greek is simpler, hard to render: νᾶες ἄναες ἄναες, literally "ships, no-ships, no-ships."[23] The anguished invocation of the "no-ships," the losses of the vaunted Persian navy, in three words literally negated, brings up the ghost that scrambles time, presence and absence.[24]

The ghost of Darius remains separate from the realm of worldly life. Painfully impotent, it cannot make anything happen directly. It does not physically intervene or interact with anyone or anything; it but reacts and prophesies. This rigid separation emerged in a delectable moment from a National Theatre of Greece production of *Persians* at the ancient theatre of the Asclepeion at Epidaurus on July 25, 2020.[25] In traditional style, Atossa and the ghost face the audience, not each other, during much of their dialogue, and when Atossa moves as if to touch, the ghost puts up a hand. As Phillip Zapkin wrote in a review, "In his gesture stopping her, we see the reminder that he is dead, and they cannot comfort one another."[26]

But the living can afflict the dead. They burden the ghost of Darius with their suffering and shame. Perhaps that is really why the ghost was desired— as in many rituals conjuring with the otherworldly, the living seek a vessel for their agonies. Earlier, Atossa called the defeat at Salamis "a disgrace to the

Persians,"[27] and the Messenger said that the best Persian soldiers "have fallen dishonorably by a shameful fate."[28] The ghost has not heard of the defeat, or of Xerxes's incredible technological innovation, a pontoon bridge across the Hellespont. When told, it is stunned, particularly at the bridge. Atossa seems proud of her son's achievement, saying that "some *daimon* must have helped him in his project." In a telling moment, the ghost corrects her: "Alas, some great *daimon* must have taken him over so he did not think rightly."[29]

These two Persian reactions could not be more Greek. *Daimon*, like many Greek words for the otherworldly, is not so much a term of narrow denotation as a bristling gradient of possible meanings. In *daimon*, both Atossa and the ghost of Darius gesture to anonymous supernatural entities that intervene in human thinking and fate. People have personal *daimones* that can arouse both good moments and bad, a flash of brilliance (as the more generous Atossa means to say) or an explosion of *ate*, muddled, bad thinking (as the ghost does).[30]

What terrifies this ghost is the spectacle of Xerxes's disordered thinking, the *daimones* and *ate* at work in his mind. Worse, he has insulted the greatest of the gods. The Hellespont bridge strikes the ghost as especially sacrilegious: "A mortal, he thought he would gain mastery over all the gods—foolishly— even Poseidon. Wasn't this a soul disease that possessed my son?"[31] Later, as if to illustrate, the Xerxes that comes on-stage shows little insight into his predicament; he but staggers in amazed pain. This is what *nemesis* looks like. The Chorus, meanwhile, has taken on the ghost's viewpoint: "Alas, alas, *diamones*, you brought evil on us, unforeseen, easy to see, like the glance of disaster."[32]

What the Ghost does for the Living

Perhaps it functions as a catharsis—taking on terror or sorrow, raising them to their keenest, purest pitch. Faced with Salamis, further, it prophecies even worse to come: defeat for the troops Xerxes left behind. As the audience knows, the ghost is right: a little less than a year after Salamis,[33] the general Mardonius and his troops were massacred at Plataea. That is the unfinished business.

Ultimately, the ghost of Darius is answering that agonized *Why did it happen?* in the ritual hymn. The ghost points to the uncontrollable interventions of gods and spirits in human choice and action. The ghost knows Xerxes is responsible, that he has shown pride and chaotic judgment. He is the cause and will suffer for it, as he should. If this intersects with the will of spirits and gods, that too is to be expected, as the ghost says in the superbly epigrammatic line 742: "When a man rushes toward his own undoing, the god joins in."

We lack the two other plays in the trilogy that once contained *Persians*, so it is hazardous to speculate on how it struck original audiences. As we have it today, however, this tragedy—for all its implicit tribute to Athens and its armies, all its demarcation of "them" from "us," Asia from Europe—raises the Persian catastrophe out of the merely factual into the abstract. This is not a particular disaster; this is disaster itself. Such can befall any would-be Xerxes. Doom, assisted by the sightless operations of fate, awaits any man rushing toward his own undoing. *Persians* speaks to the anxieties of a victorious people, indeed of any warrior people. The ghost speaks in Greek to Greeks in the voice of *anangke*.

The ghosts of Darius and Clytemnestra are portrayed at the moment they are being left behind. History is literally pivoting away from them as they speak, and what they do helps it pivot. Where the ghost of Darius presides at the collapse of the Persian invasions, that of Clytemnestra in *The Eumenides* helps close both the epic tragedy of the House of Atreus, and the historic (and in the tragedy, largely idealized) shift in Athens away from ancient aristocratic values of honor, prestige, and ritual violence toward democratic values of institutional law. The laws of Athens, domesticating revenge itself, will settle the case of *Clytemnestra's Ghost v. Orestes*. In the process, the ghost of Clytemnestra evokes anxieties intrinsic to democracy itself.

The Ghost That Wasn't There

Agamemnon's non-apparent ghost exerts a powerful influence. *The Libation Bearers* is largely an agon over the correct way to address his spirit and gain its favor, and in *The Eumenides* the father's supra-mortal protection helps Orestes win his case. In a trilogy working out the appropriate places for male and female, Agamemnon is the unspoken (or ventriloquized) voice of the side that wins.

As *The Libation Bearers* opens, Orestes, under cover, is at the grave of his father. His personal ritual is carefully crafted. In line 1, Orestes calls on "Hermes of the underworld, who guards his father's sovereignty," appealing as one reverent son to another. He also leaves a lock of hair for the river-god Inachus, an animist obeisance that recalls Atossa's reverence toward the earth while calling for the ghost of Darius. Orestes, however, never asks the ghost of Agamemnon to appear, only "to hear, to listen."[34]

Apollo—who goaded Orestes to murder the queen and who now supports Orestes's quest to be exonerated—causes a ghostly event to visit both

Figure 1.1 In *Eumenides*, the third play of three in the *Oresteia* trilogy, Orestes asks for Apollo's aid at Delphi in the MacMillan Films production of *The Oresteia* (2014). Courtesy James MacMillan, available under a CC BY-SA 4.0 license.

Clytemnestra and his oracle at Delphi. It comes to Clytemnestra as a screaming nightmare in which she gives birth to a snake. Terrified, she sends out libation bearers to the grave to appease the earth and Agamemnon's spirit. The queen's offerings clot and do not sink into the earth, a sign of rejection. At the oracle, the prophets say "that those beneath the earth threw enraged reproaches and fury against their murderers."[35] Although not spelled out, this may be the one sign of the ghost of Agamemnon. Why would "those beneath the earth" make this cry now, unless on its behalf?

"Man-Minded" Woman

Few ghosts were ever made of more anxieties than that of Clytemnestra in *The Eumenides*. Clytemnestra herself, so vivid in *Agamemnon* and *The Libation Bearers*, is an amalgam of worries: tyrant, disobedient wife,[36] over-powerful woman, woman bent on revenge, family-savaging stranger. Her ghost in *The Eumenides* is supercharged with woman's feared potential for disorder.

Anton Bierl memorably has called Clytemnestra the queen "a perverted anti-model within the gender-regulated political system" of Greek society.[37] Bullying the council elders, ruling Agamemnon's kingdom in his absence, she takes Aegisthus, his cousin, as a lover. With his own reasons for killing the king,[38] Aegisthus helps Clytemnestra plan the murder. In *Agamemnon*, the queen does the killing,[39] with Aegisthus hanging around more or less idly. Genders reverse. The Watchman calls Clytemnestra "a man-minded woman"[40] and the Chorus of city elders disdains Aegisthus as a "woman"[41] for lacking the courage to do the deed himself.

Warrior-like, the queen glories in having slain Agamemnon and his Trojan consort, Cassandra. Aggressively, unforgettably, she takes full responsibility:

> I stand where I struck. My purpose is perfected. Thus have I acted; I will not deny it ... as for me, I rejoice in the act ... with fearless heart I tell you, who know it well—it doesn't matter whether you praise or blame me—here is Agamemnon, my husband, dead, the work of this right hand, a just craftsman."[42]

Poetry blazes here. The "I stand where I struck" line is a rapid fire of initial -ε sounds: ἕστηκα δ' ἔνθ' ἔπαισ' ἐπ' ἐξειργασμένοις.

Speaking and acting in masculine register, Clytemnestra steps into the place of the male warrior-ruler, joining the ranks of wives or mothers acting badly in Greek tragedy. As Fiona McHardy has shown, "the predominance of stories about wives and mothers show that this was a key area of anxiety in Athenian society."[43] In tragedy, drawn to dramatizing the abnormal or excessive, mapping what is expected and allowed, and delineating thresholds, female characters embody the place of anger, unruled by reason, liable to escape and destroy.[44]

The Ghost's Claim

Where the ghost of Darius makes no request of mortals on earth, that of Clytemnestra in *The Eumenides* has a strident agenda. It strikes a figure familiar in literature of the West: the soul of the dead crying for vengeance, ultimate image of anxiety over our obligations to our ancestors. The ghost comes uncalled-for in a dream sent to the sleeping Furies, who are supposed to be hunting Orestes to punish him. Neither quite there nor here, not in Hades, not on earth, the ghost inhabits an oneiric space in the minds of the slumberous Furies. While living people behold the ghost of Darius, none but the audience beholds that of Clytemnestra. The Furies awake with frustration and guilt—"Blame, coming to me in a dream, stabbed me like a charioteer with tight-gripped spur, under my heart, under my liver"[45]—but they do not say they have seen a ghost or that it is Clytemnestra's. Thus the audience has a privileged view that imparts irony to all that follows, since the audience knows, even if Clytemnestra is never named, whose ghost set off these events.

As soon as the Furies awake, Clytemnestra, name and ghost, are gone from the play. Nevertheless, the ghost's claim—a momentous one—haunts all else that transpires. With the extraordinary power of absent desire, a ghost's claim drives the decisions of gods and people.

The queen was murdered by her son for murdering his father, and the ghost expects the Furies to hunt this son down. The destination for matricides, as the Furies say later, is Hades, where "the word *joy* is used nowhere."[46] To the ghost's wrath, however, the Furies fall asleep in the Delphic temple. "It is thanks to you," the ghost says in their sleeping ears, "that I am shamed this way among the other dead. Because of my murders the dead never stop blaming me, and I wander disgraced."[47] Blood-revenge is what this honor-obsessed ghost wants; in this it is distinctively aristocratic, hearkening back to the (imagined) archaic ethic of eye-for-eye violent revenge.

Distinctively tragic, too, and distinctively female. Greek tragedy "in particular delights in exceptional and problematic revenge acts" among kin.[48] Literature of the age tends to link women with blood-revenge, although there is little historical evidence to suggest women actually took it.[49] On stage, women push it to the unthinkable edge. The ghost pushes for it, as the queen's daughter Electra had in her prayer to Agamemnon's spirit in *The Libation Bearers*: "I ask that your revenger come to our enemies, father, and that the killers be killed in just return."[50] It is not that women did press for such revenge in society so much as anxiety that, out of control, they might. This leads, McHardy writes, to women's literary depiction as "bloody avengers."[51]

Taking a Ghost to Court

Clytemnestra's Ghost v. Orestes is resolved when Athena creates a permanent democratic murder court to hear the charges and testimony. *The Eumenides* celebrates the supposed evolution of Athenian law away from a more violent past, personified in the ghost. That past is a romance of violence, an imagined (and largely literary) former age where blood-revenge was routinely sought, whereas things are better "now." It is only fair to observe that the settlement of violent disputes in the archaic age was not inevitably mortal. There were avenues to nonviolent settlement. Arbitration by local elders or lords might be available, as might material recompense. Aspects of these older dispute-resolution measures had existed in Greek systems of justice since at least the sixth century BCE.[52] The Greek word *dike*, most often translated as "justice," carries the sense of "balance" or "settlement," suggesting that heritage.

Writers in the Greek-speaking world wanted to believe in an idealized notion of justice, one that softens or does away with the reflexive turn to violence. Thus Hesiod writes in *Works and Days* that "justice beats violence when the race is run."[53] *The Eumenides* dramatizes the Athenian wish to believe that reformed institutions, including the courts, improved on the old ways, sublimated and redirected the supposed anger and violence of former times, and represented the triumph of democracy.

The court voting on Orestes's fate is located at the Areopagus, the "Hill of Ares,"[54] site of an ancient court made up of aristocrats known as archons. According to a myth mentioned by Demosthenes, the gods themselves adjudicated disputes at the site: "Only in this court did the gods deign to both exact and demand satisfaction for homicide," including a case in which twelve gods ruled in the case between the Eumenides and Orestes.[55] Aeschylus gently modifies the myth, replacing the twelve-god jury with a dozen Athenian citizens.

The choice of this court is remarkable, perhaps even brave. In 462 BCE, only four years before the *Oresteia* debuted, the politician Ephialtes had managed to strip the aristocratic Areopagus of nearly all its jurisdictions except for murder. His were just the latest in a series of reforms that had begun with Draco six generations before. Reforms of the Areopagus tended to favor widened access to the law and the courts, a diversity of views and participants (in other words, easing the former aristocratic hold), and equality under the law. The court was thus a real-life synecdoche for the constant tug-of-war between aristocratic and democratic interests. Ephialtes would be assassinated in 461 BCE for his efforts. Despite such recent history and the enduring controversy over the court, Aeschylus makes it central to the resolution of the *Oresteia* and the ghost's case.

Aeschylus navigates this sensitive strait by ensuring that, while *The Eumenides* celebrates democratic court reform, aristocratic values (embodied in the Furies) find a place of honor as well. The Furies had a confused provenance in myth, associated with both punishment of murder and mercy to killers. A temple at the foot of the Areopagus was built to them, and murderers were said to take sanctuary there to protect them from reprisals. That temple will play a role in the resolution.

Fear, Anger, and Violence

Wholly on the basis of the older ethics, the Furies insist on their authority, taking as sacred their ancient charge as "upright witnesses on behalf of the dead."[56] When Athena announces her citizen jury plan, the Furies see it for what it is, "a revolution of new laws."[57] They defend their role on ancient grounds, the place of fear in making people shun evil: "There are times when fear is good and should stay firm as guardian of the heart. It is fitting to learn wisdom under stress." Who, they ask, "if he did not educate his heart in fear, would still honor justice the same way?"[58] This, too, has force in the new Athens as in the old. As if to assure the Furies they've been heard, Athena endorses the continuing role of fear: "what mortal could be just if he was afraid of nothing?"[59]

Discomfort runs throughout *The Eumenides* over getting between matricide and punishment. The ghost of Clytemnestra, victim of the taboo crime, demands what it assumes archaic courts, presided over by aristocrats, would have voted for: the death of the murderer. The ghost's claim is strong and Athena knows it. "This issue is too weighty for any mortal to judge," she tells Orestes, "nor is it even lawful for me to decide on murder cases inciting the rage of the Furies."[60] They, she says, have a charge "that does not permit them to be dismissed lightly," not only because of the issues of pollution and punishment involved, but also because revenge may continue beyond the verdict: "if they lose their case, the venom of resentment will soak the ground, a horrific, perpetual plague in the land."[61]

In a tense, dark dialogue with Athena, the Furies rage in "shame" and "anger" at being, as they rightly sense, sidetracked in favor of a court of mortals. This interplay drills to the core of all the anxieties unleashed by the ghost of Clytemnestra: anger and violence themselves. The ghost cries out for violent retribution, and every other character, even Orestes, feels a grain of justice therein. The Furies seem poised to wreak havoc throughout the land if their cause loses. As advocates (essentially) for the ghost, they embody the potentially uncontainable nature of anger, its perpetual threat to harmony in social life.

Athenian courts of law, as perhaps all courts do, harbored a great irony. Brought into existence out of the hatred of violence, law seeks to limit violence, prevent it, or distinguish between the righteous and unrighteous in violent clashes. The court restrains the hand, prevents battles, seizes property, sometimes kills for the sake of justice. But in punishing violence, the courts, especially murder courts such as the Areopagus, represent the state's monopoly of violence.[62] As Heraclitus noted, justice (*dike*) is strife or contention (*eris*)—including, among much else, the clash of interests in court and the improvisational way justice sometimes is achieved, through consensus, compromise, and equity.

René Girard memorably pointed out the complexity of justice in the tragedies: "The obligation never to shed blood cannot be distinguished from the obligation to exact vengeance on those who shed it."[63] Hatred of violence, no matter how apparently justified, is itself violence. The circle is perhaps inescapable, especially for those who seek justice or seek to enact it. Girard concludes that the essence of tragedy is not "a coherent theory of vengeance" but rather the clash of viewpoints and desires regarding it, since "in tragedy each character passionately embraces or rejects vengeance depending on the position he occupies at any given moment in the scheme of the drama."[64] That passionate contention is what the ghost of Clytemnestra has ignited.

There is no solution—only management. Agnes Callard, writing in an April 2020 *Boston Review* roundtable on the proper place of anger in society, drives the point home: while anger is "morally corrupting," it nevertheless can often be "completely correct." Her "simple, devastating conclusion" is that it is impossible for people "to respond rightly to being treated wrongly. We can't be good in a bad world."[65] Anger and violence have their uses, indeed their indispensable roles; human beings must find a way to contain or divert their potential for chaos and guide anger into safer directions. Accordingly, *The Eumenides* does not seek to banish anger or violence—it seeks to domesticate them in the courts and focus them outwardly, on enemies of Athens.

The Decision

The citizen jury of Athenian citizens is hung in a six-six deadlock—an acknowledgment of the solemnity of the crime—so the decision falls to the goddess. The case for Orestes is first religious, next political, and only finally legal. As for the religious aspect, the Furies track his blood-spoor wherever he goes, assuming it bears the trace of pollution. But Orestes has (apparently unknown to the Furies or the ghost) been cleansed through "many purifying rituals."[66] So much for that aspect of punishment.

The political aspect all but outweighs the other two. The sponsorship of Apollo and Athena is dispositive. Whenever you have gods as star witness and judge, things are looking good for your case. "This man," Apollo testifies, "was a lawful suppliant, a guest in my sanctuary, and I was his purification from bloodshed."[67] Then there is the absent ghost of Agamemnon. Just as the Furies represent Clytemnestra's ghost, Orestes's case represents the slain king's. Grilled by the Furies at trial, Orestes, having openly admitted to killing his mother, says, "I am confident Father will send me protection from the grave."[68] In this agon between two ghosts and two genders, the decision favoring Orestes is the triumph of one ghostly will.

There remains the legal question, whether Orestes must pay the "debt" for matricide. Resolution rests first on Apollo's argument based on the father's line: the father is parent to the child, but the mother is not, better seen as a stranger who "is nurse to the newly-implanted embryo."[69] Therefore, murder of the father is kin-murder but murder of the mother is not. Clytemnestra is thus reduced, in effect, to a stranger who murders the head of the family, and a son would have been expected to kill such a murderer without further penalty.[70] Athena seconds this patrilineal argument: "in all things save marriage, I am absolutely for the male and entirely on the father's side."[71]

With verdict issued, Athena must turn the Furies away from continued pursuit. This she does by appealing to their aristocratic values. It was, after all, on those very grounds that they had allowed her to take the lead in resolving the case: "We honor you because you are well-born and of honorable parentage."[72] The goddess persuades them that, while they have lost honor in the decision, they will gain even more in their new position, as The Kindly Ones installed at their temple at the Areopagus. "I promise you solemnly," Athena says, that "you will have an immense sanctuary in a just land where you will preside on shining thrones at your fires, worshipped and honored by my citizens."[73] She knows her audience. The Furies ask eagerly, "What place do you say I will have?"[74] and "What honor will be mine?"[75] Athena calls on them to redirect anger and violence, not to madden the land with "keen goads to bloodshed"[76] or sow among the people "the spirit of tribal war and aggression."[77] She counsels the Furies-turned-Kindly-Ones to direct anger outward: "let war be with foreign foes."[78] At last, they relent: "It seems you've won me over with your spells. I let my anger go."[79] Athena's legal and nonlegal solutions, the institution of a secular jury system to decide issues of murder and revenge, and the reinvention of the Furies as The Kindly Ones or Eumenides draws a line under an epoch.

In neither play nor reality was the transition that definitive. There would be plenty of retributive law and extralegal retribution; elements of honor and revenge persisted in the Athens judicial system, as such elements still do in the courts. Danielle Allen writes that the courts in effect allowed Athenian citizens to compete publicly. A man convicted in court lost honor while his victim gained it. Revenge, in court or out, was ever a bid to restore balance to perceived levels of honor.[80] Rightly has David Cohen written that litigation in Athens can be seen as an extension of feuds outside the courts. Cohen's book *Law, Violence and Community in Classical Athens* insists that courts were not apart from society, but rather that social values in that agonistic community continued to saturate the practice of law, even as the courts grew more democratic. Courts, Cohen writes, "rather than finally resolving conflicts, may provide yet another arena where they are pursued."[81]

If there is a "sacrifice" in *The Eumenides*, it may be the ghost of Clytemnestra. At the end of the *Oresteia*, it and the ghost of Agamemnon are silent and nowhere. Orestes will assume the throne for which he killed his mother. Patrilineality has triumphed, and the male domain is firmly on top. The Furies accept a new place of honor within a democratic system of law; aristocratic values are honored even as they are absorbed into a democratic bureaucracy. We are left in the Athens of an idealized "now," when the "revolution of laws" has banished the old ways. And the old ghosts.

Such an ending democratizes the courts, silences a ghost, and placates the Furies, but *The Eumenides* remains an anxious tragedy. Athenian law evolved along with the democracy itself; as with that democracy, the city-state's legal institutions reflected the power-struggle between wealthy, powerful interests and the wider citizenry, a struggle that never really ended. Perhaps definitions should always recognize such struggle as an intimate engine of democracies, rendering them perpetually unstable but also forcing perpetual improvisation and refreshment. Perhaps, too, the main subject of the tragedies of Aeschylus was always Athens, where it is "now," how it had gotten "here," what lay ahead. On his stages he enacted what most moved and frightened his audience, distancing it in other voices, characters, and contexts. So the ghost of Darius bespeaks the fears of the winner, that fate could take all away at one false decision, that *daimones* from within and without might prompt a misstep that brings down all. And the ghost of Clytemnestra is woven out of anxiety over pollution, gender, violence, and that continual, fruitful anxiety integral to democracies: instability, experiment, agon among interests, the ever-present feeling and fact and threat of unfinished business.

Notes

1   The *choregos* or sponsor/producer of the trilogy was Pericles himself, then around twenty-three.
2   Salamis was fought in September 480 BCE, and the Dionysia took place in the spring.
3   The usual setting of the House of Atreus stories was Mycenae, but Aeschylus sets them in Argos, possibly in honor of a recent alliance between that city and Athens. The democratic element in Athenian politics favored this alliance, and the aristocratic element did not.
4   Fiona McHardy, *The Ideology of Revenge in Ancient Greek Culture: A Study of Ancient Athenian Revenge Ethics* (Exeter: University of Exeter Press, 1999), 108.
5   Jacques Derrida, *Specters of Marx*, trans. by Peggy Kamuf (New York: Routledge, 2006), 220.
6   E.R. Dodds, *The Greeks and the Irrational* (Berkeley: University of California Berkeley Press, 1951), 2–13.
7   Derrida, 11.
8   Dodds, 103–105, 109.
9   Aeschylus, *Persians*, vol. 1, trans. Herbert Weir Smith (Cambridge, MA: Harvard University Press, 1926), 202. The texts of *Agamemnon*, *The Libation Bearers*, and *The Eumenides* are those of *Aeschylus*, vol. 2, trans. Herbert Weir Smith (Cambridge, MA: Harvard University Press, 1926). Accessed at Tufts

University, *Perseus Digital Library 4.0*, http://www.perseus.tufts.edu/hopper. Translations are mine except where noted.

10 *Persians*, 266–267.

11 Ibid., 296.

12 Ibid., 302–310. See also Mary Ebbot, "The List of the War Dead in Aeschylus's 'Persians,'" *Harvard Studies in Classical Philology* 100 (2000): 83–96.

13 *Persians*, 603.

14 Ibid., 609.

15 H.R. Rose, "Ghost Ritual in Aeschylus," *Harvard Theological Review* 43: 4 (October 1950): 263. Rose notes that Atossa in *Persians* performs this ritual very much the way Odysseus does in contacting the dead in the Circe episode of the *Odyssey*.

16 Atossa, the only queen Darius ever had, may have had a reputation for being able to get her husband Darius to do anything. Herodotus, writing about twenty years after the debut of *Persians*, remarks that "there was no limit . . . to the influence wielded by Atossa." Herodotus, *The Histories*, trans. Tom Holland (New York: Viking, 2013), 466.

17 *Persians*, 620–621.

18 Ibid., 633.

19 Ibid., 644.

20 Ibid., 660.

21 Andrew Buse and Peter Stott, *Ghosts: Deconstruction, Psychoanalysis, History* (London: Palgrave Macmillan, 1999), 11.

22 Ibid.

23 *Persians*, 679–680.

24 The ghost's last words constitute, with the "no-ships" line, a firm bookend. At its exit, the ghost bids the elders a goodbye with strangely little connection to the matter at hand, as if it were just an old man speaking to other old men: "To you, then, elders, farewell, and in spite of your troubles, take pleasure in each day you have, for wealth is worth nothing to the dead." Ibid., 840–842.

25 Reviewed in Elisabeth Vincentelli, "'Persians' Review: Aeschylus's Ancient Portrait of Defeat," *New York Times* July 26, 2020. https://www.nytimes.com/2020/07/26/theater/the-persians-review-aeschylus.html.

26 Phillip Zapkin, "Persians, by Aeschylus, 25 July 2020," *Theatre Reviews Blog.* https://phillipzapkin.wordpress.com/2020/07/26/the-persians-by-aeschylus-25-july-2020. The agonizing distance between Darius and Atossa is eloquently captured in Marilena Anastasiadou's lead photograph for Elisabeth Venticelli, "'The Persians' Review." See note 25.

27 *Persians*, 331.

28 Ibid., 445.

29 Ibid., 724–725.

30 Dodds, 11–12.

31 *Persians*, 749–751. Xerxes, in the ghost's view, has shown sinful hubris that seeks to dishonor another by asserting superiority, which in turn may bring

retribution to restore the balance of honor. See Nick Fisher, *Hybris: A Study of the Values of Honour and Shame in Ancient Greece* (Liverpool: University of Liverpool Press, 1992): 1.

32 *Persians*, 1005–1007.

33 Sometime in August 479 BCE.

34 *Libation Bearers*, 50 (κλύειν, ἀκοῦσαι).

35 Ibid., 39–41

36 Fiona McHardy, in *Revenge in Athenian Culture* (London: Bloomsbury Academic, 2008), remarks that in Homer, the Clytemnestra story involves "the anxiety felt by men unable to offer adequate protection for their wives. An adulterous wife, it is implied, does not only create anxiety about the paternity of her husband's children. She can also become involved in plots to kill him" (108).

37 Anton Bierl, "*Klytaimestra Tyrannos*: Fear and Tyranny in Aeschylus' *Oresteia* (with a Brief Comparison to *Macbeth*)," *Comparative Drama* 51: 4 (2017), 528.

38 In some versions of the myth, Agamemnon drives Aegisthus out of the kingship. In any event, the grievances of Aegisthus extend back generations. In *Agamemnon*, his motives are notably internecine: he says Agamemnon's murder is just, since he has now paid with his life for the evil deeds of his father, Atreus.

39 Aeschylus chooses this version; some have Aegisthus striking the blow.

40 *The Eumenides*, 11.

41 Ibid., 1625.

42 Ibid., 1372–1406.

43 McHardy, *Ideology*, 101.

44 Danielle Allen, *The World of Prometheus: The Politics of Punishing in Democratic Athens* (Princeton, NJ: Princeton University Press, 2000), 134.

45 *The Eumenides*, 154.

46 Ibid., 423.

47 Ibid., 95–98.

48 McHardy, *Revenge*, 8.

49 McHardy (*Revenge*, 40) remarks that "although there is no evidence of women ever approaching the violence level of men in any society and no evidence of any culture in which men are less violent than women, Greek literary texts often depict women as more bloodthirsty than their male counterparts."

50 *The Libation Bearers*, 143–144.

51 McHardy, *Revenge*, 40.

52 Michael Gagarin, "Early Greek Law," in *The Cambridge Companion to Ancient Greek Law*, eds. Michael Gagarin and David Cohen (Cambridge: Cambridge University Press 2005), 82–94.

53 Hesiod, "Works and Days" in *The Homeric Hymns and Homerica*, trans. by Hugh G. Evelyn-White (Cambridge, MA: Harvard University Press, 1914),

217–218. http://www.perseus.tufts.edu/hopper/text?doc=Perseus%3Atext%3A1999.01.0131%3Acard%3D202.

54 That may be a folk etymology. The rock may have been dedicated originally to the Furies themselves.

55 Demosthenes, "Against Aristocrates [23.66]," in *Demosthenes with an English Translation*, trans. by A.T. Murray (Cambridge, MA: Harvard University Press, 1939). http://www.perseus.tufts.edu/hopper/text?doc=Perseus%3Atext%3A1999.01.0074%3Aspeech%3D23%3Asection%3D66.

56 *The Eumenides*, 320.

57 Ibid., 470.

58 Ibid., 517–526.

59 Ibid., 698.

60 Ibid., 470–472.

61 Ibid., 475–479.

62 Max Weber, in "Politics as a Vocation," speaks of the evolution of social organization from a past in which the use of physical violence by groups such as the clan was completely normal, to the modern state, which successfully "lays claim to the monopoly of legitimate violence within the community." In *The Vocation Lectures*, trans. by Rodney Livingstone (Indianapolis: Hackett, 2004), 33. *The Eumenides* seems to portray democratic Athens as being in the midst of a comparable evolution.

63 René Girard, *Violence and the Sacred* (New York: Bloomsbury, 2005), 15.

64 Ibid., 15–16.

65 Agnes Callard, "The Philosophy of Anger," *Boston Review*, April 22, 2020. http://bostonreview.net/forum/agnes-callard-philosophy-anger.

66 *The Eumenides,* 276.

67 Ibid., 576–579.

68 Ibid., 599.

69 Ibid., 659.

70 McHardy, *Ideology*, 13. This ethic of "kin solidarity" is one of those bedrock principles that also can lead, as in Orestes's case, to all but insoluble complexities.

71 *The Eumenides*, 737–738.

72 Ibid., 435.

73 Ibid., 803–807.

74 Ibid., 892.

75 Ibid., 894.

76 Ibid., 858.

77 Ibid., 863–864.

78 Ibid., 864.

79 Ibid., 900.

80 Allen, 60–61.

81 David Cohen, *Law, Violence and Community in Classical Athens: Key Themes in Ancient History* (Cambridge: Cambridge University Press, 1995), 23–24.

Works Cited

Aeschylus. *The Persians*, in *Aeschylus*, volume 1, trans. Herbert Weir Smith. Cambridge, MA: Harvard University Press, 1926. Accessed at Tufts University, *Perseus Digital Library 4.0*, http://www.perseus.tufts.edu/hopper.

Aeschylus. *Agamemnon, The Libation Bearers,* and *The Eumenides*, in *Aeschylus*, volume 2, trans. Herbert Weir Smith. Cambridge, MA: Harvard University Press 1926. Accessed at Tufts University, *Perseus Digital Library 4.0*, http://www.perseus.tufts.edu/hopper.

Allen, Danielle. *The World of Prometheus: The Politics of Punishing in Democratic Athens.* Princeton, NJ: Princeton University Press, 2000.

Bierl, Anton. "*Klytaimestra Tyrannos*: Fear and Tyranny in Aeschylus's *Oresteia* (with a Brief Comparison to *Macbeth*)." *Comparative Drama* 51:4 (Winter 2017): 528–563.

Buse, Andrew and Peter Stott. *Ghosts: Deconstruction, Psychoanalysis, History.* London: Palgrave Macmillan, 1999.

Callard, Agnes. "The Philosophy of Anger." *Boston Review*, April 22, 2020. http://bostonreview.net/forum/agnes-callard-philosophy-anger.

Cohen, David. *Law, Violence and Community in Classical Athens: Key Themes in Ancient History.* Cambridge: Cambridge University Press, 1995.

Demosthenes. *Against Aristocrates* [23.66]. *Demosthenes with an English Translation*, trans. A.T. Murray. Cambridge, MA: Harvard University Press, 1939, http://www.perseus.tufts.edu/hopper/text?doc=Perseus%3Atext%3A1999.01.0074%3Aspeech%3D23%3Asection%3D66.

Derrida, Jacques. *Specters of Marx*, trans. Peggy Kamuf. New York: Routledge, 2006.

Dodds, E.R. *The Greeks and the Irrational.* Berkeley: University of California Berkeley Press, 1951.

Ebbot, Mary. "The List of the War Dead in Aeschylus's '*Persians*.'" *Harvard Studies in Classical Philology* 100 (2000): 83–96.

Fisher, Nick. *Hybris: A Study of the Values of Honour and Shame in Ancient Greece.* Liverpool: University of Liverpool Press, 1992.

Gagarin, Michael. "Early Greek Law." In *The Cambridge Companion to Ancient Greek Law*, eds. Michael Gagarin and David Cohen. Cambridge: Cambridge University Press, 2005: 82–94.

Girard, René. *Violence and the Sacred.* New York: Bloomsbury, 2005.

Herodotus. *The Histories*, trans. Tom Holland. New York: Viking, 2013.

Hesiod. *The Homeric Hymns and Homerica*, trans. Hugh G. Evelyn-White. Cambridge, MA: Harvard University Press, 1914, http://www.perseus.tufts.edu/hopper/text?doc=Perseus%3Atext%3A1999.01.0131%3Acard%3D202.

McHardy, Fiona. *The Ideology of Revenge in Ancient Greek Culture: A Study of Ancient Athenian Revenge Ethics.* Exeter: University of Exeter Press, 1999.

McHardy, Fiona. *Revenge in Athenian Culture.* London: Bloomsbury Academic, 2008.

Rose, H.R. "Ghost Ritual in Aeschylus." *Harvard Theological Review* 43:4 (October 1950): 257–280.

Vincentelli, Elisabeth. "'The Persians' Review: Aeschylus's Ancient Portrait of Defeat." *New York Times* July 26, 2020. https://www.nytimes.com/2020/07/26/theater/the-persians-review-aeschylus.html.

Weber, Max. *The Vocation Lectures*, trans. Rodney Livingstone. Indianapolis: Hackett, 2004.

Zapkin, Phillip. "The Persians, by Aeschylus, 25 July 2020." In *Theatre Reviews Blog*. Available from https://phillipzapkin.wordpress.com/2020/07/26/the-persians-by-aeschylus-25-july-2020.

2

A Theatre of Ghosts: Spirits on the Traditional Japanese Stage

Kevin J. Wetmore, Jr.

Of the variety of traditional Japanese theatres, the four major types form linked pairs: nō and kyōgen developed and are performed together, and kabuki and bunraku developed simultaneously, influenced each other, and share a common dramatic repertory. Nō (also written as noh) and kyōgen developed in the fourteenth century as a theatre of the elite, arising out of court dance, dramatic narratives, and Zen Buddhist aesthetics. Kabuki and bunraku developed separately in the seventeenth century as a theatre of the commoners, the former a dance drama and the latter a puppet theatre.

From their inceptions, linked with rituals to propitiate the dead, the theatres of Japan regarded ghosts as a major subject and dramatized apparitions in sundry ways. Japanese theatre is inherently ghostly, linked with the return and remembering of the dead in its origins and subject matter, frequently depicting ghosts, even as it grew out of memorial rituals for the departed.[1] As with all drama, Japanese stage ghosts indicate the culture's attitudes towards death. The samurai—a warrior caste, pledged to serve unto death, even to the point of committing ritual suicide (*seppuku*) to atone for failure or dishonor—developed plays featuring tragic ghosts seeking release from this world. Kabuki and bunraku, theatre for the middle class and working poor, featured supernatural entities (usually women) who achieved retribution against those who wronged them, often as a result of living in squalor. Nō ghosts are sad and regretful; kabuki and bunraku ghosts vengeful, angry and violent; kyōgen ghosts, parodying nō ghosts, reduce nō's tragic apparitions to ludicrous extremes.

Marjorie Garber reminds us, "A ghost is an embodiment of the disembodied, a re-membering of the dismembered, an articulation of the disarticulated and inarticulate."[2] This metaphor is literalized on stage. The ghosts of Japanese theatre, embodied by actors, speak, sing and dance, and exist within the dramatic world as memories come to life, assuming a remarkable variety of forms. This essay shall examine each form in light of why the ghosts appear, how they are represented, and to what end are they depicted.

Nō: Tragic Ghosts

Developed in the late fourteenth century by dancer Zeami Motokiyo (*c.* 363–
*c.*1443),[3] nō grew out of court dance and music, stories from the *Heike
Monogatari* (*Tale of the Heike*, *c.*1330, which tells the history of the Genpei
war, 1180–1185) and the *Genji Monogatari* (*Tale of Genji*, *c.*1008, a novel of
the life and loves of the eponymous "shining prince"), and Zen Buddhist
aesthetic philosophy. Because Buddhist theology maintains that we are
attached to this world through desire and can only be released from it by
relinquishing that which holds us to the world, the plays often require a
Buddhist monk or priest to pray for the release of the ghost. An elite theatre
for the court, nō tells tales of warriors and the women who love them,
focusing on the impermanence of things and the idea that suggestion is more
powerful than statement.[4]

Nō literally begins in the rites designed to appease ghosts, and two leading
scholars of the art form, Akima Toshio[5] and Umehara Takeshi, agree that the
origin of nō, other than in court dance, lies in rituals for the dead. Toshio
argues that the Motokiyo family, from which nō creators Zeami and his father
Kan'ami came, lived among the Asobi-be, who conducted funeral rites.
Akima, locating the origin of ghosts in this background, states that nō itself
descends from performed funeral rites with a focus on death and the repose
of the spirit. Takeshi, on the other hand, argues that Zeami, professional
performer of ceremonies to pacify souls of the dead (a *chinkonsha*), used
those rituals as a model for *mugen nō*, that is, plays about phantasmal subjects
(ghosts, demons, monsters and gods), as opposed to *genzai nō*, which are
plays about living humans.

In mugen nō, all the narratives follow a similar plot. At the outset, a priest
or other wanderer, called the *waki*, arrives at the site of a famous event, where
he meets a strange old man or woman, the *shite*, who is connected to the
place. In an interlude, a local resident, the *ai-kyogen*, explains the history of
the place and the famous event that caused it to be haunted. In the second
part, the shite returns, revealing that he or she is actually a *yūrei*, the ghost
of the famous person who died there. The shite bemoans his or her own
death and torment, often because they are still attached to either the event,
the people, or their life at the time. The priest then prays for the release of
the ghost. Mugen nō thus is structured as a chance encounter with a ghost
in the place where it died and/or was buried without realizing its true nature,
followed by the revelation of that ghost *qua* ghost, which, by admitting its
attachment to the world, begins the process of being released from it.

The majority of Zeami's plays, according to Thomas Blenman Hare, are
mugen nō,[6] which implies that the creator of the form was especially

interested in presenting ghosts on stage. Four Zeami plays—*Atsumori*, *Tadanori*, *Sumidagawa* and *Matsukaze*—illuminate the variety of ghost stories within mugen nō, each revealing a ghost still attached to the place of its death, needing help to be released from the world of desire, in order to enter Buddha's paradise.

Atsumori is an example of a *shura mono*, a warrior play in which, as is often the case, the warrior is already dead. Atsumori was a young warrior during the Genpei War, killed at the Battle of Ichi-no-Tani by Kumagai, who, sickened by death and war, then becomes the monk Renshō. This story is found in the *Heike Monogatari*. In the play, decades after the battle, Renshō arrives at Ichi-no-Tani and reminisces while grass cutters tend the plants in the fields where the battle was fought. One youth stays behind and asks Renshō who he is and what happened at the site. A villager then tells the story of the death of young Atsumori, Atsumori's gifted flute playing in life, and the abjuring of the samurai life by Kumagai, who became a monk after the death of Atsumori. The youth then returns in full battle regalia, revealing himself as Atsumori was when he died. Renshō prays for him, and the play ends with Atsumori's ghost begging, "Pray for me, O pray for my return."[7] A popular play in the nō repertory, probably because it resonates with samurai life, *Atsumori* exposes Atsumori's attachment to life and regret for his death, paralleling Kumagai's regret for killing a young and beautiful artist who had been left behind by his army. Neither scary nor similar to spirits in Western theatre, the ghost is a tragic remnant of a life cut short, who clings to its past too tenaciously to move on.

A similar spirit is found in *Tadanori*, whose eponymous warrior has a very different concern. Like Atsumori, Tadanori died on the losing side at Ichi-no-Tani. His ghost lingers because before his death he published a poem anonymously and, seeking fame as a poet in his afterlife, he wants his name attached to it. His ghost, appearing as a monk who has come to the site of his death, sings:

> I am ashamed! Here where death took me,
> a dream recalls my form into vision,
> real as waking. My heart roams once more
> the past that old tale I shall tell you now:
> for this my spirit, transformed, has come.[8]

He begs the monk to have his name attached to his poem: "Do this, I beg you, and give my spirit peace."[9] Once his ghost knows that future generations will see his name when they read the emperor's collection of poems, he will in this way live forever. His desire to be known evinces yet again a form of attachment.

The monk agrees to try to get the poem attributed to Tadanori so that the ghost may move on from this world. In this play, as in *Atsumori*, the ghost's purpose is to provoke sympathy rather than fear or terror, and thereby remind the audience of life's impermanence and the need to let go of all attachments, lest one linger behind in sadness.

There are other types of ghost than dead warrior. *Sumidagawa* features the ghost of a dead child. A ferryman by the Sumida River tells the story of how last year Yoshida, a twelve-year-old boy, collapsed on the bank of the river and died. His mother, looking for him, prays at his tomb. She cries out: "For his own death, he left his birthplace. / Deep in the East, / he became earth by the side of the road. / There he lies buried, / With only the new growth of spring / To cover his tomb."[10] After the mother hears a voice that she is certain is her child's, the boy's ghost appears. The mother touches his shoulder and takes his hand, but then boy's spirit, having seen his mother, calls on Amida Buddha and "his shape fades and is gone."[11] Released from his ghostly existence, however, his memory now haunts his mother, who has lost her only child. Like many mugen nō, this play suggests that although ghosts may appear to characters in dreams, the fact that the character is uncertain if she or he is dreaming renders the ghost no less real. Again, the play underscores the danger of all attachments: while the boy has been released, his mother lives on, driven to madness by her loss.

Female ghosts appear as well. *Aoi no Ue* (*The Lady Aoi*) features a female *onryō* (a vengeful type of *yūrei* more common to kabuki), the Lady Rokujō, from the *Genji Monogatari*, tormented by jealousy even after death, a character whose ghost is also the protagonist in the play *Nonomiya* (*The Shrine in the Country*). *Izutsu* also features the ghost of a dead woman, the eponymous lady who, in a dream, appears to a monk, lamenting her dead lover and begging for the monk's help to find release. Arguably, however, the most famous of the *kazura-mono* (woman plays) is *Matsukaze* (originally *Matsukaze Murasame*).

In *Matsukaze*, a Buddhist monk travels to Suma Bay near Kobe, finds a tablet commemorating two sisters, Matsukaze and Murasame ("Pining Wind" and "Autumn Rain"), nailed to a pine tree. The sisters were deserted lovers of Yukihira, a court official. A villager tells the monk: "There they lie buried deep in the earth, / yet their names still linger, and in sign / ever constant in hue, a single pine / leaves a green autumn."[12] Two salt makers who arrive and mourn their lives, while pouring brine to make salt, tell the monk they are the ghosts of the sisters. Matsukaze, dancing madly and possessed by her love for Yukihira, puts on the hat and cloak he left behind when he abandoned them.

At this point, remarkably, Murasame encourages Matsukaze to let go of desire and cease being a ghost: "How awful! This state you are in is exactly what drowns you in the sin of clinging! You have not yet forgotten the mad passion you felt when we still belonged to the world. That is a pine tree. Yukihira is not there."[13] Murasame, having been released from this world, then sits with the chorus, while Matsukaze continues to weep, sing, and dance around the tree. While the monk prays for them, the play ends as the sun rises, with one sister released and the other still a ghost. As in *Sumidagawa*, a pair of exemplary characters are presented, with one attaining release, and the other still attached to the world.

Although nō is a world of ghosts, inspired by Buddhist theology, some nō plays were also inspired by more recent events. Shelley Fenno Quinn, after Yonekura Toshiaki, observes that the second half of *Sanemori* dramatizes a story from the *Heike Monogatari*, but the first half is inspired "by the reported appearance in 1414 of the warrior Sanemori's ghost."[14] If ghosts represent an incursion of the past into the present, then the "actual" appearance of Sanemori and the play based on his story become the same thing: the wars, battles and the people who fought them erupt simultaneously as memory and cautionary tale.

"Noh ghosts are about memory, situated beyond, or after, the actual events," Quinn cannily observes. "More important than the events themselves in such plays is the lingering emotional residues of the ghost's story."[15] Nō ghosts, therefore, are to be pitied, rather than feared. As memories of historic tragedy and trauma, they ask, paradoxically, to be remembered and released. Interestingly, nō makes no attempt to theatrically present the ghost in a manner otherworldly, ephemerally, or as some kind of specter. The nō ghost wears a highly stylized costume and mask, with no attempt to represent the kind of ghostly qualities found in theatres in the West. The purpose of the spirit on stage in nō is to evoke the "lingering emotional residue" of individual loss, and of the pain the lost person feels at having had life cut short, unfulfilled.

Kyōgen: Parodic Ghosts

Kyōgen is the comic theatre—farcical, parodic, and satirical—that developed alongside serious and tragic nō. A typical performance evening, alternating serious drama with comic farce, would feature five nō plays, separated by kyōgen plays. As with mugen nō, *maikyōgen*, "dance kyogen", presents spirits on stage in a category that features a number of plays "which are explicitly modeled after the ghost plays of the noh drama."[16] These plays are "structurally and thematically modeled very closely on the ghost noh plays."[17] Just as with the dead warriors in shura mono nō, the protagonists of this category of kyōgen use song and dance to relate their tragic deaths and explain how they remain attached to the world through their suffering. What nō presents as the tragedy among noble characters, kyōgen presents as the folly of comedically lower-class humans, animals, and even inanimate objects.

Kyōgen ghosts are low—people such as an umbrella maker, in *Yūzen*, and a teahouse proprietor, in *Tsūen*, or even animals and plants: a clam eaten by someone in *Hamaguri*, an octopus in *Tako*, even, in *Tokoro*, the ghost of a potato that has been dug up, peeled, boiled and eaten.[18] These plays parody the language and structure of mugen nō. *Tsūen*, for example, is, as Karen Brazell asserts, "an almost line-by-line parody of the battle scene from the noh warrior play *Yorimasa*."[19] Whereas the warrior, Yorimasa, was overwhelmed by enemy soldiers and eventually killed, the teahouse proprietor is overwhelmed by too many customers and, exasperated, kills himself.

Ignoring for the moment the classist implications of samurai deaths being tragic and commoner deaths being comic, the reader might note that what creates the comedy is the application of the aesthetic, theology, and structure of mugen nō to absurd or ridiculous situations and people. While mocking the teahouse proprietor, the play also, by extension, equates a samurai with an overworked teahouse proprietor. Both classes are mocked in the play, and the result is neither the lingering emotional residues of the ghost's story of nō, nor the fear generated by the ghosts of kabuki, but comic ghosts, whose suffering creates bathos not pathos.

In *Semi*, when a traveling priest announces he has arrived at the village of Agematsu, he finds a slip of paper hung on a pine tree with a poem from the *Genji Monogatari*: "Dewdrops on a cicada's wing / lie hidden among the trees. / So, too, the tear-drenched sleeves / of my secret, secret longing" (shades of *Matsukaza*).[20] He humorously (and erroneously), concludes, "This poem seems to be a special eulogy composed a long time ago for a cicada shell."[21] A local man informs him that every summer people gather near the pine tree to listen to the cicadas. The previous summer, however, a particularly big cicada was eaten by a bird. Moved to pity, the priest promises to pray for the cicada. Touched by his prayers, the ghost of the cicada arrives and, with the help of a chorus of crows, narrates his death and torment—he was devoured by an owl. He prays that he will be released from torment and be reborn as "a bonze bug," a play on the Japanese words for priest and cicada.[22] Although the language parallels that of mugen nō plays in which a warrior's ghost laments his death and postmortem torments, instead of moving the audience to sympathy and self-reflection, it invites laughter.

Just as nō's encouragement of the audience to empathize with the ghost still attached to life is rooted in the aesthetics and beliefs of Buddhism, kyōgen's encouragement of laughter at suffering manifests, in many ways, yet another Buddhist belief embodied in a stage ghost. Haynes argues that although the difference between warrior and bug (or potato) makes kyōgen farcical, both remind the audience of its own attachments:

> While the noh protagonists are always in some way responsible for their fates, either because of violations of the prohibitions against taking life or because of the sin of attachment, by no stretch of the imagination can the non-human characters in the *maikyōgen* be considered so responsible. This is, presumably, deliberate, for responsibility would make them tragic figures, like the noh characters. It is precisely their total innocence which makes them suitable figures for farce.[23]

Haynes perhaps does not go far enough, for these plays are not only farce. They are satiric parodies that undercut the ideals and aesthetics of mugen nō. In lamenting the death and longing for release of ghosts of bugs, clams, and potatoes, the kyōgen plays undercut the emotional impact of the accompanying nō dramas. While the laments of a potato's ghost are funny, they nevertheless remind the audience that Buddhist tenets recognize no difference between a dead warrior and a dead potato.

Kabuki and Bunraku: Revengeful Ghosts (*Onryō*)

If the ghosts of nō are tragic spirits seeking release, the ghosts of kabuki and bunraku are dangerous, angry, violent, and vengeful. Although kabuki and bunraku are different theatrical forms—kabuki features human performers, bunraku features puppets—they share a dramatic repertory, visual aesthetic, and music. The plays described below, while predominantly performed by the kabuki have also been performed by the bunraku. They all feature terrifying, vengeful spirits, called *onryō*, which are different than (and a subcategory of) *yūrei* (ghost).

Kabuki began with a ghost story. As Benito Ortolani observes, the first documented performance by Okuni no Ise, the shrine maiden whose dance in the dry Kamo riverbed outside of Kyoto marked the origin of kabuki, was a variation of the shamanistic ritual of *tama-shizume*, a rite to appease an onryō, a dangerous, vengeful spirit.[24] "The very first kabuki performances were," Ortolani states, "in their essential content and dramatic structure, very similar to shamanic rituals to appease revengeful ghosts."[25] Thus, like nō, this theatre form, in part originates in placating spirits of the dead.

The plays, particularly in the early nineteenth century (Bunka-Bunsei era, 1804–1830), reflected "a growing taste for the bizarre,"[26] resulting in a flood of ghost plays. So-called *kaidan mono* are ghost plays famous for special effects (*keren*), quick costume and make-up changes (*hayagawari*), and violent murder scenes (*korishiba*), that result in the creation of an onryō. The ghosts in kaidan mono are active agents of retribution. Whereas Western ghosts are spectators (Hamlet's father watches after demanding revenge), Japanese ghosts not only torment those who killed them until they are driven into the arms of justice,[27] but also derive pleasure from watching their killers suffer.

The kabuki ghost is stylized very differently than the nō. The yūrei, designed to frighten, look more realistic than nō ghosts, like an uncanny version of their living selves. Instead of wearing masks, kabuki ghosts appear as corpses in white burial robes (replicating their appearance in paintings since the late seventeenth century), and they rely upon special makeup to render them bloody, hideous, often disfigured and terrifying. These were predominantly female (*Okiku, Oiwa, Otsuyu* and *Kasane*) ghosts; and what "contributed most to the establishment of the visual image of the female ghost was the kabuki theatre."[28] Presented on the kabuki stage in white burial robes, hair down and loose, face white and often distorted or disfigured—a look found even today in Japanese horror films—these ghosts are meant to scare the audience, rather than create lingering emotional effects.

The penchant for ghost stories on the stage began in the nineteenth century. One of the earliest plays featuring a ghost was by Tsuruya Nanboku IV (1755–1829), whose name would become synonymous with kaidan mono.[29] He wrote primarily for the kabuki, although he also composed for the bunraku, and wrote plays about each of the major female ghosts listed above. Although he had written several plays earlier, between 1804 and his death in 1829 Nanboku wrote 120 plays, many exemplifying the ghost genre and the theatrical preferences of the period.

The first, *Tenjiku Tokubei Ikoku Banashi* (*The Tale of Tokubei from India*, 1804), based on *Tenjiku Tokubeo Monogatari*, recounted the travels to India of the merchant Tenjiku Tokubei. The play tells the tale of Tenjiku Tokubei, a Korean warrior who seeks to overthrow the Bakufu (military government of Japan) through magic and monsters. The play featured quick changes, transformations and special effects, all designed to manifest the supernatural onstage. Tenjiku Tokubei summons both a monstrous tiger and a monstrous toad to battle his human enemies. The title character was played by Onoe Matsusuke I (1744–1815), an actor specializing in quick changes, who was considered to have founded kaidan mono acting.[30]

This play opened the genre's floodgates. In *Iroeiri Otogi Zōshi* (*Illustrated History in Vivid Colors*, 1808), Nanboku adapts Asada Icchō's puppet play, *Banshū sarayashiki* (*The Plate-Counting Mansion of Banshū*, 1741), an earlier bunraku play about Okiku, a maid who broke one plate from an exquisite set of ten. She was killed and her body thrown down a well that her ghost allegedly haunts.[31]

While Nanboku also wrote plays about other ghosts, such as in *Okuni gozen keshō no sugatami* (*The Make-up Mirror of Lady Okuni*, 1809), he wrote repeatedly about the allegedly real hauntings of Oiwa, Okiku and Kasane. In 1813 he composed his first take on the Kasane story, *Onoe Shōroku Sentaku Banashi* (*Onoe Shōroku's Washing Tale*), for the kabuki actor Onoe Shōroku. *Kesa Kakematsu narita no riken* (*The Pine Tree of the Priest's Robe and the Sharp Sword of Narita*, 1823), however, is generally considered Nanboku's masterpiece of kaidan mono about Kasane, and although many other writers have written versions of the story for kabuki, Nanboku's remains definitive.

Although the original story concerns a farmer and his wife, Nanboku makes Kasane a lady-in-waiting in love with Yoemon, a samurai who, unbeknownst to her, once had an affair with her mother, Kiku. When her father, Suke, discovered Yoemon and Kiku together, the lovers killed him, after which, Suke's ghost possesses Kasane, making her lame and disfigured. Years later, Yoemon meets Kasane on a riverbank where she believes they have come to commit love suicide (*shinju*). Suke's skull floats out of the river with a sickle in it. The chorus sings, "How strange! In the river, a skull comes floating. Joined are the spirit of Suke and a rusty sickle."[32] As Kasane screams and starts becoming deformed before the eyes of the audience, Yoemon realizes the ghost of Suke is again possessing her. Although she steals his sword, he murders her with the sickle as he dances. The act's final image (often still performed) is Kasane's dead body "standing beneath the willow tree, hands limp like a ghost, the sickle sticking out of her body...."[33] Interestingly, the play has two ghosts, Kasane and her father, who possesses and deforms her, both of whom want justice against Yoemon for killing them.

Arguably the most important and significant kaidan mono is Nanboku's *Tōkaidō Yotsuya Kaidan* (*The Ghost Story of Yotsuya on the Tokyo Highway*, 1825), based on an allegedly true (to this day companies perform rituals asking permission and forgiveness of Oiwa's ghost to ensure she does not harm the players or the production) story of supernatural horror. In the play, Iemon, a *ronin* (masterless samurai) marries Oiwa (after secretly killing her father), but, repulsed by Oiwa's appearance after she gives birth to their child and offered a better life if he marries a neighbor's daughter, he allows his neighbor to disfigure Oiwa with a poison. She is subsequently killed and mutilated when, in darkness, she runs into a sword Iemon has embedded in a post in their house. Blaming her death on the servant, Kohei, Iemon also kills him and nails both bodies to opposite sides of a door, which he throws into a canal. In one of the most famous scenes in kabuki—not least of which because the same actor plays both Kohei and Oiwa—the door pulled out of the canal displays each body in turn, as it comes to life before turning into a skeleton.[34]

Brandon and Leiter argue that Act 5 "resembles a nō play in structure"[35] inasmuch as Oiwa appears as a "beautiful country maiden" at the hermitage to which Iemon has fled, and he does not recognize her ghost, nor even that she is a ghost.[36] "You sound like that lunatic Oiwa" he tells her, "that everyone's gossiping about."[37] When she reveals herself to be Oiwa's vengeful ghost, he attacks but is unable to harm her. Oiwa then takes action that leads to the death of Iemon's bride, father-in-law, and mother-in-law. In the next scene we see him dreaming of Oiwa every night, exhausted and sinking into madness. His limp, twisted face, and shaking hands, "all indicate physical torment by the ghost of OIWA."[38] As the monks of the hermitage gather and pray, an eerie flute begins to play, the bell tolls, and the large lantern lighting the room drops into darkness before relighting to show the silhouette of Oiwa. The lantern then splits in half, and Oiwa's ghostly, disfigured head emerges, followed by her body. Iemon calls her a "vindictive ghost."[39] Iemon's servant, Chōbei, arrives and is told, "The ghost of Oiwa is here,"[40] after which Oiwa emerges from the altar and strangles Chōbei, then "drags the corpse to the compartment at the altar's rear" where his blood begins to drip off the altar.[41]

Only Iemon and his mother, Okuma, surrounded by praying monks, can see Oiwa. When Iemon threatens Oiwa with a sword, she tears Okuma's throat with her teeth, and then hangs upside down behind him. Slashing at her, he cuts open a screen to reveal the corpse of his stepfather, while Oiwa exits through a wall. She continues to torment and physically harass him, while he tells the monks, "A murderer haunted by a ghost can't escape heaven's net but I'll try anyway."[42] In short, after Oiwa's orchestrated accident, the play stages uncanny manifestations of her spirit, using special effects to horrify and delight the audience.

Finally, Yomoshichi, the husband of Oiwa's sister, arrives and announces, "I am her avenger!"[43] Iemon and Yomoshichi duel, but Oiwa, still inflicting pain on Iemon, summons rats to swarm up his sword. Once Iemon is disarmed, Yomoshichi kills him and Oiwa to find rebirth in Buddha's paradise since she is now avenged. Thus, the play ultimately presents its horrifying images in the service of justice being done.

Our last female ghost in this survey is Otsuyu, an amorous ghost who drains her lovers of life. Like the stories of Okiku, Kasane, and Oiwa, aspects of Otsuyu's story form a cautionary tale. The best-known version of her tale is *Kaidan botan dōrō* (*Peony Lantern Ghost Story*, 1884) by Sanyūtei Enchō (1839–1900), who also wrote *Shincho Kasane ga Fuchi* (*The True Story of Kasane Swamp*), another version of the Kasane story. In *Kaidan botan dōrō*, Saburo, a young man, falls in love with Otsuya, the daughter of his father's

Figure 2.1 Kabuki actor Arashi Rikan II as Iemon, confronted by an image of his murdered wife, Oiwa, on a broken lantern, referring to Katsushika Hokusai's *Hyaku monogatari* (*One Hundred Ghost Stories*) by Shunbaisai Hokuei, *c.*1832. Courtesy Metropolitan Museum of Art.

friend. They meet in secret, until he falls ill and is unable to see her for a long period. When he finally can look for her, he finds she is dead, but then she appears to him, explaining that her alleged death was an ugly rumor started by her aunt, who did not want them to marry, and they resume their relationship. One night his servant, seeing him making love to a decaying corpse, tells Saburo his love is actually a ghost. A Buddhist priest is summoned to help exorcise Otsuya, but Saburo cannot stay away from her, even though she is slowly draining his life. After one final night together, the servants find Saburo's smiling body holding Otsuya's skeleton. A key difference between *Kaidan botan dōrō* and the previous plays is that because Otsuya pines away for a lost love, rather than suffering violent death, this is the only kaidan mono play about the danger of attachment, rather than justice from beyond the grave.

Kabuki/bunraku drama also features male ghosts, as in *Tsuta Momiji Utsunoya Tōge* (*Ivy Autumn Leaves in the Utsunoya Pass*, 1856) by Kawatake Mokuami. In that play, Jūbei murders a masseur, Bunya, in order to steal Bunya's money. Bunya's ghost possesses Jūbei's wife, who attacks Jūbei leading Jūbei to kill his possessed wife. Jūbei also kills a criminal named Daiba no Nisa, who witnessed Bunya's murder and is attempting to blackmail Jūbei. The final murder leads to Jūbei's arrest.[44] Like the other ghosts who cannot achieve justice in this life, the murder victim's spirit drives the murderer crazy, ensuring that the murderer is either avenged (as in the case of *Tokaido Yotsuya Kaidan*), or punished. All of these plays link a tortured life to a haunting and early death, showing how horrific murder and torture convert its victim into a tormentor. Because kabuki/bunraku ghosts haunt a world where justice is often denied to women and to middle and lower class men, they embody a terrifying vengeance as the only means to justice.

Conclusion

A wide variety of ghosts haunt the traditional stages of Japan, from the lost, tragic ghosts of the nō to the vengeful onyrō of kabuki and bunraku. Each form of theatre has its own apparitions, distinguished by how they are represented on stage, why they haunt, how they interact with the living, and what they want. Both nō and kyōgen are aimed at an audience from the ruling and warrior classes, for whom death in battle is a real possibility, but nō spirits are internalized—invoked memories that seek to be released of their attachments—while kyōgen ghosts are mock-nō ghosts, trivializing and satirizing what nō takes seriously. Kabuki and bunraku, on the other hand, offer violent, externalized ghosts, aimed outward at the people who have harmed them. They seek vengeance and justice.

What ties all these ghosts together is rebellion against the status quo: they all want to resolve conditions that keep them from passing on. As Gillian Beers reminds us, "Ghost stories are to do with the insurrection, not the resurrection of the dead."[45] The spirits of Japanese theatre come back from the dead, regardless of form, to protest, to make things right, and to enforce justice before they finally leave this plane. A theatre originating in rituals to propitiate the dead thus also ironically tells stories about that very activity, whether by praying for the repose of a warrior who died too young or by watching the spirit of a wronged woman torment the man who wronged her.

Notes

1 See Gondō Yoshikazu, Nakagawa Akira, and Tsuyuno Gorō, *Nihon no yūrei: Nō kabuki rakugo* (Ōsaka: Ōsaka Shoseki), 1983.

2 Marjorie Garber, *Shakespeare's Ghost Writers: Literature as Uncanny Causality* (New York: Routledge, 1987), 15.

3 All Japanese names are given Japanese style, with surname first and given name second.

4 Through a series of treatises, Zeami outlines how one should write and perform nō plays. See Zeami Motokiyo, *On the Art of the Nō Drama: The Major Treatises of Zeami*, trans. J. Thomas Rimer and Yamazaki Masakazu (Princeton, NJ: Princeton University Press, 1984).

5 Toshio Akima, "The Songs of the Dead: Poetry, Drama, and Ancient Rituals in Japan," *Journal of Asian Studies* 41.3 (1982): 502–507.

6 Thomas Blenman Hare, *Zeami's Style: The Noh Plays of Zeami Motokiyo* (Stanford, CA: Stanford University Press, 1986), 297.

7 Royall Tyler, *Japanese Nō Dramas* (New York: Penguin, 1991), 48.

8 Ibid., 273.

9 Ibid.,

10 Ibid., 261.

11 Ibid., 263.

12 Ibid., 193.

13 Ibid., 202.

14 Shelley Fenno Quinn, *Developing Zeami: The Noh Actor's Attunement in Practice* (Honolulu: University of Hawai'i Press, 2005), 127.

15 Ibid., 14.

16 Carolyn Haynes. "Comic Inversion in Kyōgen: Ghosts and the Nether World," *The Journal of the Association of Teachers of Japanese* 22.1 (1988), 29.

17 Ibid., 34.

18 Ibid.; Karen Brazell, ed. "Semi," trans. Carolyn Haynes, in *Traditional Japanese Theatre* (New York: Columbia University Press, 1998), 284.

19 Brazell, 284.

20 Ibid., 287.

21 Ibid.

22 Ibid., 291.

23 Haynes, 37.

24 Benito Ortolani, *The Japanese Theatre: From Shamanistic Ritual to Contemporary Plurality* (Princeton, NJ: Princeton University Press, 1990), 173.

25 Ibid.

26 Samuel L. Leiter, *The Kabuki Encyclopedia: An English-Language Adaptation of Kabuki Jiten* (Westport, CT: Greenwood, 1979), 92.

27 Kevin J. Wetmore, Jr. "'Avenge Me!': Ghosts in English Renaissance and Kabuki Revenge Drama," in *Revenge Drama in European Renaissance and Japanese Theatre*, ed. Kevin J. Wetmore, Jr. (New York: Palgrave Macmillan, 2008), 75, 83.

28 Satoko Shimazaki, "Japan's Ghosts," in *The Ashgate Encyclopedia of Literary and Cinematic Monsters*, ed. J.A. Weinstock (Farnham: Ashgate Publishing, 2014), 274. Komatsu Kazuhiko, after Ema Tsutomu, sees the shaping hand of kabuki in visual representations of ghosts beginning in the Edo period, when kabuki began. Komatsu Kazuhiko, *An Introduction to Yōkai Culture*, trans. Hiroko Yoda and Matt Alt (Tokyo: Japan Publishing Industry Foundation, 2017), 142.

29 Nanboku was the first of two great writers of kaidan mono for the kabuki, the other being Kawatake Mokuami (1816–1893).

30 Leiter, 296.

31 Shimizaki, 274. Other plays about Okiku include Kawatake Mokuami's *Shin sarayashiki tsuki no amagasa* (*A New "Plate-Counting Mansion": An Umbrella on a Moonlight Night*, 1883).

32 James R. Brandon and Samuel L. Leiter, *Kabuki Plays on Stage Volume 3: Darkness and Desire, 1804-1863* (Honolulu: University of Hawai'i Press, 2002), 127.

33 Ibid., 133.

34 See ibid., 137.

35 Ibid.

36 Ibid., 148.

37 Ibid., 151.

38 Ibid., 156.

39 Ibid., 158.

40 Ibid., 159.

41 Ibid.

42 Ibid., 162.

43 Ibid.

44 Leiter, 414.

45 Gilliam Beers. "Ghosts," *Essays in Criticism* 28.3 (1978), 260.

Works Cited

Beers, Gillian. "Ghosts," *Essays in Criticism* 28.3 (1978): 259–264.

Brandon, James R. and Samuel L. Leiter. *Kabuki Plays on Stage Volume 3: Darkness and Desire, 1804-1863*. Honolulu: University of Hawai'i Press (2002).

Brazell, Karen, ed. "Semi," trans. Carolyn Haynes. *Traditional Japanese Theatre*. New York: Columbia University Press (1998).

Garber, Marjorie. *Shakespeare's Ghost Writers: Literature as Uncanny Causality*. New York: Routledge (1987).

Gondō Yoshikazu, Nakagawa Akira and Tsuyuno Gorō. *Nihon no yūrei: Noō kabuki rakugo*. Ōsaka: Ōsaka Shoseki (1983).

Hare, Thomas Blenman. *Zeami's Style: The Noh Plays of Zeami Motokiyo*. Stanford, CA: Stanford University Press (1986).

Haynes, Carolyn. "Comic Inversion in Kyōgen: Ghosts and the Nether World." *The Journal of the Association of Teachers of Japanese* 22.1 (1988): 29–40.

Komatsu Kazuhiko. *An Introduction to Yōkai Culture*, trans. Hiroko Yoda and Matt Alt. Tokyo: Japan Publishing Industry Foundation (2017).

Leiter, Samuel L. *The Kabuki Encyclopedia: An English-Language Adaptation of Kabuki Jiten*. Westport: Greenwood (1979).

Noma Shoji. *Japanese Theatre: From the Origin to the Present*. Osaka: Osaka Kyoiku Tosho (1998).

Ortolani, Benito. *The Japanese Theatre: From Shamanistic Ritual to Contemporary Plurality*. Princeton, NJ: Princeton University Press (1990).

Quinn, Shelley Fenno. *Developing Zeami: The Noh Actor's Attunement in Process*. Honolulu: University of Hawai'i Press (2005).

Shimazaki, Satoko. "Japan's ghosts," in *The Ashgate Encyclopedia of Literary and Cinematic Monsters*, ed. J.A. Weinstock. Surrey, UK: Ashgate Publishing (2014).

Toshio, Akima. "The Songs of the Dead: Poetry, Drama, and Ancient Death Rituals of Japan." *The Journal of Asian Studies* 41.3 (1982): 485–509.

Tyler, Royall. *Japanese Nō Dramas*. New York: Penguin (1991).

Umehara Takeshi. *Kakusareta jūjika: Hōryūjiron*. Tokyo: Shinchōbunko (1972).

Wetmore, Jr., Kevin J. "'Avenge Me!': Ghosts in English Renaissance and Kabuki Revenge Drama," in *Revenge Drama in European Renaissance and Japanese Theatre*, ed. Kevin J. Wetmore, Jr. New York: Palgrave Macmillan (2008).

Zeami Motokiyo. *On the Art of the Nō Drama: The Major Treatises of Zeami*, trans J. Thomas Rimer and Yamazaki Masakazu. Princeton, NJ: Princeton University Press (1984).

3

The Holiest of Ghosts: Staging the Supernatural in the Early Middle Ages

Andrew Rabin

The spiritual, cultural, and at times even physical world of the early middle ages was shaped by the omnipresence of death.[1] From the holy relics of saints to the walking corpses of the damned—the former venerated on feast days and petitioned in times of need; the latter feared as a source of plague or crop failure—death was understood not as an end but as a transition into what Patrick Geary labels its own "age group,"[2] a stage of self-conscious existence during which the dead could intervene in both positive and negative ways in the affairs of the living.

Accordingly, for those witnessing the *Visitatio sepulchri*, a representation of the discovery of Christ's resurrection that survives as England's earliest documented dramatic performance, the associations raised by the portrayal of Jesus's empty tomb extended well beyond the early Church's orthodox theology; rather, the *Visitatio* and its representation of the Christian triumph over death existed within a rich cultural context that shaped both its performance and reception. Indeed, as this chapter will argue, viewing the *Visitatio* solely as liturgical ritual overlooks the complex web of belief, social norm, and cultural practice that shaped its composition and reception.

Using the text of the *Visitatio* preserved in the *Regularis Concordia* (*RC*) as a case study, this chapter considers how the ritual representation of Christ's resurrection drew from contemporary narratives concerning the unquiet dead in order to extend the performance's narrative potential beyond its liturgical setting. The *Visitatio* should not be viewed as somehow outside or in opposition to non-liturgical accounts of animate bodies; rather, narratives of this sort provide an interpretive frame designed to shape the audience's understanding of the performance and their internalization of its message. Reading the *Visitatio* in this context thus explores how early medieval ecclesiastics not only staged the supernatural but also drew upon non-liturgical and secular influences to enhance the impact of the performance on their flock.

Visitatio Sepulchri as Ghost Story

The *Visitatio sepulchri*, was, in its own way, a ghost story. Staged as part of the Easter liturgy, it reenacted the visit of the Virgin Mary, Mary Magdelene, and Mary, sister of Lazarus, to Christ's grave, where they encounter a vacant tomb and an angel proclaiming the resurrection.[3] This part of the liturgy was performed by monks in symbolic, if not necessarily fully imitative, garb and involved both a limited set (to represent the sepulcher) and a "prop" in the form of a cloth, meant to represent Jesus's now empty funeral shroud. The interaction between the angel and the Marys took the form of a chanted dialogue based on John 18:4–5 ("Again therefore he asked them: Whom seek ye? And they said, Jesus of Nazareth.").[4] The dialogue itself, however, comes not from John's account of the resurrection but from the arrest of Jesus in the Garden of Gethsemane: Jesus himself questions the Roman soldiers sent to arrest him. The text thus transforms liturgical celebration into a performance using stagecraft to unite the entire Passion narrative from initial arrest to final resurrection. In so doing, it presents not the risen Christ but the space from which the protagonist is conspicuously absent. Only an angel and a cloth remain to signify Christ's missing body. Represented to the congregation in the form of symbolic remnants rather than corporeal reality, Christ is simultaneously present and absent, dead and alive, natural man and supernatural being.[5] He must, therefore, be conjured in the minds of the congregation through a mixture of faith and narrative. For the worshippers, he exists as an incorporeal presence—a ghost.

Versions of the *Visitatio sepulchri* survive in more than a thousand manuscripts from across Europe, with the earliest detailed account of its performance occurring in the *RC*, a monastic rule composed c.973, possibly by Bishop Æthelwold of Winchester.[6] Yet despite its popularity and numerous manuscript attestations, much about the *Visitatio* remains controversial. Many scholars question whether the dramatic liturgy of the early Middle Ages—the *Visitatio* being the foremost example—can be properly considered "drama," in the same theatrical tradition as the Mystery and Morality plays of the fifteenth century.[7] But even if viewed more as ritual than drama, the *Visitatio sepulchri* employed familiar representational and performative strategies to convey the miracle of resurrection. Although the extent to which these strategies derived from many liturgical sources has been well documented, less well understood is how performances of the *Visitatio sepulchri* also drew upon non-liturgical texts and traditions, especially upon popular notions of the supernatural and the afterlife.

While recent debates over the *Visitatio*'s place in the history of European drama have hinged on whether it should be understood as mimetic (and therefore "theatre") or symbolic (and therefore "ritual"),[8] this issue of categorization may create an artificial binary, for little evidence suggests distinctions of this sort existed in the minds of either performers or audience.[9] Indeed, both ritual and theatre generated emotional and intellectual responses using similar strategies of representation. Accordingly, we need to unpack the features of early medieval liturgical performance that intersect with conceptions of death and the afterlife.

The clerics leading the ritual well understood the integral role of performance. Although the *Visitatio* was the most elaborate example of liturgical performance, it was hardly the only one. Elsewhere in the *RC*, for instance, the text incorporates performative elements into the liturgical commemoration of the rending of Christ's robes by Roman soldiers following the crucifixion (John 19:24): once the celebrant has read the relevant Biblical passage, the text instructs that "immediately, two deacons shall—in the manner of thieves—remove from the altar the cloth which had previously been placed under the Gospels".[10] Among the most striking features of this passage is its characterization of the two deacons acting "in the manner of thieves." The prepositional *in modum* introduces a performative aspect to the ritual, implicitly distinguishing the deacons' clerical identity—presumably well-known to the worshippers—from their actions at this particular moment. The deacons are not acting *in modum diaconi* but *in modum furantes*. Joyce Hill has suggested that the phrase *in modum furantes* is meant to "elicit some kind of representation of underhandedness or shameful behaviour in the movements of the two enacting deacons,"[11] but it is also possible that the deacons' performance *in modo furantis* recalls the thieves crucified alongside Jesus, whose different fates (one repents his sins and is saved, the other does not and is damned) dramatize the mindset necessary to understand the liturgy properly. Neither reading of this passage is necessarily "correct"—other liturgical texts are similarly multivalent—but in either case, the deacons' actions call for audience engagement that is interpretive as well as emotional. Performances of this sort, Hill explains, were intended to break through "the normal tenor of the liturgy as a shocking, if stylized, ritual and must have had the effect of concentrating the mind on the seriousness and even horror of the physical event of the Crucifixion and the treatment of the Son of God by man."[12] In such a context, performance integrates the liturgy's didactic, interpretive, and emotional components, conditioning the audience to experience prayer from outward action to inward acceptance.

Performative liturgy was no less important for its effect on the performers themselves. As described by Ælfric, the prominent tenth-century abbot of the community at Eynsham, divergences from the strict order of the service for the purpose of representing, rather than simply relating, narrative was as much a matter of participation as performance. Citing the ninth-century theologian Amalarius of Metz, Ælfric suggests that when celebrating Epiphany, "we leave out the invitatory, that we [in making the invitation] may be distinguished from the invitation of Herod, who assembled the scribes and the high priests in order to learn from them where Christ would be born, whom he was planning to kill."[13] Likewise, at Nocturnes, the monks are to sing Psalm 46 out of sequence, "because the Magi came to worship the Lord before he had been baptized;"[14] therefore Psalm 94 should be sung in its place. In both cases, the celebrants' actions are understood not merely as praise, but as a performance designed to represent particular gospel narratives and to draw the participants into those narratives through imitative worship. The celebrants' emotional response to such performances was expected to be profound: in setting forth the instructions for a similar ritual of performative liturgy for the nocturnes service on Maundy Thursday, the author of *RC* writes, "this means of evoking religious compunction was, I believe, designed by Christians to plainly evoke the fear of that darkness which fell upon the whole world at our Lord's Passion."[15] The impact of such a moment was such that the *RC* cautions that "truly, no one shall be compelled to perform this ritual against his will."[16] It appears, then, that for both worshipper and celebrant, performative liturgy was designed to induce a powerful emotional response by making the participants actors in the gospel. As with the figurative rending of Christ's robes, it did so symbolically, substituting sacred history for the celebrants and congregation's immediate context.[17] More than simply representing Biblical events, performative liturgy compelled worshippers, by reenacting those events, to experience the power and terror of God.

Although such liturgical performances intended to prepare the congregation to receive the Eucharist, it is important to note that, unlike the representative elements elsewhere in the liturgy, the Eucharist in the early medieval church was more than mere representation. In the words of Ælfric, "truly, the bread and the wine, which are made sacred by the priests' mass, appear one thing to human understanding without, and cry another thing to faithful minds within. Outside they appear as bread and wine, both in form and taste; but they are truly, Christ's body and his blood through a spiritual mystery."[18] For the clerical and the lay, transubstantiation was real, the wafer and wine were the body of Christ. For Ælfric, as Bradford Bedingfield notes, "the invoked presence of Christ is to be understood as, if not literal, just as real as if Christ were literally present."[19] Resurrection of the body on the Day of Judgment depends on recognizing this truth. Paraphrasing John 6:56, Ælfric continues: "just as Christ himself said ... 'he that eats my flesh and drinks my blood, he lives in me, and I in him, and he shall have everlasting life, and I will raise him on the last day.'" Mutivalent as the liturgy's performative elements were, the reality of transubstantiation and Christ's vow to the faithful fixed the parameters for interpretating those performances.[20] Even though this view of the Eucharist as the foundation for understanding the liturgy is central to the *RC* (which exceeds analogous service books in requiring daily communion),[21] the significance of the Eucharist and Christ's vow exceeded liturgical interpretation, for the resurrection Jesus promised was bodily resurrection.[22] Just as Christ had risen in body following the resurrection, so the faithful would rise in body on the Day of Judgment. As Jerome and Augustine argued, the resurrection of the faithful entailed both restoration of corporeal matter and renewal of bodily integrity.[23] Both Augustine and Jerome, borrowing a metaphor from Theophilus of Antioch, figures the movement of the faithful from a corruptible to an incorruptible body as a cure from illness and a return to the moral and corporeal purity enjoyed in the Garden of Paradise.[24] The significance of a performative ritual such as the *Visitatio*, then, lay in its power to unite temporalities: reenacting the past prepared the celebrants for their future resurrection, which would restore them to a state of prelapsarian innocence.

The doctrine of transubstantiation, however, was not unproblematic. In particular, associating bodily consumption with bodily resurrection intersected uncomfortably with common beliefs concerning the unquiet dead. This issue was hardly new. In its early years, the Church faced frequent accusations of cannibalism, ritual murder, and demon worship.[25] By the tenth century, though, these charges had given way not just to the establishment of transubstantiation as formal Church doctrine, but also to the creation of an "acceptable" category of unquiet dead in the form of saints whose incorruptible bodies revealed their triumph over earthly temptations and the physical consequences of mortality.[26] Yet if the Eucharist, the cult of the saints, and the promise of physical resurrection for the saved offered appropriately moral frameworks through which to view the posthumous body, they also closely paralleled less orthodox versions of the unquiet dead, which likewise emphasized the risen as essentially corporeal. Although the canon of early medieval narratives of the unquiet dead does include immaterial hauntings, the majority feature the return of a body in the form of a revenant rather than just a shade.[27] Typical is a narrative preserved in the twelfth-century *Vita sancte Moduenna virginis* (*Life of Saint Modwenna the Virgin*) by Geoffrey of Burton, who draws upon local oral tradition in his account of the saint's *miracula*. According to Geoffrey, two peasants of the town of Stapenhill had been miraculously struck dead after abandoning their lord's service. Their bodies were returned to their lord and buried:

What came next was astonishing and truly shocking. On the very same day that they were buried, they appeared at twilight ... bearing the wooden coffins in which they had been buried on their shoulders.... They spoke to the other peasants, beating on the walls of their houses and shouting, "Move quickly, move! Get going! Come!" When these incredible events had taken place every evening and every night for some time, such a sickness afflicted the village that all the peasants fell into dire straits and within a few days ... perished by sudden death in a shocking way.[28]

Similar narratives occur in the work of Thietmar of Merseburg, who includes three accounts of the risen dead in the first book of his *Chronicon*. In the first, the dead rise from their graves to inform a priest of his coming death; in the second, the dead repeatedly expel a priest from his church (where he has been sleeping at the instruction of his bishop) until, angered by his persistence, they cause his body to be burnt to ash;[29] and in the third, the dead grunt from within their graves to mark a coming death.[30] Similarly, in his *Miracula sancti Eadmundi*, Herman the Archdeacon tells of a corrupt reeve in Bury St Edmunds, "possessed by a demon in life and then likewise possessed as a cadaver in death. Not long confined by the grave's embrace, his body was sewn into a calf-skin and sunk in a lake."[31]

Several features distinguish narratives of this type. Most obviously, each emphasizes the unquiet dead's corporeality: these are bodies that rise, not souls. Indeed, in the episode from Bury St Edmunds, the text even emphasizes that the reeve's soul had been expelled from his body before his death (presumably because its extreme wickedness merited premature judgment). The creature that walked was merely the man's body, "possessed by a demon in life and then likewise possessed as a cadaver in death." An even more dramatic example appears in the *Historum rerum Anglicarum* of William of Newburgh, in which a recently deceased man returning to his wife "almost crushed her with the insupportable weight of his body."[32] Second, the dead in each case represent a real and material threat to the community, whether it is the plague spread by the runaway peasants, abuse of local (and seemingly innocent) priests, or the corruption of secular judicial authority. Most striking is the extent to which their perspective deviates from that of the texts in which they are preserved. Although two of these texts are saints' lives (the *vitae* of Edmund and Modwenna) and two ecclesiastical chronicles (the *historiae* of Thietmar and William), the salvific power of God seems strangely absent. Neither Modwenna nor Edmund intercede to protect the community, and in Thietmar's *Chronicon* the fatal attacks on the clergy go entirely unpunished, even though the priest in the second narrative had been following Church doctrine and obeying the instructions of his bishop. Indeed, following the deaths of the two priests, the *Chronicon* does not record that either of their bishops went so far as to pray for their souls or conduct an exorcism in their churches. Even further from Christian orthodoxy is the narrative of William, in which the husband's return appears to serve no other purpose than to occasion an off-color joke about his weight in bed. Despite their religious context, in these tales, faith goes unrewarded and heavenly justice offers little defense against supernatural menace.[33] For a Church seeking to represent itself as the primary agent of God's will in the world, such narratives do little to support claims of ecclesiastical power or divine favor.

In part, the absence of saintly or ecclesiastical intervention, likely reflecting origins in oral folktales (Thietmar more or less admits as much),[34] reveals the significant cross-pollination between "secular" and "religious" texts. Likewise, the focus on corporeality may reflect the Church's view of the body as the property of the physical world and the soul as the property of the spiritual. The apparent uninterest of God, saint, or bishop in protecting their flock, however, points to the Church's deeper discomfort with narratives concerning unholy resurrection, that is, the implication that bodies may rise from the grave and retain individual identity after death at the behest of a power other than God's. Since none of these narratives were taken as a threat to the truth of the resurrection, this was not a problem of faith but of reconciling narrative tradition to Christian doctrine. Christ's resurrection, his revival of Lazarus, and his promise of the physical resurrection of the saved all frame the power to conquer death as exclusively divine. To believe otherwise would contravene Christ's declaration in John 14:6: "I am the way, and the truth, and the life. No man cometh to the Father, but by me." The discomfort caused by narratives of the risen dead is indicated by the (often tenuous) attempts by medieval theologians to fit them into a Christian worldview, attempts made particularly difficult by the account in I Samuel 28 of the Witch of Endor's raising of the prophet Samuel, which suggests that resurrection was not an exclusively divine power. Bede's struggle to explain the episode indicates the complications that this passage causes. He first dismisses the witch as "a ventriloquist," then initiates an elaborate allegorical reading, claiming the passage's purpose is to communicate to Christian readers the dangers of trying to "resurrect" the Jewish beliefs of the Old Testament. However, he writes, "if there is anyone troubled as to how, by some devilish art, a woman could disturb the prophet after death and revive him again, let that person know for certain either that the devil at that point showed a false ghost to those who were asking, or, if it really was Samuel, that the devil only has as much leeway in doing such things as the Lord permits."[35] Bede's reasoning here—that the witch was merely a ventriloquist, that the passage should be read allegorically, that the risen Samuel was just an illusion of the devil, or that the raising of Samuel was permitted by God for his own inscrutable purposes—offered later authors a convenient means of explaining other narratives of the risen dead. That said, Thietmar adopted the more idiosyncratic explanation that such accounts indicate no one "may doubt the future resurrection of the dead."[36] Although it is unclear whether medieval readers accepted this or any other explanation, these explanations nevertheless highlight the Church's uneasiness about the unquiet dead. The problem, in other words, was how to represent the crucifixion and resurrection as more than just another ghost story.

This difficulty reflects the fact that the *Visitatio sepulchri* provided celebrants a broad range of potential referents, even if audiences did not necessarily view the *Visitatio* with the same interpretive framework they used for more conventional tales of the unquiet dead. Nevertheless, the *Visitatio*, whether understood as ritual or theatre, did not occur independent of other, non-liturgical influences. Indeed, these influences were so prevalent they became incorporated into the *Visitatio*, shaping both its text and its performance.

Visitatio Sepulchri as Drama

Although reception of the *Visitatio* and the influence of more secular afterlife narratives would have been determined by the experiences and expectations of its viewers, the *RC* does not specify whether the *Visitatio* was directed towards a secular or ecclesiastical audience.[37] What little evidence there is survives primarily in the text's limited stage directions, the first of which involves the location of the performance. It instructs the brethren portraying the three Marys to approach the "sepulcher," located somewhere close by the main altar.[38] It has been suggested that setting the action in the quire and altar limited the sight lines (and the audience) to those present in the parts of the church restricted to those in holy orders.[39] However, as the rood screen (the wall separating the quire from the nave) had not yet become a common feature in church construction, it is likely that the ceremony would have been visible to the whole congregation.[40] That said, the greater challenge for a lay audience may have been linguistic rather than visual. The *Visitatio*, like the rest of the Easter liturgy, was performed in Latin, which few members of the laity could be expected to know. It is, however, possible to overstate this obstacle. Other than the homily, few Church rituals were carried out in the vernacular, including those in which the lay congregation was expected to participate, such as receiving the Eucharist. Moreover, the text's directions to the performers—that the Marys should proceed "slowly, as if they were searching for something," and that the performer playing the angel should sing the antiphon *Venite et videte locum* "as if calling them back"[41]—do not suggest stages in ritual worship as much as character-focused actions designed to clarify the narrative for an audience.[42] As such, the brethren's movements appear to function in much like the performative aspects of church dedication rituals studied by Helen Gittos, in which the symbolic gestures seem designed to ensure the laity's comprehension, even if "only in an attenuated manner."[43] It thus seems logical to conclude that the *Visitatio* was performed before both clergy and laity, the latter of whom may have only partially understood the words of the ceremony but nonetheless grasped its symbolic import.

Insofar as the stage directions communicated the nature of the performance to the congregation, any attempt to understand how the *Visitatio* was viewed must include the interpretive framework that made this communication possible. That framework is most visible in departures from Biblical sources, as on repeated allusions to the Marys' ignorance of the location of Jesus's tomb, even though the Gospels never indicate that the tomb's whereabouts were unknown or that the Marys needed guidance to locate it.[44] The text, however, twice instructs the Marys to wander about the performance space "as if they were searching for something," until the angel shows them the tomb. The audience would have easily recognized the trope of the Marys' ignorance, since such ignorance in the face of the divine was common in early medieval religious writing, but awareness of the limits of human understanding extended beyond the explicitly theological. Consider Bede's famous comparison in the *Historia ecclesiastica* of human life to the brief flight of a sparrow through a hall in the midst of a winter storm: "so a person's life appears briefly, but of what will follow or what went before we know nothing at all." Christianity does not promise to calm the storm or assure comfort on the other side of it, but instead it "tells us something more certain" about what happens in the unknowable dark.[45] Bede's metaphor underlines the crucial distinction between the modern assumption that the world is knowable through observation and scientific experimentation and the medieval view that humans cannot fully comprehend the forces that shape the world around them.[46] This state of ignorance links narratives of mortal interaction with the divine to those dealing with the behavior of the unquiet dead. Thietmar's account, for example, of the innocent priest repeatedly expelled from his church and ultimately killed turns on his (and the reader's) inability to understand why the dead should behave in this fashion. The moral of this episode, according to Thietmar, is that "it is not fitting for a mortal to know more than that which encourages sobriety."[47] Human ignorance likewise underscores the villagers' suffering at the hands of the undead peasants in Geoffrey's *Vita Moduenna*, which apparently occurs without motive by the perpetrators or understanding by the victims. William of Newburgh stresses the limitations of human comprehension even more explicitly when the wickedness of a man, hitherto believed virtuous, was exposed after his corpse refused to remain in its grave. Elsewhere, he declares that he "does not know how the dead rise from their graves and wander about to the terror or destruction of the living."[48] For William, Thietmar, Geoffrey, and the author of the *Visitatio*, human failure to anticipate or comprehend the supernatural emphasize a fundamental inability to understand a world created according to God's whims and populated by creatures operating beyond the limits of human comprehension. Even if one views the Marys' actions as ceremonial rather than mimetic, the brethren's performance nonetheless dramatizes a state of mind easily recognizable to a medieval audience: it imitates human psychology as much as (if not more than) human action.

Although the Gospels differ significantly in their treatment of the resurrection, they all agree that the dialogue with the angel occurs after the Marys arrive at the tomb and find it empty, so that the angel's intervention allays any anxiety or fear caused by the body's disappearance.[49] In the *RC*, though, the Marys, having failed to find the tomb on their own, are guided to it by the angel singing the *Quem quaeritis* trope "softly and sweetly."[50] In part, this change provides a somewhat pat allegory of the transition from ignorance to true knowledge with the aid of the divine. More importantly, though, in this rendering, the Marys' prior knowledge of the miracle abrogates any fear they might experience at finding an empty tomb, thereby distancing the Gospels' accounts of the resurrection from more secular afterlife narratives, particularly those that feature graves found to be unnaturally open. Because the grave was both a vessel preserving the bodies of the saved until the Day of Judgment and a prison ensuring that the wicked could not haunt the living,[51] the danger of an empty tomb was a common theme in early medieval accounts of the supernatural.[52] When graves fail to contain the wicked, therefore, the unquiet dead become a sacrilegious parody of Christ's resurrection: even though—like Christ—the revenant has risen bodily from his tomb, because the walking corpse violates the natural boundaries between death and life instead of becoming an image of death overcome, it must be returned to the tomb. And arrangements must prevent another escape. Geoffrey of Burton writes that the corpses of the two runaway peasants were exhumed and dismembered before being returned to their graves. William of Newburgh records an episode in which the corpse can only be kept in the tomb by the laying of an episcopal dispensation upon its chest. Most extreme is Herman's *Miracula*, in which reeve's corpse had to be "sewn into a calf-skin and sunk in a lake."[53] Given the popularity of these narratives, liturgists needed to ensure that Christ's resurrection would not be similarly depicted. That Thietmar felt the need to explain his tales of the unquiet dead as evidence for the Resurrection while other theologians, such as Raymond of Saint-Foy and Amiel de Rieux, attacked them for undermining the singularity of Christ's return indicates how intertwined were Gospel narrative and traditional revenant stories.[54] The alterations to the Biblical narrative could be seen, in this light, as a need to extricate the resurrection from familiar narratives of the unquiet dead. While the *Visitatio*'s emphasis on the Marys' ignorance imbricates secular and sacred themes, its presentation of the resurrection reflects the need to differentiate between them. Hence, the guiding angel makes the Marys' arrival at the empty tomb a moment of tenderness and the discovery itself less important than the angelic intervention that made it possible.

> Arising and lifting up the veil, [the angel] shall show them the place [now] empty of the cross and with only the linen in which the cross had been wrapped. Witnessing this the three shall set down their thuribles in that same "sepulcher" and, taking the linen, shall display it to the clergy; and, as if showing that the Lord was risen and no longer wrapped in it, they shall sing this antiphon: *Surrexit Dominus de sepulchro.* Then they shall lay the linen on the altar.[55]

Hardison dismissed this passage as "awkward" and "something less than pure representation," in part because at this point that dramatic performance gave way to religious ceremony.[56] More recently, both those viewing the *Visitatio* as theatre and those viewing it as religious rite have recognized, contra Hardison, that the representational mode of the performance has not failed but shifted: the symbolic has now overtaken the literal turning a "drama" into a ritual expression of faith.[57] Appropriately enough, at this point the *Visitatio* departs from, and ultimately transcends, the expectations of a more conventual afterlife narrative. Accounts of the unquiet dead typically offer little moral instruction, so that the texts' ignorance betokens moral innocence rather than spiritual immaturity. Neither Thietmar's priest nor the villagers of Geoffrey and Herman lack faith or neglect their prayers, and insofar as their victimization appears to lack motive, the texts do little to change their audience's belief or behavior. In contrast, the ceremonial turn in the *Visitatio* follows a logic similar to that underlying the communion mass. Although still built around a series of representations—so that, for instance, the Marys are to present the linen "as if showing that the Lord was risen"—the performance demands interpretive engagement in much the same way as does the Eucharist.[58] Just as the wine and wafer "appear one thing to human understandings without, and cry another thing to believing minds within,"[59] so the ceremonial presentation of the linen demands the audience see past the rudimentary trappings of performance to the moral instruction within. Although the presentation of the linen does not involve transubstantiation, the instruction that the Marys act "as if" it proved the resurrection requires the audience—in the allegorical manner common to medieval texts—to transcend the literal (the linen as stage prop) in order to grasp the underlying truth. If they fail to do so, the *Visitatio* becomes little more than another ghost story.

Too often the early medieval liturgy is understood only with reference to its theological orientation and its Biblical or patristic sources. For those participating in the rites of the Church, however, the context encompassed far more than religious custom or Christian orthodoxy. Though rarely acknowledged, the liturgy made use of secular narrative traditions that shaped the cultural practices of its worshippers, both clerical and lay. Although not based on a specific text or narrative, the *Visitatio sepulchri* drew upon the conventions of the afterlife tale to enrich and make comprehensible its representation of Christ's resurrection. Familiar narratives of the unquiet dead, therefore, provided a crucial, if not always explicitly recognized, interpretive demarcation, supplying tropes to be adapted or, in some cases, avoided. From this perspective, the boundary between "drama" and "ritual" appears porous, and the *Visitatio*, in its diversity of referents—especially those expressed through performance—resists the confines of a single category or genre. The historian may try to bury the *Visitatio* in one spot or another, but like any good revenant, it won't stay there for long.

Notes

1   Peter Brown, *The Cult of the Saints: Its Rise and Function in Latin Christianity* (Chicago: University of Chicago Press, 1981); Nancy Mandeville Caciola, *Afterlives: The Return of the Dead in the Middle Ages* (Ithaca, NY: Cornell University Press, 2016), 23–65.

2   Patrick J. Geary, *Living with the Dead in the Middle Ages* (Ithaca, NY: Cornell University Press, 1994), 78. See also Caciola, 53–54.

3   The version of the *Visitatio sepulchri* discussed in this chapter will be that found in §51 in the *RC*. Quotations will be taken from Lucia Kornexl, *Die Regularis Concordia un ihre altenglische Interlinearversion* (Munich: Wilhelm Fink Verlag, 1993). Here and elsewhere, all translations are my own unless

otherwise indicated. The modern study of representational liturgy and the *Visitatio* more specifically, begins with O.B. Hardison, *Christian Rite and Christian Drama in the Middle Ages* (Baltimore, MD: Johns Hopkins University Press, 1965), 35–79 and 178–219. More recent responses to their work can be found in Mirosław Kocur, *The Second Birth of Theatre: Performances of Anglo-Saxon Monks*, trans. Grzegorz Czemiel. (Frankfurt-am-Main: Peter Lang, 2017), 92–110; Fletcher Collins, *The Production of Medieval Church Music-Drama* (Charlottesville: University of Virginia Press, 1972), 47–84 and 283–293; M. Bradford Bedingfield, "Ritual and Drama in Anglo-Saxon England: The Dangers of a Diachronic Perspective," in *The Liturgy of the Late Anglo-Saxon Church* (London: The Henry Bradshaw Society, 2005), 294–296; Nils Holger Petersen, "The Representational Liturgy of the *Regularis Concordia*," in *The White Mantle of Churches*, ed. Nigel Hiscock (Turnhout: Brepols, 2003), 107–117; Michael Norton, *Liturgical Drama and the Reimagining of Medieval Theatre*. (Kalamazoo: Medieval Institute Press, 2017).

4   Biblical quotations will be taken from the Latin Vulgate with translations from the Douay-Rheims.

5   Kocur, 93.

6   On the *RC* and its status as the earliest full record of the *Visitatio* and potential antecedents, see David A. Bjork, "On the Dissemination of the *Qudem Quaeritis* and the *Visitatio Sepulchri* and the Chronology of Their Early Sources," *Comparative Drama* 14, no. 1 (1980): 46–69; George B. Bryan, *Ethelwold and Medieval Music-Drama at Winchester* (Berne: Peter Lang, 1981), 101; Pamela Sheingorn, *The Easter Sepulchre in England*. (Kalamazoo, MI: Medieval Institute Publications, 1987), 18–21; Jesse D. Billett, *The Divine Office in Anglo-Saxon England*, Subsidia (London: Henry Bradshaw Society, 2014), 179–186; Lynette R. Muir, *The Biblical Drama of Medival Europe* (Cambridge: Cambridge University Press, 1995), 14–15.

7   On this debate, see Norton; M. Bradford Bedingfield, *The Dramatic Liturgy of Anglo-Saxon England* (Woodbridge: Boydell, 2002), esp. 156-170; Bedingfield, "Ritual and Drama," 291–318; C. Clifford Flanigan, "Medieval Latin Music-Drama," in *The Theatre of Medieval Europe*, ed. Simon Eckehard (Cambridge: Cambridge University Press, 1991), 21–41; Andrew Hughes, "Liturgical Drama: Falling between the Disciplines," in *The Theatre of Medieval Europe*, ed. Simon Eckehard (Cambridge: Cambridge University Press, 1991), 42–62; Petersen, 111–117; Leonard Goldstein, *The Origin of Medieval Drama* (Madison, NJ: Farleigh Dickinson Press, 2004).

8   Bedingfield, *Dramatic Liturgy*, 5–11; Bedingfield, "Ritual and Drama" 296–297; Bryan, *Medieval Music-Drama*, 113–116; Goldstein, *Origin*, 222–223.

9   Flanigan, "Medieval Latin Music-Drama," 29; Goldstein, *Origin*, 223; Dunbar H. Ogden, *The Staging of Drama in the Medieval Church* (Newark: University of Delaware Press, 2002), 17.

10 *RC* §43.

11 Joyce Hill, "Rending the Garment and Reading the Rood: *Regularis Concordia* Rituals for Men and Women," in *The Liturgy of the Late Anglo-Saxon Church*, ed. Helen Gittos and M. Bradford Bedingfield (London: The Henry Bradshaw Society, 2005), 57.

12 Hill, "Rending the Garment, 59.

13 Christopher A. Jones, *Ælfric's Letter to the Monks of Eynsham*. (Cambridge: Cambridge University Press, 1998), 118.

14 See also Bedingfield, *Dramatic Liturgy*, 44.

15 *RC* §37.

16 *RC* §37. On this passage, see Bedingfield, "Ritual and Drama," 307.

17 Bedingfield, "Ritual and Drama," 303; Kocur, *Second Birth of Theatre*, 94; John J. McGavin and Greg Walker, *Imagining Spectatorship: From the Mysteries to the Shakespearean Stage* (Oxford: Oxford University Press, 2016), 10–11; Ogden, 26.

18 Ælfric, *Sermo de Sacrificio in Die Pascae*, in M.R. Godden, ed. *Ælfric's Catholic Homilies, Second Series*. (Oxford: Oxford University Press, 1979), at 150–160.

19 Bedingfield, *Dramatic Liturgy*, 8.

20 Ibid., 9.

21 Billett, 182–183.

22 Bedingfield, *Dramatic Liturgy*, 73.

23 Caroline Walker Bynum, *The Resurrection of the Body* (New York: Columbia University Press, 1995), 95. See also Caciola, 43–47.

24 Bynum, 31.

25 Bart Wagemakers, "Incest, Infanticide, and Cannibalism: Anti-Christian Imputations in the Roman Empire," *Greece & Rome* 57, no. 2 (2010): 337–354; Bynum, 31–33.

26 Robert Bartlett, *Why Can the Dead Do Such Great Things?* (Princeton, NJ: Princeton University Press, 2013), 239–330; Brown, *Cult*; Patrick J. Geary, *Furta Sacra: Thefts of Relics in the Central Middle Ages* (Princeton, NJ: Princeton University Press, 1978), 3–28; Geary, *Living with the Dead*, 163–219.

27 Winston Black, "Animated Corpses and Bodies with Power in the Scholastic Age," in *Death in Medieval Europe: Death Scripted and Death Choreographed*, ed. Joelle Rollo-Koster (London: Routledge, 2017), 75–79.

28 Geoffrey of Burton, *Vita sancte Moduenna virginis*, §47, in Robert Bartlett, *Geoffrey of Burton: Life and Miracles of St. Modwenna*. (Oxford: Oxford University Press, 2002), 194–196.

29 The death of the priest in this instance appears to be an inversion of the conventional folktale motif in which the holy man's persistence ultimately results in a triumph over the demonic.

30 Thietmar of Merseburg, "*Chronicon Thietmari*, I.xi-xiii," in *Thietmari Merseburgensis Episcopi Chronicon*, Monumenta Germaniae Historica, ed. Robert Holtzmann. (Berlin: Weidmannschen Verlagsbuchhandlung, 1935), 16–19.

31 Herman the Archdeacon, "*Miracula sancti Eadmundi*, §3," in *Herman the Archdeacon and Goscelin of Saint-Bertin: Miracles of St. Edmund*, ed. Tom Licence. (Oxford: Oxford University Press, 2014), 12. Submersion appears to have been a common method of preventing the return of the dead. See Paul Barber, *Vampires, Burial, and Death: Folklore and Reality* (New Haven, CT: Yale University Press, 1988), 56, 74, 171–172.

32 William of Newburgh, *Historia rerum Anglicarum*, V.xxii, in Hans Claude Hamilton, *Historia Rerum Anglicarum Willelmi Parvi*, 2 vols. (London: Sumptibus Societatis, 1856), at vol. II, p. 182.

33 Caciola, 135–136.

34 Thietmar, I.xi.

35 Bede, *In primam partem Samuhelis libri IIII*, IV, commentary on *I Samuel* 28:7–17, in *Bedae venerabilis opera, pars II: Opera exigetica*, ed. D. Hurst, O.S.B., Corpus Christianorum Series Latine (Turnholt: Brepols, 1962), at 255–256.

36 Thietmar, I.xi.

37 Ogden, 39, 96.

38 Collins, 83–84.

39 See Bryan, 121–124.

40 See Helen Gittos, *Liturgy, Architecture, and Sacred Places in Anglo-Saxon England* (Oxford: Oxford University Press, 2013), 13–14; Petersen, 109–111; Ogden, 26.

41 *RC* §51.

42 See Gittos, 276–277; Ogden, 24.

43 Gittos, 18.

44 The closest analogue to this moment appears only in John, in which Mary Magdelene at first fails to recognize the risen Christ and then assumes that he is the gardener. See John 20: 14–15.

45 Bede, "*Historia ecclesiastica gens Anglorum*, II.xiii," in *Bede's Ecclesiastical History of the English People*, ed. Bertram Colgrave and R.A.B. Mynors (Oxford: Clarendon Press, 1991), at 182–184.

46 In the later middle ages, this state of ignorance would provide the foundation for a popular religious tract, *The Cloude of Unknowing*.

47 Thietmar, I.xii. Thietmar here paraphrases Romans 12:3.

48 William of Newburgh, V.xxiv.

49 See Mark 16:8, Matthew 28:8, Luke 24:5, and John 20:11.

50 *RC* §51. An analogue to this direction can be found in early Swedish versions of the *Visitatio*. Audrey Ekdahl Davidson, *Holy Week and Easter Ceremonies and Dramas from Medieval Sweden* (Kalamazoo, MI: Medieval Institute Publications, 1990), 23.

51 Andrew Reynolds, *Anglo-Saxon Deviant Burial Practices* (Oxford: Oxford University Press, 2009), 54, 90, 172–173; John Blair, "The Dangerous Dead in Early Medieval England," in *Early Medieval Studies in Memory of Patrick Wormald*, ed. Stephen Baxter, et al. (Farnham: Ashgate, 2009), 550–551; Barber, 54–55.

52 The harshest penalties in early Frankish law were reserved for those who
   disturbed the dead after burial, even if it was done without criminal intent.
   See Bonnie Effros, *Caring for Body and Soul: Burial and the Afterlife in the
   Merovingian World* (University Park: Pennsylvania State University Press,
   2002), 49.
53 Ibid.
54 Caciola, 265.
55 *RC* §51.
56 Hardison, 248.
57 Bedingfield, 163.
58 Ibid., 9.
59 Ibid.

Works Cited

Ælfric. "Sermo de Sacrificio in Die Pascae," in *Ælfric's Catholic Homilies, Second
    Series*, ed. M.R. Godden. Oxford: Oxford University Press, 1979: 150–160.
Barber, Paul. *Vampires, Burial, and Death: Folklore and Reality*. New Haven, CT:
    Yale University Press, 1988.
Bartlett, Robert. *Why Can the Dead Do Such Great Things*? Princeton, NJ:
    Princeton University Press, 2013.
Bede. "*Historia ecclesiastica gens Anglorum*, II.xiii," in Bede's Ecclesiastical
    History of the English People, ed. Bertram Colgrave and R.A.B. Mynors.
    Oxford: Clarendon Press, 1991: 182–184.
Bede, "*In primam partem Samuhelis libri IIII*, IV, commentary on I Samuel
    28:7–17," in *Bedae venerabilis opera, pars II: Opera exigetica*, ed. D. Hurst,
    O.S.B., Corpus Christianorum Series Latine. Turnholt: Brepols, 1962: 255–256.
Bedingfield, M. Bradford. "Ritual and Drama in Anglo-Saxon England: The
    Dangers of a Diachronic Perspective," in *The Liturgy of the Late Anglo-Saxon
    Church*. London: The Henry Bradshaw Society, 2005: 294–344.
Bedingfield, M. Bradford. *The Dramatic Liturgy of Anglo-Saxon England*.
    Woodbridge: Boydell, 2002.
Billett, Jesse D. *The Divine Office in Anglo-Saxon England, Subsidia*. London:
    Henry Bradshaw Society, 2014.
Bjork, David A. "On the Dissemination of the Qudem Quaeritis and the Visitatio
    Sepulchri and the Chronology of Their Early Sources." *Comparative Drama*
    14.1 (1980): 46–69.
Black, Winston. "Animated Corpses and Bodies with Power in the Scholastic
    Age," in *Death in Medieval Europe: Death Scripted and Death Choreographed*,
    ed. Joelle Rollo-Koster. London: Routledge, 2017.
Blair, John. "The Dangerous Dead in Early Medieval England," in *Early Medieval
    Studies in Memory of Patrick Wormald*, ed. Stephen Baxter, et al.. Farnham:
    Ashgate, 2009: 539–560.

Brown, Peter. *The Cult of the Saints: Its Rise and Function in Latin Christianity.* Chicago: University of Chicago Press, 1981.

Bryan, George B. *Ethelwold and Medieval Music-Drama at Winchester.* Berne: Peter Lang, 1981.

Bynum, Caroline Walker. *The Resurrection of the Body.* New York: Columbia University Press, 1995.

Caciola, Nancy Mandeville. *Afterlives: The Return of the Dead in the Middle Ages.* Ithaca, NY: Cornell University Press, 2016.

Collins, Fletcher. *The Production of Medieval Church Music-Drama.* Charlottesville: University of Virginia Press, 1972.

Davidson, Audrey Ekdahl. *Holy Week and Easter Ceremonies and Dramas from Medieval Sweden.* Kalamazoo, MI: Medieval Institute Publications, 1990.

Effros, Bonnie. *Caring for Body and Soul: Burial and the Afterlife in the Merovingian World.* University Park: Pennsylvania State University Press, 2002.

Flanigan, C. Clifford. "Medieval Latin Music-Drama," in *The Theatre of Medieval Europe,* ed. Simon Eckehard. Cambridge: Cambridge University Press, 1991: 21–41.

Geary, Patrick J. *Living with the Dead in the Middle Ages.* Ithaca, NY: Cornell University Press, 1994.

Geary, Patrick J. *Furta Sacra: Thefts of Relics in the Central Middle Ages.* Princeton, NJ: Princeton University Press, 1978.

Geoffrey of Burton, "Vita sancte Moduenna, §47," in *Geoffrey of Burton: Life and Miracles of St. Modwenna,* ed. Robert Bartlett. Oxford: Oxford University Press, 2002: 194–196.

Gittos, Helen. *Liturgy, Architecture, and Sacred Places in Anglo-Saxon England.* Oxford: Oxford University Press, 2013.

Goldstein, Leonard. *The Origin of Medieval Drama.* Madison, NJ: Farleigh Dickinson Press, 2004.

Hardison, O.B. *Christian Rite and Christian Drama in the Middle Ages.* Baltimore, MD: Johns Hopkins University Press, 1965.

Herman the Archdeacon. "Miracula sancti Eadmundi, §3," in *Herman the Archdeacon and Goscelin of Saint-Bertin: Miracles of St. Edmund,* ed. Tom Licence. Oxford: Oxford University Press, 2014: 12.

Hill, Joyce. "Rending the Garment and Reading the Rood: Regularis Concordia Rituals for Men and Women," in *The Liturgy of the Late Anglo-Saxon Church,* ed. Helen Gittos and M. Bradford Bedingfield. London: The Henry Bradshaw Society, 2005: 53–64.

Hughes, Andrew. "Liturgical Drama: Falling between the Disciplines," in *The Theatre of Medieval Europe,* ed. Simon Eckehard. Cambridge: Cambridge University Press, 1991: 42–62.

Jones, Christopher A. *Ælfric's Letter to the Monks of Eynsham,* Cambridge Studies in Anglo Saxon England. Cambridge: Cambridge University Press, 1998.

Kocur, Miroslaw. The Second Birth of Theatre: Performances of Anglo-Saxon Monks, trans. Grzegorz Czemiel. Frankfurt-am-Main: Peter Lang, 2017.

Kornexl, Lucia. *Die Regularis Concordia un ihre altenglische Interlinearversion.* Munich: Wilhelm Fink Verlag, 1993.

McGavin, John J. and Greg Walker, *Imagining Spectatorship: From the Mysteries to the Shakespearean Stage.* Oxford: Oxford University Press, 2016.

Muir, Lynette R. *The Biblical Drama of Medieval Europe.* Cambridge: Cambridge University Press, 1995.

Norton, Michael. *Liturgical Drama and the Reimagining of Medieval Theatre.* Kalamazoo, MI: Medieval Institute Press, 2017.

Ogden, Dunbar H. *The Staging of Drama in the Medieval Church.* Newark: University of Delaware Press, 2002.

Petersen, Nils Holger. "The Representational Liturgy of the Regularis Concordia," in *The White Mantle of Churches*, ed. Nigel Hiscock. Turnhout: Brepols, 2003.

Reynolds, Andrew. *Anglo-Saxon Deviant Burial Practices.* Oxford: Oxford University Press, 2009.

Schmitt, Claude. *Ghosts in the Middle Ages: The Living and the Dead in Medieval Society.* Chicago: University of Chicago Press, 1998.

Sheingorn, Pamela. *The Easter Sepulchre in England.* Kalamazoo, MI: Medieval Institute Publications, 1987.

Thietmar of Merseburg. "Chronicon Thietmari, I.xi–xiii", in *Thietmari Merseburgensis Episcopi Chronicon*, Monumenta Germaniae Historica, ed. Robert Holtzmann. Berlin: Weidmannschen Verlagsbuchhandlung, 1935: 16–19.

Wagemakers, Bart. "Incest, Infanticide, and Cannibalism." *Greece & Rome* 57.2 (2010): 337–354.

William of Newburgh. "Historia rerum Anglicarum, V.xxii", in *Historia Rerum Anglicarum Willelmi Parvi*, ed. Hans Claude Hamilton, 2 vols. London: Sumptibus Societatis, 1856: vol. II, 182.

4

"I Am Not Here": Staging the (Un)Dead and the Thresholds of Theatrical Performance

Christopher Salamone

In Thomas Middleton's *The Second Maiden's Tragedy* (c.1611), the ghost of Lady, having committed suicide to save her virginity, returns as a spectral voice to tell her true love, Govianus, that her body has been stolen from its tomb. She adopts, by way of verbal entrance, a decidedly cryptic revelation of sepulchral absence:

VOICE WITHIN

I am not here.

GOVIANUS
What's that? Who is not here? I'm forced to question it.[1]

Present in spirit to declare her body robbed, Lady drops Govianus into the supernatural paradox implicit to every haunting: that the deceased is simultaneously absent and present. His response posits hermeneutic uncertainty and confronts a contradiction, for not only must he both clarify the speaker's identity—indeed ontology—by asking further questions, but also, as a spectator, question the truth-value of the statement itself, bewildered by its self-cancelling declaration of absence. I shall return to Middleton's play but, by way of introduction, I want to appropriate Govianus's central question—"Who is not here?"—to ask, quite simply, who or what is perceived to be present and absent when an actor performs a ghost on the early modern stage?

"Yet was his Soul but Flown Beyond ...":
Prologues and Inductions

Early modern drama between 1560 and 1610 was saturated with the spirits of revenge tragedy, and Caroline dramatists repeatedly re-worked the conceit of haunting for sundry generic ends.[2] This abundance can be traced to Renaissance translations of Seneca's tragedies, the earliest of which, Jasper Heywood's *Troas* (1559), augments the original with an Act 2 prologue delivered by the spirit of Achilles.[3] The invention, consistent with the prologue-ghosts of other Senecan tragedies that would soon after be translated, such as Heywood's *Thyestes* (1560) and Studley's *Agamemnon* (1566), speaks to a spirit of creative imitation—and an attraction to the trope itself—that would feed a native tradition of revenge tragedy. By the close of the 1580s, the vengeful Ghost of Gorlois is opening Thomas Hughes's *The Misfortunes of Arthur* (c.1587), and in Kyd's *The Spanish Tragedy* (c.1587), the Ghost of Andrea and Revenge start proceedings with an Induction indebted, as Lukas Erne observes, to the ghost of Tantalus and Fury in *Thyestes*'s prologue.[4]

The proliferation of prologues and Inductions spoken by ghosts from the 1590s onwards, indicating the popularity and influence of Kyd's play,[5] also attests to the metaphoric valency of these metatheatrical threshold devices, which playfully disrupt the illusion of fictional presence with speakers who are neither entirely "here," in the audience's reality, or "there," in the fictional stage-world. Inductions and prologues, as Bruster and Weimann observe, took up a "position before and apparently 'outside' the world of the play," serving as a nexus between "text" and "event," between "imaginary and material modes of representation."[6] As "boundary breaking entities," they "negotiated charged thresholds between and among, variously, playwrights, characters, audience members, play-worlds, and the world outside the playhouse."[7] The liminality of these devices, introductory go-betweens ushering spectators in with the flickering absent-presence of both player and character, becomes emphasized when spoken or inhabited by specters. Thus, while popularized by *The Spanish Tragedy*, the association between dramatic threshold devices and the liminal ghost extended to genres beyond tragedy. William Haughton's comedy, *Grim the Collier of Croydon* (1600, published 1662), for example, is introduced by a framing scene wherein Pluto and the court of Hell hear the arraignment of Malbecco's Ghost, who blames his wife for his suicide; William Percy's *Cuckqeans and Cuckolds Errants* (c.1601) opens with the Ghost of Richard Tarlton (1530–1588), the popular stage clown; and Thomas Nashe resurrects the spirit of Will Summers, fool to Henry VIII, to induct us into and comment upon *Summer's Last Will and Testament* (1592; published 1600).

These threshold devices, temporally and spatially "out of joint," belong neither wholly in the audience's present, nor in the play's fictional temporality.[8] Christopher Marlowe's prologue to *The Jew of Malta* (c.1589), spoken by the spirit of Niccolo Machiavelli (1469–1527), typifies this dislocation. Machiavelli's ghost oscillates between states of absence and presence. Upon entering, "Machiavel" identifies himself though a dissociative third-person: "The world think Machiavel is dead," the player remarks, "Yet was his soul but flown beyond the Alps," and now "is come from France / To view this land and frolic with his friends."[9] Not until the seventh line does the speaker identify with the "soul" of Machiavelli ("let them know that I am Machiavel"), delaying the perception of the spirit's presence, which is then partially absented near the Prologue's close, as the speaker admits to their dramatic function: "I come not," they remember, "To read a lecture here in Britainy, / But to present the tragedy of a Jew."[10] The mask of "Machiavel," temporarily dropping in and out of presence, allows for an awareness of the performer's purpose as prologue, intensifying the spectrality of the moment through shifting degrees of visibility.

"So this Likeness of Samuel, is Called Samuel": Discerning Dissemblance

Although the liminality of prologues and inductions makes them hospitable haunts for specters, the early modern stage ghost frequently walks beyond those threshold devices. Breaking free from the prologue, the trope shifts away from motifs of the Classical underworld, which marked the Senecan tradition, towards more eclectic instantiations informed by contemporary culture. Scenes of haunting are inflected by a mixture of popular folklore and recent intertheatrical conventions, as well as a complex range of contextual, theological disputes over the authenticity and ontological status of ghostly presence.[11] The prevalent questions each spirit initially meets in their stage hauntings, in turn, concern an ontology de-stabilized and compounded by this gallimaufry of interpretative frameworks. Who or what, the haunted character asks, is present before me? And to what extent is the apparition actually present?

The early modern ghost controversy revolves, we might say, around Govianus's question of "Who is not here," finding scriptural and classical precedents for the idea that ghosts may, for example, be counterfeits undertaken by diabolic (or living Catholic) entities, or by hallucinatory shadows, conjured by an overactively melancholic imagination. The debate over whether a specter was authentically the absent dead or a demonic or theatrical counterfeit no doubt informs the hermeneutic uncertainty depicted in the reactions of early modern drama's haunted characters. But in what ways might the character's contestation and questioning of spectral presence apply to the early modern audience? In so asking, my intent is not so much to excavate the theological beliefs or superstitions held by audiences, as to foreground the stress that the contested figure of the ghost put on modes of early modern dramatic representation and spectatorship.

Cultural historians have much surveyed the controversy in the period over the nature of apparitions, not least with a view to shedding light on the multifarious ghost beliefs that manifest in *Hamlet*, and the presentation of that ghost's "questionable shape,"[12] which elicits enquiries of ontology from characters and literary critics alike.[13] Rather than rehearse these positions in their entirety, I will focus briefly on one aspect of the period's demonological discourse pertaining to the problematic perception—and representation—of a counterfeit absent presence. Moving beyond Stephen Greenblatt's elucidation of the parallel that Protestant polemicists made between early modern theatrical ghosts and supposed hauntings counterfeited by dissembling Catholics,[14] I want to highlight the language used to describe diabolic dissemblance, through which the notion of feigned appearances most frequently unites ghosts and drama. Although confessional division is clearly evident in the dispute surrounding the dead's ability to haunt the living, Catholic and Protestant demonological positions both accept that an apparition may be a demon in the semblance of an absent, deceased loved one.

This interpretative suspicion extends far beyond *Hamlet*'s uncertainty about whether his father's apparition is "spirit of health or goblin damn'd."[15] The advice given by Nemo in Robert Wilson's *The Three Lordes and Three Ladies of London* (*c*.1588, published 1590) that a "Ghost may walke to mocke the people rude: / Ghostes are but shadowes, and doe sense delude," is paralleled in Thomas Kyd's 1594 closet-drama translation of Robert Garnier's *Cornélie*, where the Chorus warns Cornelia that her husband's ghost, who, we are told, appears in a dream, must be, if not a figment of "vaine thoughts, or meloncholie shows," then surely "some false *Dæmon* that beguild your sight."[16] Under the reign of James I, a monarch so interested in discerning the supernatural, the staging of demonological interpretations increased significantly: the status of Asdruball's ghost, necromantically summoned by Syphax in John Marston's *Sophonisba* (*c*.1605: published 1606), is called into question by Syphax himself, who asks what "damn'd ayre is form'd / Into that shape."[17] This habit of thought persists into Caroline drama: Wallace, in J.W.'s *The Valiant Scot* (*c*.1626, published 1637), for example, suspects demonic dissemblance when confronted with Friar Gertrid's Ghost (the first in a *Richard III*-style parade of specters), dismissing his warning of impending death on the grounds that "Thou art a lying spirit" or "some *English* damned witch, / That from a reverend Fryer has stoln his shape / To abuse me."[18]

The apparition's mockery of those who witness it mimics the impersonations performed on stage, a parallel repeatedly drawn upon by contributors to the early modern ghost controversy. Although actors and apparitions have often been seen as simulacra signifying absent entities, in the sixteenth and seventeenth centuries the analogy was specifically mobilized for theological arguments concerning the discernment of spirits. Theologians turned to the rhetoric of representation and similitude when discussing the apparition of Samuel summoned by the witch of Endor before Saul in 1 Samuel 28:4–28. Thomas Bilson, Bishop of Winchester (1547–1616), poses the question as to "whether it were *Samuel* in deede that rose or spake, or whether it were the divell transforming himself into the likenesse of *Samuel* to drive *Saul* into dispaire."[19] Interpreting the apparition of Samuel as truly being his returned spirit would be, Protestants argued, to invest overly in illusory signs—to interpret as present something that is absent, merely signified—like a naïve spectator at the theatre. William Perkins invokes this theatrical parallel when explaining the scriptural description of Samuel's apparition:

> The name of the thing signified is given to the signe, as upon a stage he is called a king that represents the king. And Augustine saith, that images are woont to be called by the names of things whereof they are images, as the counterfeit of Samuel is called Samuel.[20]

Comparing spectral and theatrical counterfeits for this purpose was a commonly rehearsed trope by the end of the sixteenth century. Henry Smith had likewise argued that "he which playeth the King upon a stage, is called a King ... so this likenesse of Samuel, is called Samuell, though it was not Samuel in deede, but a counterfeit shape of Samuel.[21] The diabolic deception of the dead's presence, Perkins and Smith suggest, relies upon the haunted spectator misconstruing the counterfeiting signifier for the signified; and our misreading of 1 Samuel 28, they argue, derives from the naive inability to recognize a metaphor. Their anxiety circles around the misperception and faulty reading of authentic presence in acts of signification. It is therefore no surprise that Philip Stubbes, having explained away a contemporary anecdote of a ghostly pauper in 1581 as nothing but a demonic deception in the manner of Satan "counterfeit[ing] the body of Samuell," extends his hyper-awareness and demonization of signifying practice to his outlook on theatres.[22] In 1583, Stubbes portrayed theatrical shadow-play in demonological terms, hysterically decrying the stage's counterfeit presentations as diabolically seductive to the senses, "sucked out of the Devills teates."[23] Shifting between identities, evoking both belief and disbelief, truth and falsehood, aligned players in anti-theatrical discourse with deceptive, shape-shifting apparitions.

The polyvalence of the term "shadow" in this period facilitated that parallel: it could signify both actors and spirits, with the theatrical perspective, informed by Platonic theory, articulating the idea that performers function as shadows or representations of characters.[24] Thus, William Prynne argues that a spectator is "Cheated, with shadowes instead of substance" in theatres that are "nought else but feining, but counterfeiting, but palpable hypocrisies and dissimulation."[25] A rhetoric of spectrality in the period's condemnation of illusory theatrical presence—implied by this shadows imagery and made explicit with references to the diabolic—aligned the seductive, dissembling spirit with the player who supposedly seduced spectators to vice. Daniel Dyke invokes that parallel by following his advice for actors to repent (by "turning shows into substance, shadowes into truth, a double heart, into a hart of simplicity") with a report that "when among a company of counterfeit divels, on the stage, the true Divell shall come in and chase away the fained."[26]

"We are not here": The Actor as Medium

Illusion and deception unite stage-players, therefore, not just in the feigning of spectral presence supposedly perpetrated by Catholic dissemblers, but in the deceptive apparition itself, as conceived across the period's confessional divide. Prynne's Puritan disdain for the "ontological queasiness" of actors— "always *acting* [as] *others*, not themselves"—stems from the same anxiety about which demonologists warn: "the crafty pollicie" of the Devil who "counterfaite[s] and fayne[s] him selfe to be some holy man, by resembling his words, voice, gesture," transforms "himselfe into an Angell of lyght, and fashioneth hys Ministers like unto the Ministers of righteousnesse."[27]

Just under two decades prior to Prynne's attack on the stage, John Stephens similarly argued that players were riddled by ontological subversions enacted on stage: "He is but a shifting companion; for he lives effectually by putting on, and putting off.... His owne [profession] therefore is compounded of all Natures, all Humours, all professions."[28] The performer's presence is, he suggests, problematically plural, changeable, and untrustworthy. In its multiplicity and self-erasure, the protean player aligns rhetorically with the deceptive spirits we find, for instance, in Greville's closet-drama, *Alaham* (*c*.1598–1603), who are "Varieinge in all but this," that they "can never longe be one," adopting "masked artes," that deceive the credulous and make "this diverse world a stage for blood-enammell'd shows."[29] The parallel— underscored by Greville's theatrical metaphors—inflects depictions of acting in the period. In the Induction to John Marston's romantic comedy, *Antonio and Mellida* (*c*.1599, published 1601), a boy-player's despair that his multiple roles would be a "right part for Proteus," is filtered through demonological rhetoric: "Unless I were possessed with a legion of spirits, 'tis impossible to be made perspicuous by any utterance."[30]

Whereas early modern anti-theatricalist polemics appropriated the rhetoric of haunting shadows to demonize the theatre for its ontological subversions, for Marston the conceits of spirit possession or shape-shifting apparitions playfully and ironically articulate the skills of the player and the limits of dramatic representation.[31] The physical body of the performer, "possessed" with the spirits of absent characters, becomes the site of a self-effacement, resembling the notion of dramatic representation as the "mediumship or ventriloquism" theorized by Michael Goldman.[32] Early modern manifestations of this are found, too, in commendatory descriptions of actors: Richard Flecknoe's praise of Richard Burbage, for example, admiringly portrays theatrical representation as a process of self-effacing possession, with the tragedian lauded as such "a delightful *Proteus*, so wholly transforming himself" that he "never (not so much in the Tyring-House) assum'd himself again until the play was done."[33] The eulogizing praise of the actor valorizes his perceived ability to absent his identity. It is an early modern instantiation of what Goldman has termed an actor's "ecstasy of self surrender," whereby, as Jonathan Holme notes, mimetic acts are "only possible if identity is simultaneously negated and pluralized, whether this be through fragmentation or multiplication, while remaining unfixed and impermanent."[34] *A Midsummer Night's Dream*, of course, articulates this conception of theatrical representation when Quince optimistically tells his onstage audience, with unknowing self-critique, that "All for your delight / We are not here."[35]

And yet, again, like Govianus, we are "forced to question" who or what is "not here." After all, the Mechanicals' performance is metatheatrically comedic because the amateur players are unavoidably there, ineptly drawing attention to their presence as (bad) actors. Indeed, instead of simply overlooking the disconnect between the signifying body and character, early modern spectatorship partook in the imaginative frisson between the performer's partially absented presence and the counterfeited manifestation of an absent signified. The above-mentioned *Antonio and Mellida* revels, like its sequel, *Antonio's Revenge* (*c*.1601, published 1602), in self-consciously foregrounding the boy players at St. Paul's for whom it was written.[36] Thomas Nashe's defense of theatres, particularly history plays, suggests this dual perspective when he describes how "our forefathers valiant acts (that have line long buried in rustie brasse and worme-eaten books) are revived, and they themselves raised from the Grave of Oblivion, and brought to pleade their aged Honours in open presence." Turning to *1 Henry VI*, which he co-authored with Shakespeare, Nashe wonders:

> How would it have joyed brave *Talbot* to thinke that after he had lyne two hundred years in his Tombe, hee should triumphe againe on the Stage,

and have his bones newe embalmed with the teares of ten thousand spectators at least (at several times), who, in the Tragedian that represents his person, imagine they behold him fresh bleeding.[37]

Nashe's lingering figuration of theatre as a necromantic medium conjuring the dead breaks down the process of spectatorship and mimesis, drawing attention to "the Tragedian that represents his person." The subsequent effect, Brian Walsh notes, is an acknowledgment of the audience's double-perspective.[38] Theatrical moral didacticism here requires, rather than negates, a virtuous mode of spectatorship, one aware of the effort and identity of the tragedian effecting an act of similitude in which an audience imaginatively collaborates. Keeping one eye on the metaphorical structure of signifying "shadows" thus redeems the stage from charges of falsehood. The Catholic demonologist, Pierre Le Loyer, makes a similar conceptual point regarding divine apparitions that appear as representations of deceased friends and family members. Just "as *Metaphorras* speeches are not therefore any whit the sooner to be reputed false, in which by the similitude of things, other significations are comprehended," so too, he argues, "the figures and formes of Angells are not false, because they are taken and assumed to the similitude and semblance of men."[39]

"A Robe for to Goo Invisibell": Seeing and Unseeing

In the theatre, the embodied quality of the signifying medium—the perceivable presence of a "Tragedian that represents"—cannot avoid underscoring how dramatic "similitude and semblance" are metaphorically constructed. The player's body, as Anthony B. Dawson remarks, "exists under erasure, and yet that elision of the body, that move toward discourse, is a direct result of the body's presence."[40] Early modern dramatists, by staging ghosts, explore and ironically stress-test this tension on the experience of spectatorship, for a player's physicality is most perceptible—and most incongruently present—when disturbing the specter's feigned insubstantiality. Dramatic hauntings thereby turn the actor's absent-presence into a spectacle for scrutiny, mirrored in the reactions of characters onstage, who question who or what is present. The theatrical trope of a spirit's invisibility puts particular stress on the material means of presenting absence and the disjunction between signifier and signified. In George Peele's *The Old Wives Tale* (c.1591–4, published 1595), for example, the ghost of Jack is initially invisible to all but the audience,[41] with Eumenides unable to fathom who or what is pinching him, yet within four lines he makes his visible presence known.[42] To shift from invisibility to appearance, as Charles Whitworth remarks, "is scarcely within an actor's capability."[43] But the purchase of a "robe for to goo invisibell" in 1598 by the Admiral's Men suggests that invisibility could be signified paradoxically by a material, visible costume.[44] This kind of representational convention cues a mode of spectatorship that simultaneously sees and imaginatively unsees the actor's signifying presence.[45] The actor's disruptive physical presence is particularly perceptible when the spectral dead are apparently invisible only to certain characters, as when Jack's ghost appears unseen to the evil sorcerer, Sacrapant (*"Enter Jack, invisible, and taketh off* Sacrapant's *wreath from his head,"*) but is visible to Eumenides, whom he is assisting in gratitude for payment towards re-burying his body on sanctified ground.[46] The Ghost of Young Bateman in William Sampson's *The Vow Breaker* (published 1636), likewise appears only to his former lover, Anne Boote, whose betrayal of their promised marriage drove the jilted Bateman to suicide:

ANNE

>Are you blind, or will you make yourselves so?
>See! How like a dreadful magistrate it stands
>Still pointing at me, the black offender;
>...
>It stares, beckons, points, to the piece of gold
>We brake between us. Look! Look there! Here! There!

BOOTE

>I see nothing, perceive nothing, feel nothing.

URSULA

>Nor I. No quick thing, neither clothed nor naked.[47]

Returning to remind Anne of her broken promise—the "piece of gold / We brake between us"—and to manifest his dying threat that "My airy ghost shall find her where she lies / And to her face divulge her perjuries,"[48] his absent-presence solicits intertextual shadows that adumbrate the play's concern with visual spectacle. In its beckoning and pointing, it summons echoes of *Macbeth*'s Banquo, the gory-locked spirit first visible only to Macbeth amidst the banquet, who later smiles, pointing to a line of spectral, regal descendants that prophesizes, by contradistinction, the failure of Macbeth's bloodline. Subjected to a fearful ekphrasis, Anne rhetorically traces the visual presence of Batemen's ghost with literary reference points for the benefit of those characters perceiving only absence: it stands, she explains, as a "dreadful magistrate," returning to call out those who wronged him in the manner of the poetic spectral complainants in William Baldwin's *Mirror for Magistrates* (1559).

Those who cannot see the spirit echo, of course, more familiar characters who "see nothing, perceive nothing, feel nothing":[49] Gertrude in *Hamlet's* bedroom scene, who sees "Nothing at all,"[50] and Lady Macbeth ("When all's done, / You look but on a stool").[51] In these moments of selective invisibility in early modern dramatic hauntings, offstage spectators are asked to imagine a perspective from which they may view "no quick thing, neither clothed nor naked," simultaneously with the apparent sight before them onstage, both the signified returning dead and the actor, who may or may not be adorned with a "cloak to go invisibell." These dizzying multiple perspectives are catalyzed by a language of repeated and self-cancelling deixis that characterizes private hauntings. Anne's plea to those for whom the ghost is not visible ("Look! Look there! Here! There!"), which she repeats to Old Bateman during his son's later haunting ("Why, 'tis your son, / Just as he died. Look! Look! There! Here! There!"),[52] draws attention to the physical presence of the player and channels us through her viewpoint; yet in each instance this viewpoint is haunted by contradiction. Is the spirit "here" or "there," if at all? For beneath this confusion, Anne's desperate discernment of presence echoes not just the maddening cries of Lear before the corpse of his absent, lifeless daughter ("Look there, look there")[53] but the deluded madmen of Thomas Dekker and Thomas Middleton's *The Honest Whore* (1604) ("ha ha ha ha, no no, looke there, looke there, looke there").[54]

"Enter Lady: Rich Robinson"

Drama embodying the spectral—at times invisible—dead invites audiences into a reflective viewpoint whereby we witness theatre deconstruct its mode of representation as it puts the personating body in tension with the imaginary, discursive character. It prompts a hyper-alertness to the material reality of the stage and the habits of spectatorship. This is why, as Drew Milne suggests, representations of death and the dead, or any form of absence on stage, can "descend into farce" when audiences are "amused by signs of life."[55] Early modern stage ghosts similarly bring attention to the means of representation, evoking metatheatrical scrutiny of the distance between sign and signified. Such scrutiny can mock satirically, as in the anonymous tragedy *A Warning for Fair Women* (1599), wherein the figure of Comedy derides the farcical materiality of Tragedy's favorite trope, the "filthie whining ghost" that, "Lapt in some fowle sheete, or a leather pelch," cries "Vindicta, revenge,

revenge" to the accompaniment of a "little Rosen [that] flasheth forth, / Like smoke out of a Tabacco pipe, or a boyes squib."[56] Emphasizing the underwhelming pyrotechnics, and the disparity between the "fowle sheete" and the insubstantial specter it signifies, the passage ridicules the incongruous corporeality of these stage ghosts.

Yet that incongruity can also be usefully harnessed. For instance, awareness of an actor's stage history creates, in early modern culture, as it does today, ironic parallels and significations. Marvin Carlson has theorized that audiences perceive an actor's body as a site of intertextual signification, haunted by previous roles.[57] Surviving early modern play-texts—printed and manuscript—indicate this double-vision in staging ghosts. While Govianus's skeptical response to Maria's paradoxical declaration of absence in Middleton's *Second Maiden's Tragedy* articulates comic puzzlement, the stage directions marking the ghost's subsequent appearance ("*Enter Lady: Rich Robinson*") put into textual form the metatheatrical virtues of an audience's dual perception of actor and character.[58] Rich Robinson, who performed the unnamed "Lady," is one of two players from the King's Men identified in the manuscript, the other being Robert Gough. A boy apprentice in the King's Men, also appearing in the cast list for Ben Jonson's *Catiline* (1611), Robinson by 1616 had a reputation for playing female parts, being praised for such talents in Jonson's *The Devil is an Ass*.[59] His identity here intrudes into the text —"who is (not) here, Rich Robinson or the Lady?"—at the moment his signifying onstage body disrupts the sense of the female ghost's insubstantiality while also facilitating the mimetic act by soliciting the audience's familiarity with his female roles.

The Second Maiden's Tragedy invokes a metatheatrical awareness of Rich Robinson's signifying body most forcibly in his final scene, for here the Lady's ghost is present at the same time as her cosmetically adorned corpse, the latter having been subjected to idolatrous veneration by the play's necrophile tyrant. Middleton's splitting of body and soul exceeds the limits of dramatic representation. For her to "*Enter . . . in the same form as the Lady is dressed in the chair*,"[60] necessitating the use of a dummy, requires spectatorship that imagines corporeal flesh in the fleshless prop, and incorporeality in Robinson's substantial, living body, while sustaining a satirical (indeed anti-Catholic) perspective on the Tyrant's idolatrous and delusional perception of a living presence in its beautified counterfeit. The play satirically sends up Catholic idolatry—the worship of spiritual presence in material objects—via a metatheatrical foregrounding of representational practices, in this case the co-presence of real and unreal bodies that both signify problematically in a piece of spectacular stage business that lays itself open to scrutiny.

"It would not Seem so Ghostly in these Eyes": Discerning (Im)materiality

The body that signifies spectral (absent) presence is, in Sampson's *The Vow Breaker*, similarly duplicated, albeit through portraiture, and is repeatedly the subject of spectatorial inspection. Early descriptions of Young Bateman's ghost stress, even whilst denying, his substantiality: although "it wants the rosy-coloured face" of the living, Anne states, "It would not seem so ghostly in these eyes, / [For] It bears the perfect form it used to do."[61] When the ghost eventually appears onstage, Sampson playfully highlights the apparent contradiction between its assumed, fictional immateriality and the player's corporeality. "There is," the spirit warns Anne, "no cavern in the earth's vast entrails / But I can [pass] through as perceant as the light / And find thee."[62] Emanuel Stelzer notes the "phantasmatic body" under construction here: the Ghost's penetrating ("perceant") freedom is granted by a supposed immateriality that contrasts with, and cannot be contained by, the corporeal "entrails" within the earth.[63] Unconstrained by fleshly limits, the ghost advises his former love that "Thou canst not catch my unsubstantial part, / For I am air, and am not to be touched."[64] When spoken by the performer, such statements are self-deconstructing, drawing attention to how impersonation, in this period, is limited to the substantial, touchable "part" of performance, the material player. The metatheatrical contradiction, perceptible to the audience, inflects Anne's response: "I know not whether I see, hear, or speak," she cries, for her "intellectual parts are frozen up / At the sight of thee, thou fiery effigies / Of my wronged Bateman."[65] At once embodied (for on- and offstage spectators) yet asserting ethereality, a physical effigy with a "fiery" intangibility, the ghost presents an aporia that forces the haunted subject to question the ontology of the spirit, its presence, and the condition of her own spectatorial senses. When the spirit next appears, in Old Bateman's house, before a portrait duplicating his once-living image, it seems so substantially present, manifesting "In every limb as perfect as he lived," that Anne moves to "hug and embrace it."[66] She is denied, however, by the ghost's foreboding revelation that "Thy time is not yet come; I'm now exiled / I may not touch thee while thou art with child."[67] The warning, which prophesizes Anne's suicide and post-parturition union with the vengeful spirit, allows Sampson to justify a common theatrical trope using a wry explanatory narrative logic: the performers must not touch lest they further disestablish the simulation of the ghost's self-proclaimed airy quality.

The incongruity between performer's body and disembodied ghost thus provides dramatists a source of arch comic irony across genres. These double-edged declarations of immateriality on the Renaissance stage cause haunted characters and offstage audiences to reflect on evidence to the contrary. The actor's bodily presence, in other words, causes incredulity as it becomes the subject of questioning within the play-world. In J.W.'s *The Valiant Scot*, for example, Wallace queries the spectrality of a prophesizing ghost on the basis that if it "hast a voyce," then "th'art bloud and bone, / As I am."[68] Wallace is a spectator for whom the assertion, "I am not here," would be wholly unsatisfactory. As it would be for Cleander in *The Lovers' Progress*, Philip Massinger's 1634 revision of John Fletcher's *The Wandering Lovers* (c.1624): he is initially perplexed by the (un)ghostly corporeality of a singing spectral Host, whom he meets at a tavern, remarking flatly, "He is not dead, he's here."[69]

Hermeneutic confusion could also be comically prompted by foregrounding the material cosmetics that acting companies conventionally used to portray ghosts. In William Heminge's *The Jews' Tragedy* (c.1626, no Caroline record of performance), we find Eleazer portrayed, in his madness, as fully aware of the flour conventionally signifying a spectral presence:

> *Enter his* FATHER'S GHOST *in white.*

> . . .

> GHOST
> Fool: thou art posting to the stage of death!
> Adiew, adiew, adiew: expect thy doom.

> *Exit* GHOST

> ELEAZER
> By this light a rare miller.
> Wo, ho, ho, wo, ho, ho: Miller, Miller.[70]

Eleazer perceives not ghostliness, but the actor's miller-like floured face.[71] While his lunacy attains a clear-sighted metatheatrical perspective, his dismissal of the ghost's presence fails to correctly accord with the representational conventions of his play-world. By contrast, in Sampson's *The Vow Breaker*, Old Boote is too invested in the material conventions of theatrical representation, interpreting Miles, the flour-covered miller of Ruddington, as a ghost in the play's final Act:

> MILES [*Aside*]
> Ha, Ha! No fool to th'old one! He takes me for a ghost!
> OLD BOOTE
> Art thou of air, of earth, heaven or hell
> Or art thou of some incubus's breed?
> Are there more walking Batemans? Answer me

I will beat thy carcass into a form
That is full substantial and has feeling!
Seeing, hearing, smelling and sweet-tasting ghost
I'll thunder thee![72]

The (albeit absurd) plausibility of Old Boote's confusion—a comic recalibration of Hieronimo's mistaking of Bazulto for a vengeful spirit in *The Spanish Tragedy*—conforms to the play's narrative logic because spectators must acknowledge that, even in the same play, the "authentic" ghost of Young Bateman was tangibly signified by a performer no less meal-faced than Miles.[73] Old Boote's delusion is one that audience members have themselves already willfully indulged.

"What Art Thou. . .": The Absent-presence of Intertheatricality

The representational conventions signifying the absent-presence of a spirit in early modern theatre—floured face, trapdoors, white-sheets, "robe to go invisbell," or (even more enigmatically) a "gostes sewt [suit]" and "gostes bodeyes [bodice]"—rely on intertheatrical cultural memory.[74] These signs spur memories of previous theatrical tropes to help spectators constitute the fiction before them. Representational conventions in this way work as a form of haunting. I have throughout this chapter been spotlighting intertheatrical connections to the ghost scenes of *Hamlet*, *Richard III*, and *Macbeth*: just as they offer the critic reference points, so too they provided dramatists efficient absent-present signposts by which audiences could be directed (or misdirected). The ghost in early modern drama solicits, even requires, frequent intertheatrical reference points.

Such cases productively complicate the notion of presence—"who is (not) here?"—through augmentation. Some non-spectral characters in fact undertake this themselves, overlaying intertheatrical markers to counterfeit a ghostly identity that augments the onstage spectator's reality: Borgias in John Mason's *Mulleasses, or The Turk* (1606, published 1610), fraudulently persuades Timoclea that he is an avenging spirit by co-opting the cultural memory of King Hamlet's Ghost.[75] The approach of morning that will end the ghostly visitation, which *Hamlet*'s Ghost signifies through the glow-worm that "gins to pale his uneffectual fire,"[76] finds new form in Borgias's image of the night's fading stars, which "gin to twinckle and take in their fires."[77] Borgias's strategy exemplifies a metatheatrical practice fairly ubiquitous amongst seventeenth century dramatists writing scenes of real or feigned haunting. Thomas Heywood's *The Second Part of The Iron Age* (1612–13, published 1632), for instance, may invoke a sense of déjà vu when the vengeful ghost of Agamemnon appears solely visible to his son, Orestes, as the latter confronts his mother about the father's death.[78] Audiences in 1612 would recognize the scene: so far, so *Hamlet*. But intertheatrical ghostings work through networks of similarity and difference. Although Agamemnon's specter, in contrast to King Hamlet's, haunts the bedroom to inspire Orestes's vengeful murder of his mother, the allusion to *Hamlet*'s closet-scene reminds audiences of Hamlet the Elder's failure to prohibit his son from directing vengeful energy toward Gertrude. Heywood is, moreover, asking audiences to acknowledge Shakespeare's "original" scene as, itself, a haunted palimpsest, making visible, as Claire Kenward puts it, "Shakespeare's submerged conflation of Clytemnestra/Gertrude and Orestes/Hamlet."[79] Agamemnon's vengeful son was, Tanya Pollard evocatively suggests, a "ghostly figure" in the sense that his story "haunted English stages in this period," with at least three sixteenth-century Orestes plays, and critics attuned to *Hamlet*'s classicism have, she notes, frequently discerned the absent-present "shadow of Orestes" in Shakespeare's play.[80]

Such layered references occur, too, in the reactions of early modern characters subjected to hauntings. Their responses are constructed through literary precedents that give representational efficiency to dramatists portraying the perplexity of characters beholding puzzling sights. Some achieve this with extreme economy. Aeneas's opening words to Hector's ghost in Heywood's *The Second Part of The Iron Age*—"What art thou …?"— efficiently prompt spectators to Horatio's fearful uncertainty from the opening scene of *Hamlet*,[81] although, as Catherine Belsey notes, it is "Banquo who features in the ghost's reply: 'I shooke these lockes, now knotted all, / As bak'd in blood.'"[82] That the phrase became synonymous with *Hamlet*'s opening ghost scene is evident in William Heminge's *The Fatal Contract* (*c.*1639), where Clotair adopts the language used on the battlements of Elsinore castle when he fearfully asks a counterfeited ghost, "What art thou that usurp'st this dead of night, / In metal like the age?"[83]

Some dramatists, by contrast, compose extended intertheatrical hauntings. In *The Roman Actor* (performed 1626, published 1629) Philip Massinger layers the audience's memory of the haunting from Shakespeare's *Richard III* on top of his presentation of Caesar's reaction to the vengeful spirits of his former opponents, Palphurius Sura and Rusticus, who appear to him onstage while he sleeps.[84] Plagued by internal debate, Caesar re-performs Richard's frightened awakening: "What accuser," he asks, "Within me cries aloud … Who dares speake this?"[85] Positing the vision and accusation as his own guilty conscience, his language, as with Richard's,[86] stages self-contestation.

One side cries, "Presumptuous traytor thou shalt dye," the other asks, "what traytor?" for "who can sit / A competent Judge ore *Cæsar*?"[87] only to settle upon the authority of his own moral judgment: "*Cæsar*. Yes / *Cæsar* by *Cæsar's*, sentenc'd, and must suffer."[88] Massinger calls for a mode of spectatorship that interprets onstage events mediated through familiar literary precursors. Whom do spectators perceive as present in these intertheatrical hauntings? Not just Caesar, or the member of Queen Henrietta's Men performing at the Salisbury Court Theatre in 1630: for "presence" here is a palimpsest, additionally layered with both the spectral absent-presence of Shakespeare's Plantagenet tyrant and the early modern spectator's memory of the tragedian who convincingly performed the haunted king, Richard Burbage.

"So did I Guess. . .": Speculative Projections

Early modern audiences had a host of superstitious, theological and dramaturgical conventions available to aid and complicate a stage-ghost's ontological presence and its purpose within the play-world. While documentary evidence of how audiences responded to these theatrical hauntings is scant, the texts discussed in this essay indicate models of spectatorship within the plays themselves. Characters who read and misread the ghost-as-spectacle repeatedly channeled their responses not just through demonological beliefs, but also through dramaturgical frameworks and precedents. Although the haunted characters typically received prophetic or commanding messages, from a dramaturgical perspective their relationship with the ghost is reciprocal; the onstage spectator's fearful, scrutinizing, chastened responses, contributed to the representational illusion of the ghost's absent-presence. In *The Vow Breaker*, Anne's sense of guilt informs her conjectural construction of the apparition's features in the midst of its haunting: "So did I guess," she explains "a flux of brinish tears / Came from this airy and unfathomed ghost."[89] Our offstage perception of a spirit is thus formed by the sight of its performer and the onstage spectatorship that scrutinize the threshold between presence and absence, visibility and invisibility. As a spectator—in the act of articulated perception—Anne gives back to the ghost a paradoxical ontology that exceeds available methods of representation. She perceives it as airy and, simultaneously, capable of bodily, tearful response, thereby reflecting her expectations and remorse. A "guess" augments what is "unfathomed" to bridge the gap between signifying body and absent-present signified. The early modern stage ghost draws attention to this mode of spectating that involves a dialectical exchange motivated by affect.

One of the few extant early modern accounts of a spectator responding to a stage-ghost suggests this dialectic. In *a Warning for Fair Women* we find the apocryphal tale of a woman who murdered her husband and subsequently beheld onstage "a tragedy / At Linne a towne in Norfolke," in which "a woman that had murtherd hers / Was ever haunted with her husbands ghost": "She was so moved with the sight thereof, / As she cryed out, the Play was made by her, / And openly confesst her husbands murder."[90] The stage accommodates haunting projections not simply because we witness impersonations of the dead, à la Nashe's necromantic history plays, or because actors dissemble the presence of those who are absent, but because spectators construct their own ghosts, providing interpretations overlain on the players' signifying bodies. The stage-ghost at Norfolk, after all, was "made by her" that viewed it through layers of guilt, remembrance, and fear of her husband's vengeful spirit.

The anecdote suggests that Govianus's query—"Who is not here?"—might be met with another: who is asking? For the foregrounded and at times comic representational insufficiency of sixteenth- and seventeenth-century stage-ghosts, too solid in their flesh, provoked and called attention to an audience's imaginative involvement in dramatic signification. Govianus's question foregrounds the fluctuating states of spectral absent presence that unite player, spirit, and theatrical memory. The answer to his ontological enquiry turns out then to be legion, with stage-ghosts and players alike subjected to imaginative processes of erasure and projection that respond to competing and overlapping personal, theological, and intertheatrical frameworks of interpretation. The theatrical ghost, so accustomed to instructing the haunted, called early modern audiences into an awareness of their own role in conjuring the shadows of the stage.

Notes

1   4.4.40–41. Julia Briggs, the play's recent editor, adopts the title "*The Lady's Tragedy.*" See Julia Briggs, ed., *The Lady's Tragedy*, in *Thomas Middleton: The Collected Works*, ed. Gary Taylor (Oxford: Oxford University Press, 2007), 833–906. I adopt the more commonly used title, *The Second Maiden's Tragedy*.

2   See Eleanor Prosser, *Hamlet and Revenge* (Stanford, CA: Stanford University Press, 1967). Prosser counts fifty-two ghosts in revenge tragedies from 1560 to 1610 (156–157).

3   See Susan Braund, "Haunted by Horror: The Ghost of Seneca in Renaissance Drama," in *Companion to the Neronian Age*, ed. Emma Buckley and Martin Dinter (Oxford: Wiley-Blackwell, 2013), 432.

4   Lukas Erne, *Beyond "The Spanish Tragedy": A Study of the Works of Thomas Kyd* (Manchester: Manchester University Press, 2001), 81.

5   Kyd's play went through ten separate editions between 1594 and 1610 and was performed twenty-nine times during the 1590s, making it the third most performed play of the era. See D.F. Rowan, "The Staging of *The Spanish Tragedy*," in *The Elizabethan Theatre V*, ed. G.R. Hibbard (London: Macmillan, 1975), 112–123.

6   Douglas Bruster and Robert Weimann, *Shakespeare's Prologues: Performance and Liminality in Early Drama* (London: Routledge, 2004), 2; ix.

7   Ibid., 2.

8   *Hamlet*, 1.5.189. All Shakespeare quotations are from John Jowett, William Montgomery, Gary Taylor, and Stanley Wells, eds. *The Oxford Shakespeare: The Complete Works*, 2nd ed. (Oxford: Clarendon Press, 1986, 2005).

9   Prologue, lines 1–4. Christopher Marlowe, *The Jew of Malta*, in *The Complete Works of Christopher Marlowe*, ed. Roma Gill et al. (Oxford: Oxford University Press, 1987), 5 vols: IV.

10 Ibid., 28–30.

11 On intertheatrical networks in this period, and in relation to dramatic ghosts, see William W. West, "Intertheatricality", in Henry Turner, ed., *Early Modern Theatricality* (Oxford: Oxford University Press, 2013), 166–170.

12 *Hamlet*, 1.4.24.

13 On the early modern ghost controversy, see Peter Marshall, "Deceptive appearances: Ghosts and Reformers in Elizabethan and Jacobean England," in *Religion and Superstition in Reformation Europe*, ed. Helen Parish and William G. Naphy (Manchester: Manchester University Press, 2002), 188–208.

14 See Stephen Greenblatt, *Hamlet in Purgatory* (Princeton, NJ: Princeton University Press, 2001), 255–257.

15 *Hamlet*, 1.3.21.

16 Robert Wilson, *The Pleasant and Stately Morall, of the Three Lordes and Three Ladies of London* (London: 1590), sig. J3; Thomas Kyd, *Cornelia* (London: 1594), sigs. E1^{r-v}.

17 John Marston, *Sophonisba*, in Macdonald P. Jackson & Michael Neil, eds., *The Selected Plays of John Marston* (Cambridge: Cambridge University Press, 1986), 5.1.39–40.

18 J.W. *The Valiant Scot* (London: 1637), sig. J4.

19 Thomas Bilson, *The effect of certaine sermons touching the full redemption of mankind by the death and bloud of Christ Jesus.* (London: 1599), 204.

20 William Perkins, *A Reformed Catholike* (London: 1598), 184.

21 Henry Smith, *The Sermons of Maister Henrie Smith gathered into one volume* (London: 1593), 535.

22 Philip Stubbes, *Two wunderfull and rare examples, of the undeferred and present approching judgement of the Lord our God* [...]. (London: 1581), sig. A3.

23 Philip Stubbes, *The Anatomie of Abuses* (London: 1583), sig. L4.

24 See *OED* shadow, *n.* 6b. On this linguistic link between actors and ghosts, see Sarah Outterson-Murphy, "Remember Me: The Ghost and Its Spectators in *Hamlet*," *Shakespeare Bulletin* 34. 2 (2016): 254.

25 William Prynne, *Histrio-Mastix. The Players Scourge, or, Actors Tragedy* (London: 1633), sig. X3; X2ᵛ.

26 Daniel Dyke, *The Mystery of Selfe-Deceiving* (London: 1614), sigs. D2ʳ⁻ᵛ; D2ᵛ. Prynne, sig. X2ᵛ.

27 Jonas Barish, *The Antitheatrical Prejudice* (Berkeley: University of California Press, 1981), 3; Prynne, sig. X2ᵛ; Ludwig Lavater, *Of Ghostes and Spirits Walking By Night, translated into Englyshe by R.H* (London: 1572), 141.

28 John Stephens, *Satyrical essayes, characters and others* (London: 1615), sigs. R4ᵛ–R5.

29 Fulke Greville, *Alaham* (c.1598–1603), in *The Complete Poems and Plays of Fulke Greville, Lord Brooke (1554–1628) in Two Volumes*, 2 vols. ed., G. A. Wilkes (New York: Edwin Mellen Press, 2008), I.181–398; Chor.III.75–77, 97–98.

30 John Marston, *Antonio and Mellida* in *The Selected Plays of John Marston*, eds., Macdonald P. Jackson & Michael Neill (Cambridge: Cambridge University Press, 1986), Induction. l.158; ll.139–141.

31 On the rhetorical intersection between possession and theatrical representation, see Jan Frans van Dijkhuizen, *Devil Theatre: Demonic Possession and Exorcism in English Renaissance Drama, 1558-1641* (Cambridge: D.S. Brewer, 2007), 153–184.

32 Michael Goldman, *The Actor's Freedom: Toward a Theory of Drama* (New York: Viking, 1975), 9. See also Mary Luckhurst, "Giving Up the Ghost: The Actor's Body as Haunted House," in *Theatre and Ghosts: Materiality, Performance and Modernity*, ed. Mary Luckhurst and Emilie Morin (Basingstoke: Palgrave, 2014), 166–168.

33 Richard Flecknoe, *Love's kingdom a pastoral trage-comedy with a short treatise of the English stage, &c* [...]. (1664), sigs. H2ᵛ–3.

34 Goldman, 15; Jonathan Holmes, "'Sometime a Paradox': Shakespeare, Diderot and the Problem of Character," *Shakespeare Survey* 59 (2006): 289–290.

35 *A Midsummer Night's Dream*, 5.1.118–119.

36 See Rebecca Yearling, *Ben Jonson, John Marston and Early Modern Drama: Satire and the Audience* (Basingstoke: Palgrave, 2016), 166–168.

37 Thomas Nashe, *Pierce Penilesse*, in *The Works of Thomas Nashe*, ed., R. B. McKerrow (Oxford: Blackwell, 1958), I.212.

38 See Brian Walsh, *Shakespeare, the Queen's Men, and The Elizabethan Performance of History* (Cambridge: Cambridge University Press, 2000), 108–138.

39 Pierre Le Loyer, *IIII Livres de Spectres* (Angers: 1586), trans. Z. Jones, *A Treatise of Specters or Straunge Sights* (London: 1605), sigs. N1ᵛ–N2.

40 Anthony B. Dawson, "Performance and Participation: Desdemona, Foucault, and the Actor's Body," in *Shakespeare, Theory and Performance*, ed. C.J. Bulman (London: Routledge, 1996): 29–42; 36.

41 George Peele, *The Old Wife's Tale* (1595), ed. Charles Whitworth (London: New Mermaid, 1996), ll.674–678. I follow critical tradition in referring to Peele's play as *The Old Wives Tale*.

42 Ibid.

43 Ibid.

44 Philip Henslowe, *Henslowe's Diary*, ed. R.A. Foakes and R.T. Rickert (Cambridge: Cambridge University Press, 1961), 325.

45 On costume conventions for staging spirits and the "embarrassing materiality of the immaterial Ghost" (245), see Rosalind Jones and Peter Stallybrass, *Renaissance Clothing and the Materials of Memory* (Cambridge: Cambridge University Press, 2000).

46 *Old Wives Tale*, line 1783 SD.

47 William Sampson, *The Vow Breaker*, in *A Critical edition of William Sampson's The Vow Breaker (1636)*, ed. Patricia A. Griffin. Doctoral Thesis (Sheffield Hallam University, 2009), 3.1.89–97.

48 Ibid., 2.4.36–37.

49 Ibid., 3.1.96.

50 *Hamlet*, 3.4.123.

51 *Macbeth*, 3.4.66–67.

52 *The Vow Breaker* 3.3.74–75.

53 *King Lear*, 5.4.286.

54 Thomas Dekker and Thomas Middleton, *The Honest Whore* (London: 1604), sig. J4^v.

55 Drew Milne, "What Becomes of the Broken-Hearted: *King Lear* and the Dissociation of Sensibility," *Shakespeare Survey* 55 (2002): 57, 55.

56 Anonymous, *A Warning for Faire Women* (London: 1599), sig. A2^v.

57 Marvin Carlson, *The Haunted Stage* (University of Michigan Press, 2003).

58 *Second Maiden's Tragedy*, 4.4.42 SD.

59 See E.K. Chambers, *The Elizabethan Stage* (Oxford; Clarendon, 1923, 1961), Vol. II, 336–337; Ben Jonson, *The Devil is an Ass*, ed., Peter Happé (Manchester University Press, 1994), 2.7.57–75.

60 *Second Maiden's Tragedy*, 5.2.153 SD.

61 *The Vow Breaker* 3.1.13–16.

62 Ibid., 3.1.60–61.

63 Emanuel Stelzer, *Portraits in Early Modern English Drama: Visual Culture, Play-Texts, and Performances* (Abingdon: Routledge, 2019), 200.

64 *The Vow Breaker*, 3.1.63–64.

65 Ibid., 3.1.81–84.

66 Ibid., 3.1.106; 3.1.101.

67 Ibid., 3.1.103–104.

68 J.W., *The Valiant Scot* (London: 1637), sig. J4.

69 John Fletcher and Philip Massinger, *The Lover's Progress*, in *The Dramatic Works in the Beaumont and Fletcher Canon*, vol X, ed. George Walton Williams (Cambridge University Press, 1996), 425–552; 3.5.68.

70 William Heminge, *The Jewes Tragedy* (London: 1662), sig. J3^v.

71 See Edmund Gayton's anecdote of two actors playing ghosts, "Faces meal'd, and Torches in their hands, and some flashes of Sulphur made at their entrance," in *Pleasant Notes Upon Don Quixot* (London: 1654), 94–95.

72 *The Vow Breaker*, 5.2.91–99.

73 Thomas Kyd, *The Spanish Tragedy*, ed. Philip Edwards (London: Methuen, 1959), 3.13.132–160.

74 *Henslowe's Diary*, 318–321.

75 Linda Woodbridge (*English Revenge Drama: Money, Resistance, Equality*, Cambridge: Cambridge University Press, 2010) suggests the "preposterous incident[s]" that abound in *Mulleases the Turk*, including its "phony vengeance-craving ghosts," are indicative of how "popular genres tend to tip into parody" (45).

76 *Hamlet*, 1.5.90.

77 John Mason, *Mulleases the Turke* (London: 1610), sig. J2.

78 Thomas Heywood, *The Second Part of the Iron Age*, in *The Dramatic Works of Thomas Heywood*, ed., R.H. Shepherd (London: 1874), III. 347–431; 384. Cf. *Hamlet*, 3.4.49–50.

79 Claire Kenward, "The Reception of Greek Drama in Early Modern England," in *A Handbook to the Reception of Greek Drama*, ed. Betine van Zyl Smit (Wiley Blackwell, 2016), 179.

80 Tanya Pollard, *Greek Tragic Women on Shakespearean Stages* (Oxford: Oxford University Press, 2016), 132, 117.

81 *Hamlet*, 1.1.53.

82 Heywood, 383–384; Catherine Belsey, "Beyond Reason: *Hamlet* and Early Modern Stage Ghosts," in *Gothic Renaissance: A Reassessment*, ed. Elizabeth Bronfen and Beate Neumeier (Manchester: Manchester University Press, 2014), 41.

83 William Heminge, *The Fatal Contract* (London: 1653), sig. E1.

84 Philip Massinger, *The Roman Actor*, ed. Martin White (Manchester: Manchester University Press, 2007), 5.1.180 SD. See *Richard III*, 5.3.128–210.

85 Ibid., ll.189–191.

86 *Richard III*, 5.3.186–207.

87 *The Roman Actor*, 5.1.193, 195–196.

88 Ibid., ll.196–197.

89 *The Vow Breaker*, 3.1.23–24.

90 *Warning for Fair Women* sig. A2.

Works Cited

Anonymous. *A Warning for Faire Women*. London: 1599.

Barish, Jonas. *The Antitheatrical Prejudice*. Berkeley: University of California Press, 1981.

Belsey, Catherine. "Beyond Reason: *Hamlet* and Early Modern Stage Ghosts," in *Gothic Renaissance: A Reassessment*, ed. Elizabeth Bronfen and Beate Neumeier. Manchester: Manchester University Press, 2014: 32–54.

Bilson, Thomas. *The effect of certaine sermons touching the full redemption of mankind by the death and bloud of Christ Jesus*. London: 1599.

Braund, Susan. "Haunted by Horror: The Ghost of Seneca in Renaissance Drama," in *A Companion to the Neronian Age*, ed. Emma Buckley and Martin Dinter. Oxford: Wiley-Blackwell, 2013: 425–443.

Bruster, Douglas and Robert Weimann. *Shakespeare's Prologues: Performance and Liminality in Early Drama*. London: Routledge, 2004.

Carlson, Marvin. *The Haunted Stage*. Ann Arbor: University of Michigan Press, 2003.

Chambers, E.K. *The Elizabethan Stage*, 4 vols. Oxford; Clarendon, 1923, 1961.

Dawson, Anthony B. "Performance and Participation: Desdemona, Foucault, and the Actor's Body," in *Shakespeare, Theory and Performance*, ed. C.J. Bulman. London: Routledge, 1996: 29–42.

Dekker, Thomas and Thomas Middleton. *The Honest Whore*. London: 1604.

Dyke, Daniel. *The Mystery of Selfe-Deceiving*. London: 1614.

Erne, Lukas. *Beyond "The Spanish Tragedy": A Study of the Works of Thomas Kyd*. Manchester: Manchester University Press, 2001.

Flecknoe, Richard. *Love's kingdom a pastoral trage-comedy with a short treatise of the English stage, &c*. 1664.

Fletcher, John & Philip Massinger, *The Lover's Progress*, in *The Dramatic Works in the Beaumont and Fletcher Canon*, vol X, ed. George Walton Williams. Cambridge University Press, 1996: 425–552.

Gayton, Edmund. *Pleasant Notes Upon Don Quixot*. London: 1654.

Goldman, Michael. *The Actor's Freedom: Toward a Theory of Drama*. New York: Viking, 1975.

Greenblatt, Stephen. *Hamlet in Purgatory*. Princeton, NJ: Princeton University Press, 2001.

Greville, Fulke. *Alaham*, in *The Complete Poems and Plays of Fulke Greville, Lord Brooke (1554–1628) in Two Volumes*, ed., G.A. Wilkes. New York: Edwin Mellen Press, 2008.

Heminge, William. *The Jewes Tragedy*. London: 1662.

Heminge, William. *The Fatal Contract*. London: 1653.

Henslowe, Philip. *Henslowe's Diary*, ed. R.A. Foakes and R.T. Rickert. Cambridge: Cambridge University Press, 1961.

Heywood, Thomas. *The Second Part of the Iron Age*, in *The Dramatic Works of Thomas Heywood*, ed., R.H. Shepherd. London: 1874.

Holmes, Jonathan. "'Sometime a Paradox': Shakespeare, Diderot and the Problem of Character," *Shakespeare Survey* 59 (2006): 285–297.

J.W. *The Valiant Scot*. London: 1637.

Jonson, Ben. *The Devil is an Ass*, ed., Peter Happé. Manchester University Press, 1994.

Jones, Rosalind and Peter Stallybrass, *Renaissance Clothing and the Materials of Memory*. Cambridge: Cambridge University Press, 2000.

Jowett, John, William Montgomery, Gary Taylor, and Stanley Wells, eds. *The Oxford Shakespeare: The Complete Works*, 2nd edn. Oxford: Clarendon Press, 1986, 2005.

Kenward, Claire. "The Reception of Greek Drama in Early Modern England," in *A Handbook to the Reception of Greek Drama*, ed. Betine van Zyl Smit. Malden, MA: Wiley Blackwell, 2016: 173–198.

Kyd, Thomas. *Cornelia*. London: 1594.

Kyd, Thomas. *The Spanish Tragedy*, ed. Philip Edwards. London: Methuen, 1959.

Lavater, Ludwig. *Of Ghostes and Spirits Walking By Night, translated into Englyshe by R.H.* London: 1572.

Le Loyer, Pierre. *IIII Livres de Spectres* (Angers: 1586), trans. Z. Jones, *A Treatise of Specters or Straunge Sights*. London: 1605.

Luckhurst, Mary. "Giving Up the Ghost: The Actor's Body as Haunted House," in *Theatre and Ghosts: Materiality, Performance and Modernity*, ed. Mary Luckhurst and Emilie Morin. Basingstoke: Palgrave, 2014: 163–177.

Marlowe, Christopher. *The Jew of Malta*, in *The Complete Works of Christopher Marlowe*, ed. Roma Gill et al. Oxford: Oxford University Press, 1987.

Marshall, Peter. "Deceptive Appearances: Ghosts and Reformers in Elizabethan and Jacobean England," in *Religion and Superstition in Reformation Europe*, ed. Helen Parish and William G. Naphy. Manchester University Press, 2002:188–208.

Marston, John. *Sophonisba*, in *The Selected Plays of John Marston*, ed. Macdonald P. Jackson and Michael Neil. Cambridge: Cambridge University Press, 1986.

Marston, John. *Antonio and Mellida*, in *The Selected Plays of John Marston*, ed. Macdonald P. Jackson and Michael Neill. Cambridge: Cambridge University Press, 1986.

Mason, John. *Mulleases the Turke*. London: 1610.

Massinger, Philip. *The Roman Actor*, ed. Martin White. Manchester: Manchester University Press, 2007.

Middleton, Thomas, *The Lady's Tragedy*, ed. Julia Briggs, in *Thomas Middleton: The Collected Works*, eds. Gary Taylor and John Lavagnino. Oxford: Oxford University Press, 2007: 833–906.

Milne, Drew. "What Becomes of the Broken-Hearted: *King Lear* and the Dissociation of Sensibility," *Shakespeare Survey* 55 (2002): 53–66.

Nashe, Thomas. *Pierce Penilesse*, in *The Works of Thomas Nashe*, 5 vols, ed., R.B. McKerrow. Oxford: Blackwell, 1958, vol. I, 137–245.

Outterson-Murphy, Sarah. "Remember Me; The Ghost and Its Spectators in *Hamlet*," *Shakespeare Bulletin*, 34. 2 (2016): 253–275.

Peele, George. *The Old Wife's Tale*, ed. Charles Whitworth. London: New Mermaid, 1996.

Perkins, William. *A Reformed Catholike*. London: 1598.

Pollard, Tanya. *Greek Tragic Women on Shakespearean Stages*. Oxford: Oxford University Press, 2016.

Prosser, Eleanor. *Hamlet and Revenge*. Stanford, CA: Stanford University Press, 1967.

Prynne, William. *Histrio-Mastix. The Players Scourge, or, Actors Tragedy*. London: 1633.

Rowan, D.F. "The Staging of *The Spanish Tragedy*," in *The Elizabethan Theatre V*, ed. G.R. Hibbard. London: Macmillan, 1975: 112–123.

Sampson, William. *The Vow Breaker*, in *A Critical edition of William Sampson's The Vow Breaker (1636)*, ed. Patricia A. Griffin. Doctoral Thesis. Sheffield Hallam University, 2009.

Smith, Henry. *The Sermons of Maister Henrie Smith gathered into one volume.* London: 1593.

Stelzer, Emanuel. *Portraits in Early Modern English Drama: Visual Culture, Play-Texts, and Performances.* Abingdon: Routledge, 2019.

Stephens, John. *Satyrical essayes, characters and others.* London: 1615.

Stubbes, Philip. *The Anatomie of Abuses.* London: 1583.

Stubbes, Philip. *Two wunderfull and rare examples, of the undeferred and present approching judgement of the Lord our God.* London: 1581.

van Dijkhuizen, Jan Frans. *Devil Theatre: Demonic Possession and Exorcism in English Renaissance Drama, 1558–1641.* Cambridge: D.S. Brewer, 2007.

Walsh, Brian. *Shakespeare, the Queen's Men, and The Elizabethan Performance of History.* Cambridge: Cambridge University Press, 2000.

West, William W. "Intertheatricality," in *Early Modern Theatricality*, ed. Henry Turner. Oxford: Oxford University Press, 2013: 151–172.

Wilson, Robert. *The Pleasant and Stately Morall, of the Three Lordes and Three Ladies of London.* London: 1590.

Woodbridge, Linda. *English Revenge Drama: Money, Resistance, Equality.* Cambridge: Cambridge University Press, 2010.

Yearling, Rebecca. *Ben Jonson, John Marston and Early Modern Drama: Satire and the Audience.* Basingstoke: Palgrave, 2016.

5

Creating Stage Ghosts: The Archeology of Spectral Illusion

Beth A. Kattelman

From Shakespeare's plays to gothic melodramas to Broadway musicals, ghosts have been popular characters in theatrical productions and performances. Although the figure of the ghost on stage has been widely studied and theorized, the technologies deployed to create theatrical specters have received less attention, with scholarship focusing chiefly on the mechanics of presenting ghosts, using Victorian-era spectacle and machinery.[1] Little work, however, has offered insight into the material culture and the cultural zeitgeist that supported and made these effects desirable at a particular time. This chapter, therefore, will explore the archeology of spectral illusion and the tools and materials used to "create" onstage ghosts, including mechanical apparatuses, luminous materials, projections, and reflections. Examining newspaper reports and theatrical reviews, the chapter will further theorize how the reception of these effects reflects ideological preoccupations with the nature of reality, sensory perception, and rational thought. Effects such as the phantasmagoria, the Corsican trap, and Pepper's Ghost not only reveal the social values of their time, but also provide potent insights into attitudes toward advances in science, improved manufacturing techniques, and a preoccupation with ideas about the veracity of the senses.

Early Ghosts

The question of how to present a ghost effectively onstage arises each time a director confronts a spectral character in the dramatis personae. The director must make sure that the specter can adequately convey an unearthly presence and that the ghostly effects can be executed surely and consistently. A mishap or miscalculation can disrupt the illusion and engender laughter rather than support the intensity of a melodramatic climax or a dramatic moment in a Shakespearean tragedy. To maintain maximum control over the presentation of a ghost, many directors opt for the simplest techniques, ones that employ no special machines, mechanics, or optical illusions, thus keeping costs low and the possibility of technical failure to a minimum. While often the otherworldliness of a stage ghost may be indicated by nothing more than makeup, some directors employ technologies that can render a spectral character unique or even astounding.

While we cannot pinpoint the first appearance of a stage ghost, by the late 1500s the character was a standard theatrical figure. If we do not know exactly how Elizabethan theatres presented ghosts, we do know that, by the late-seventeenth and eighteenth centuries, they were usually dressed in white, and the actors' hands and faces were whitened with makeup. As one commentator noted:

> The dress of the ghost should be the dress of most other ghosts, and that is *white*, at least so says ancient tradition; let him then be clad in such a garment as the managers would take care should adorn a ghost in a modern melo-drame: in fact, let him *look like a ghost*: then the face should be whitened, as should the hands . . .[2]

If makeup, according to this commentator, fulfilled standard expectations, other stage conventions occasionally dictated that spectral characters don costumes reminiscent of their station in life. In some mid-nineteenth-century productions of *Hamlet*, for example, the ghost of Hamlet's father wore an actual suit of armor, despite its potential to encumber and restrict movement. One actor, according to an apocryphal story, was "overcome by the weight of his harness, fell down on the stage and rolled towards the foot-lights, the pit raising an alarm lest the poor apparition should indeed be burnt by the fires of the lamps."[3] In such cases, the ghost exhibited all-too-present corporeality along with an opportunity for unexpected hilarity (or injury).

When performers embody a ghost, disguising the performer's corporeality is always a challenge. To this end, some directors have helped the performer seem amorphous by adding gauze or flowing material or having the character appear behind a scrim, thus blurring the outline of the human form. This technique was already in use in sixteenth-century Italy, as evidenced by the following description from Angelo Ingegneri's 1594 treatise on the theatre:

> If the spirit be not already upon the stage when the curtain rises, it should enter at the far end, behind a thin black veil which should wear the semblance or give the idea of a dark cloud or dense body of air, such as may be supposed to surround an inhabitant of the internal regions during its temporary sojourn upon earth. Through this veil the shade

should be seen in perpetual motion; for, in my opinion, a ghost should never stand still. The dress or drapery I would recommend is black taffety [*sic*] or sarsenet, which should fall over and conceal the face, hands, and feet, so that the figure would appear a formless form.[4]

These simple make-up and costume tricks indicated otherworldliness without employing complex machinery, and not only reduced the possibility of malfunction but lessened costs.

Another low-tech alternative was to use only a disembodied voice or represent the ghost only through the other onstage characters' reactions. Audiences who enjoyed seeing fantastic characters, however, did not always welcome these choices. For many theatregoers, ghosts were the most interesting and anticipated characters of the dramatis personae. In the 1794 Drury Lane production of *Macbeth*, for example, Banquo's ghost was left solely to the spectators' imagination. Dutton Cook reports that this atypical staging "was not found to be agreeable to the audience."[5]

A very important factor in the development of stage effects, of course, was the configuration of the performance space. Changes in theatrical architecture and seating arrangements brought new possibilities, and the advent of the proscenium arch (thought to have been introduced in early sixteenth-century Italy) increased the use of stage machinery. The framed stage allowed technicians to hide various machines behind, above, below, and on the sides of the stage. Thus, grand illusions and spectacular scene changes became the order of the day, allowing directors numerous ways to set ghosts apart from the human characters, both in how they entered the scene and how they looked on the stage.

A simple mechanism that came into wider use was the standard stage trap: a hole in the floor, usually covered by a trapdoor. Although this device had been used for centuries, it became particularly prominent during the heyday of gothic melodrama, a genre that thrived after the success of Matthew Monk Lewis's *The Castle Spectre* at Drury Lane in 1797. Gothic plays often featured hauntings and ghosts rising through a trap, their standard entrance on both sides of the Atlantic. In 1844, in the first American production of *A Christmas Carol*, at New York's Chatham Theatre, Marvin Carlson notes, "the figure of Marley rose through a trap door to the sounds of a bass drum."[6]

Phantasmagoria

In times of violence and turmoil, which often intensify fears of death and consideration of the afterlife, people often wonder if the dead may still be wandering the earth as ghosts or disembodied spirits. When reminiscences of the deceased are ubiquitous, some people seek comfort by trying to connect with the ghosts of loved ones. This was certainly the case during the era of the French Revolution (1789–1799) when hundreds of thousands of people died or were executed in the streets of Paris. Into this milieu came Étienne-Gaspard Robertson, a Belgian inventor, with his ghost show or "fantasmagorie," which featured ghostly figures—many of them celebrities of the Revolution—projected onto screens and smoke using a hidden magic lantern.

First presented January 23, 1798, at the Pavillon de l'Échiquier in Paris, Robertson's phantasmagoria intended both to frighten and to amuse. Robertson created his ghosts by using a movable magic lantern to project images from behind onto smoke, giving the images an animation impossible to achieve on a standard, planar screen. Because the lantern was on wheels, moreover, moving it forward and backward would change the size of the projections. Thus, Robertson's ghosts could grow or shrink, rush toward the audience or fade from it.

At the start of the performance, Robertson extinguished the candles in the room where the audience was gathered and then brought forth a variety of images. François Martin Poultier-Dellmotte, the editor of *L'Ami des lois*, who attended the show, described what occurred after the lights were doused:

> Robertson immediately threw upon the brazier containing lighted coals, two glasses of blood, a bottle of vitriol, a few drops of aqua fortis and two numbers of the *Journal des Homme Libris* and there instantly appeared in the midst of the smoke caused by the burning of these substances, a hideous livid phantom armed with a dagger, and wearing the red cap of Liberty.[7]

Robertson then conjured numerous other phantasmal characters, some representing audience members' lost loved ones, and some referencing major figures of the Revolution, such as Marat or Robespierre.

Robertson eventually expanded his projection techniques to create an ever-growing array of wondrous effects. In addition to the magic lantern, he employed the fantascope, which could project the reflected images of opaque objects, projections that created unique visions. Experimenting with mirrors, shadows, animated slides, crossfades, and superimpositions, he created a dazzling and somewhat spooky viewing experience consistent with the horror and trauma of the times. He also incorporated audio accompaniment and planted confederates in the audience to perform predetermined reactions to specific images. The multisensory experience was wildly popular.

Robertson continued his performances at the Pavillon de l'Échiquier until some potential political troubles forced him to leave Paris for a short time. When he returned, he resumed the performances, this time at the Convent des Capucines with great success. Running for four years, they were instrumental in establishing the Convent as a performance site[8] and led to his phantasmagorias becoming imitated throughout Europe.[9]

The phantasmagoria was made possible by Aimée Argand's invention of the Argand lamp, in the early 1780s. Recognizing the lamp's potential, Robertson was one of the first to employ it in his shows. This oil lamp's tubular wick allowed for increased airflow, giving magic lanterns much brighter light. Previously, only small audiences in intimate settings could view lantern shows, requiring lanternists to travel extensively and give numerous performances. The Argand lamp, however, enabled Robertson to accommodate larger audiences, increasing his profits and his word-of-mouth advertising exponentially.[10] His show thus became the standard by which other phantasmagoria shows were measured, and established him as the "father" of the ghost show.

Spiritualism

In addition to advances in science and material culture, social movements also significantly impacted theatrical production by bringing historically specific issues and narratives to the fore. The Spiritualism craze, for example, fostered an interest in stories featuring ghosts and other uncanny figures. The craze began in 1848, when two young girls, Kate and Margaret Fox, heard knocking noises in their Hydesville, New York, bedroom, sounds they claimed to be communications from beyond the grave. News of the phenomenon quickly spread, and soon much of the Western world was curious about communication with the dead. Newspapers reported ghost sightings, and many con artists took advantage of unsuspecting believers by setting themselves up as spirit mediums offering séance participants contact with deceased loved ones. These sham mediums became adept at employing magicians' tricks to convince the unsuspecting that they were receiving messages from the beyond. Strange sounds or voices might be heard, inanimate objects might seem to move of their own accord, and glowing, diaphanous figures might appear. Most of the phenomena associated with spirit manifestations had people rethinking the adage "seeing is believing." "As a means of reproducing and reanimating the dead," Sheri Weinstein notes, "spiritualism fostered new types of vision, new terms for vision and, overall, new conceptions of visuality."[11]

In this atmosphere, not surprisingly, mid-nineteenth century theatres capitalized on the excitement surrounding the possibility of engaging with spirits, by developing enhanced illusion techniques that drew on technologies created and perfected during the Industrial Revolution. Advances in machinery, glassmaking, and lighting facilitated theatrical experimentation by giving theatre-makers numerous new tools to create astounding visions.

Corsican Trap/Ghost Glide

One machine developed specifically to produce a "ghost" in the legitimate theatre was the Corsican Trap, a.k.a. Ghost Glide, so named because it was created for Dion Boucicault's 1852 adaptation of Alexandre Dumas's *The Corsican Brothers.* In the play, twin brothers share a psychic link. When one is killed in a duel, his ghost appears to his twin who takes it upon himself to avenge his brother's death. When the actor playing the ghost brother entered, he rose slowly through the floor while also slowly sliding across the stage. A small platform at the bottom of an inclined plane under the stage was connected to a winch and pulley system that, when cranked by stagehands, would cause the platform upon which the actor stood to slide up the incline. Directly above the incline, a slot in the stage floor ran almost the entire width of the stage. Masked with small strips of wood, this slot was attached to a movable belt that worked in the same way as a rolltop desk. The strip featured an opening just large enough for the actor's body. Because the belt concealing the slot in the floor was synchronized with the platform's movement, the opening stayed exactly above the actor. Bristles that filled the hole allowed the actor to pass through it while hiding the opening from the audience. Thus, the ghost seemed to emerge through a solid floor and to slowly drift sideways. According to one contemporary reviewer:

> First the head was seen, and then, as it slowly ascended higher and higher, the figure advanced, increasing in stature as it neared him [the actor playing his brother], and the profound silence of the audience denoted how rapt was their attention. Melodramatic effect was never more perfectly produced.[12]

The Corsican "Ghost Glide" met with both critical and audience approbation and became the expected way for the ghost in the play to enter, such that audiences were disappointed if a performance did not use the effect. The slow, majestic glide, accompanied by a melancholic "ghost melody," also provided an air of dignity and decorum lacking in most ghost entrances of the time. As one reviewer wrote:

The French dramatist, however, assisted by scenic device, has invented a ghost which does not thrust itself unnecessarily upon our presence, or like vulgar spectres, startle the audience from its propriety, by suddenly popping up through a trap and then display all the hideous ghastliness that red paint and fire can create.[13]

Pepper's Ghost

As the Corsican Trap demonstrates, advancements in technology provided opportunities to create or enhance stage illusions. The advent of inexpensive plate glass further advanced techniques for creating stage ghosts. While plate glass had been available in Europe since the early 1700s, it was expensive and full of imperfections that hampered transparency and clarity. In 1834, however, a cylinder sheet process imported from Germany allowed the British to manufacture large sheets of higher-quality glass inexpensively.[14] This improvement greatly increased the demand for glass and, by 1869, there were six plate glass factories in England.[15] Glass grabbed the Victorian imagination, offering new visual experiences both in the theatre and on the street. With the spread of plate glass and mirrors in buildings, the public acquired prolific opportunities for viewing reflections of themselves. As Isobel Armstrong points out, a "glass culture" came into being:

> Glass culture's material form was generated from the glass panel, vitreous squares larger than ever before, translucent, or silvered as a public mirror. These surfaces, recording the random, dispersed, and evanescent images of the body in the world, gave a new publicity to the subject, who could exist outside itself in these traces.[16]

Victorians enjoyed being able to see themselves reflected in the shop windows and watching the play of lights and images on the shiny surfaces. The availability of plate glass also encouraged optical experimentation.

Equally influential in theatre and performance was the limelight, an incandescent calcium oxide light invented by Thomas Drummond in 1816, which directed an oxyhydrogen flame onto a cylinder of lime. Because this very bright light could be directed and focused, the limelight led to the creation of the first theatrical spotlights. This technology, introduced at Covent Garden in 1837, was used widely in theatres by the 1860s. Limelight, in conjunction with plate glass, made possible one of the most influential ghost-creating illusions of the nineteenth-century, one that came to be known as "Pepper's Ghost."

Figure 5.1 Stage setup for Pepper's Ghost, *c.*1862. Le Monde Illustré.

John Henry Pepper first premiered Pepper's Ghost at the London Polytechnic Institute in 1862. Based on an idea presented to him by Henry Dircks, it cleverly exploited the fact that plate glass is simultaneously transparent and reflective. Because a windowpane can reflect any object in a room, when one looks out a window, he or she can see a translucent reflection of the items in the room as well as the world outside. This fact allowed the Pepper's Ghost setup to reflect "ghost" performers interacting with "live" performers, with whom they appeared to occupy a common space. The illusion was created by placing a sheet of glass near the front of a proscenium stage, tilted toward the audience at forty-five degrees, which could thus reflect objects and people in the theatre's pit. If a performer in the pit is illuminated with a sufficiently bright light, his image will appear on the plate glass and thus be superimposed onto the playing area. With the correct angles, the audience sees only the "ghost's" reflection and the stage beyond. The only other required adjustment was that the ghost performer be tilted at an angle parallel to the plate glass sheet, putting him in a position to appear as if he were upright on the stage. A review by one of the attendants of the initial demonstration stated:

> On Monday evening I went to see Professor Pepper's Ghost. The appearance of the Ghost, as an optical illusion, is one of the most remarkable discoveries of modern science. The apparent reality of the spectre puts into dim shade the living individual, who performs his part in the haunted chamber, rendering him more like the dark shadowy representative of a ghost, than the ghost itself. The contrast is wonderful! I feel but little doubt the exhibition might be so arranged, under favourable conditions, for an effect, that an assemblage of persons at first witnessing the illusion, might remain for some time in doubt, as to which is the living being, and which the spectre. The whole exhibition tends to prove the surprising effect of light and shade.[17]

In response to public interest, magazines and newspapers often explained how stage illusions were accomplished, much to the chagrin of the showmen who could make more money by keeping their setups proprietary. Such was the case with Pepper's Ghost. Several press outlets quickly revealed the secret, and even Dircks himself published a how-to book in 1863 because he felt that Pepper was not giving him due credit for the creation of the illusion.[18] When information on the mechanics of Pepper's Ghost became widely available, numerous showmen copied the illusion, and it quickly found its way into many stage performances, fairs, and festivals.

In order to adapt the illusion to as many venues as possible, several ingenious technicians experimented with alternative setups. In some theatres, for example, the pit was too shallow to hide the ghost performer there, thus making it impossible to recreate the configuration employed at the Polytechnic. Enterprising showmen, therefore, placed the ghost performer in the wings. In this case, the pane of glass stood upright, placed at forty-five degrees to the front edge of the stage. This created the same superimposition effect by allowing brightly lit objects on the side-stage to be reflected in the glass. Magician Henri Robin used this setup for his very popular ghost illusion performance, *Robin's Spectres*, at the Châtelet in Paris in 1866.[19]

Magician Harry Kellar created the Blue Room illusion, loosely based on the Pepper's Ghost principle. It employed several superimpositions to make it appear that magical transformations were occurring within the said small room. For this trick, Kellar devised a mirror that gradually progressed from completely silvered at one end to completely transparent at the other, so that, as the mirror slid into place, objects behind it gradually "disappeared," and the reflected objects in the wings slowly came into view. This careful control of the audience's point of view created an extremely convincing transformation effect.

Luminous Paint

The chemical development figuring most prominently in the production of stage ghosts was luminous paint. In 1870, Balmain's—the first, well-recognized luminous paint—entered the market.[20] This paint's phosphorous substance could be "charged" by a light source so that in the dark, the object glowed by emitting the light it had absorbed. The ability to make props and costumes visible in the dark was very opportune for those interested in creating glowing, otherworldly figures for séances, magic shows, and other popular entertainments. Designers found applications for luminescent paint in sundry stage productions. The *Ziegfeld Follies of 1922*, for example, prominently employed the paint in a spectacular number called "Laceland," featuring dresses of glowing lace.[21] Magicians also used it to create the phantoms and other objects that filled the theatre during the blackout sequences of the very popular midnight ghost shows, which played in film houses throughout much of the twentieth century.[22]

Conclusion

Ghosts that "materialize" through a stage floor, glide and ascend, appear translucent, or glow in the dark provide a visual metaphor for questions related to materiality, epistemology, and ontology. The most effective ghost illusions not only serve the performance, but also signify what is happening outside the theatre. As Jonathan Gil Harris and Natasha Korda have noted, "Stage properties encode networks of material relations that are the stuff of drama and society alike."[23] Theatrical illusion also encodes networks of material relations: new materials, gadgets, architecture, inventions, and social movements are just a few of the things that have influenced theatre history and played a major role in how ghosts have been presented on stage. By looking at tools and techniques such as these, researchers can gain a broader insight into the synergy that is ever-present between the theatre and society.

Notes

1   See Ray Johnson, "Tricks, Traps and Transformations: Illusion in Victorian Spectacular Theatre," *Early Popular Visual Culture* 5.2 (2007): 151–165; Iwan

Rhys Morus, "Illuminating Illusions, or, the Victorian Art of Seeing Things," *Early Popular Visual Culture*, 10.1 (2012), 37–50.

2   "The Ghost in Macbeth," *The Drama; or, Theatrical Pocket Magazine*, No. 1, Vol. VII, October 1824: 14–15.

3   Dutton Cook, *A Book of the Play: Studies and Illustrations of Histrionic Story, Life and Character*, 4th edn. (London: Sampson Low, Marston, Searle, and Rivington, 1882), 180.

4   Angelo Ingegneri, qtd. in W.J. Lawrence, "Stage Ghosts," *The Gentleman's Magazine*, Vol 263, 1887: 546.

5   Cook, 181.

6   Marvin Carlson, "Charles Dickens and the Invention of the Modern Stage Ghost," in *Theatre and Ghosts: Materiality, Performance and Modernity*, ed. Mary Luckhurst and Emilie Morin (New York: Palgrave Macmillan, 2014), 35.

7   François Martin Poultier-Dellmotte, qtd. In Mervyn Heard, *Phantasmagoria: The Secret Life of the Magic Lantern* (Hastings: The Projection Box, 2006), 92.

8   Ibid., 112.

9   Terry Castle, *The Female Thermometer: Eighteenth-Century Culture and the Invention of the Uncanny* (New York: Oxford University Press, 1995), 144.

10 For a complete history of the phantasmagoria and similar ghost shows, see Heard.

11 Sheri Weinstein, "Technologies of Vision: Spiritualism and Science in Nineteenth-Century America," in *Spectral America: Phantoms and the National Imagination*, ed. Jeffrey Andrew Weinstock (Madison: University of Wisconsin Press, 2004), 125.

12 "Theatres, &c," *Era*, February 29, 1852: 11.

13 "The Drama, Music, &c." *Reynold's Newspaper*, London, February 29, 1852: 9.

14 Jess Sharman, "Windows, Glass, Glazing – A Brief History," NBS.com, https://www.thenbs.com/knowledge/windows-glass-glazing-a-brief-history. Accessed December 31, 2019.

15 Thos Lockwoode, "The Manufacture of Plate Glass in England and the United States," *Scientific American* 21.13 (1869): 199.

16 Isobel Armstrong, *Victorian Glassworlds: Glass Culture and the Imagination 1830–1880* (Oxford: Oxford University Press, 2008), 95.

17 "Professor Pepper's Ghost," *Nottinghamshire Guardian*, Friday, July 17, 1863: 3.

18 Henry Dircks, *The Ghost: As Produced in the Spectre Drama* (London: E and F.N. Spon, 1863).

19 Henry Ridgely Evans, *The Old and New Magic* (London: Kegan Paul, Trench, Trübner and Co., 1906), 100.

20 E. Newton Harvey, *A History of Luminescence from the Earliest Times until 1900* (Philadelphia: American Philosophical Society, 1957), 347.

21 Jonas Westover, *The Shuberts and Their Passing Shows: The Untold Tale of Ziegfeld's Rivals* (New York: Oxford University Press, 2016), 210.

22 For more information on midnight ghost shows see Beth Kattelman, "Where Were You When the Lights Went Out?: American Ghost Shows of the Twentieth Century," in *Theatre and Ghosts: Materiality, Performance and Modernity*, ed. Mary Luckhurst and Emilie Morin (New York: Palgrave Macmillan, 2014), 96–110.

23 Jonathan Gil Harris and Natasha Korda, "Introduction: Towards a Materialist Account of Stage Properties," in *Staged Properties in Early Modern English Drama*, ed. Jonathan Gil Harris and Natasha Korda (New York: Cambridge University Press, 2002), 1.

Works Cited

Isobel Armstrong, *Victorian Glassworlds: Glass Culture and the Imagination 1830–1880*. Oxford: Oxford University Press, 2008.

Carlson, Marvin. "Charles Dickens and the Invention of the Modern Stage Ghost," in *Theatre and Ghosts: Materiality, Performance and Modernity*, ed. Mary Luckhurst and Emilie Morin, New York: Palgrave Macmillan, 2014: 27–45.

Castle, Terry. *The Female Thermometer: Eighteenth-Century Culture and the Invention of the Uncanny*. New York: Oxford University Press, 1995.

Cook, Dutton. *A Book of the Play: Studies and Illustrations of Histrionic Story, Life and Character*, 4th edn. London: Sampson Low, Marston, Searle, and Rivington, 1882.

Dircks, Henry. *The Ghost: As Produced in the Spectre Drama*. London: E and F.N. Spon, 1863.

"The Drama, Music, &c." *Reynold's Newspaper*, London, February 29, 1852.

Evans, Henry Ridgely. *The Old and New Magic*. London: Kegan Paul, Trench, Trübner and Co., 1906.

"The Ghost in Macbeth," *The Drama; or, Theatrical Pocket Magazine*, No. 1, Vol. VII, October 1824: 14–15.

Harris, Jonathan Gil and Natasha Korda, "Introduction: Towards a Materialist Account of Stage Properties," in *Staged Properties in Early Modern English Drama*, ed. Jonathan Gil Harris and Natasha Korda. New York: Cambridge University Press, 2002: 1–34.

Harvey, E. Newton. *A History of Luminescence from the Earliest Times until 1900*. Philadelphia: American Philosophical Society, 1957.

Heard, Mervyn. *Phantasmagoria: The Secret Life of the Magic Lantern*. Hastings: The Projection Box, 2006.

Johnson, Ray. "Tricks, Traps and Transformations: Illusion in Victorian Spectacular Theatre," *Early Popular Visual Culture* 5.2 (2007): 151–165.

Kattelman, Beth. "Where Were You When the Lights Went Out?: American Ghost Shows of the Twentieth Century," in *Theatre and Ghosts: Materiality, Performance and Modernity*, ed. Mary Luckhurst and Emilie Morin. New York: Palgrave Macmillan, 2014: 96–110.

Lawrence, W.J. "Stage Ghosts," *The Gentleman's Magazine*, Vol. 263, 1887.

Lockwoode, Thos. "The Manufacture of Plate Glass in England and the United States," *Scientific American*, 21.13 (1869): 199.

Morus, Iwan Rhys. "Illuminating Illusions, or, the Victorian Art of Seeing Things," *Early Popular Visual Culture*, 10.1 (2012), 37–50.

"Professor Pepper's Ghost," *Nottinghamshire Guardian*, Friday, July 17, 1863.

Sharman, Jess. "Windows, Glass, Glazing – A Brief History," NBS.com, https://www.thenbs.com/knowledge/windows-glass-glazing-a-brief-history. Accessed December 31, 2019.

"Theatres, &c," *Era*, February 29, 1852.

Weinstein, Sheri. "Technologies of Vision: Spiritualism and Science in Nineteenth-Century America," in *Spectral America: Phantoms and the National Imagination*, ed. Jeffrey Andrew Weinstock, Madison: University of Wisconsin Press, 2004: 124–140.

Westover, Jonas. *The Shuberts and Their Passing Shows: The Untold Tale of Ziegfeld's Rivals.* New York: Oxford University Press, 2016.

6

Blithe Spirit: A Spectral Anatomy of Astral Bigamy

Judith Roof

"Hail to thee, blithe spirit/Bird thou never wert"
Percy Bysshe Shelley, "To a Skylark"

A record player plays on stage. The record has preserved the sound waves of a voice singing a song at some other time and place. The lyrics of the song, Irving Berlin's "Always," assure the song's addressee of the singer's undying, timeless love. The play, Noël Coward's 1941 *Blithe Spirit*, extends the phenomenon of those preserved waves of extra-temporal co-presence as well as the recording's message of perennial devotion via the performative protocols of the spirit world. *Blithe Spirit* was first staged at the Piccadilly Theatre on July 2, 1941, for the longest run in a London theatre to that date. It was also produced on Broadway from 1941–1942. There were London revivals in 1970, 1976 (directed by Harold Pinter), 1986 (with Joanna Lumley as Elvira), 2010, 2014, and 2019–2020 (Starring Jennifer Saunders). In the United States, there were revivals in 1987, 2009 (with Angela Lansbury as Madame Arcati), and 2014.[1]

Blithe Spirit plays out what happens to the living when a "medium," Madame Arcati, brings back the preserved waves of the deceased, the ghostly manifestations of "historical" beings who have passed. Just as the Berlin record opens the stage to another world, so *Blithe Spirit*'s "medium" opens both the stage world and the entire theatre to the imaginary co-presence of present and past, a lover/husband together with his once-beloved and his now-beloved wives. Although the unworldly spousal encounter is the effect of dramatic conventions insofar as the play itself defines the hauntological status of the characters who appear, the onstage clash between the reappearance of an offstage past and the onstage present, between the dead and the living. In the process, *Blithe Spirit* explores the capacity of theatre both to define its spatio-temporal locus and to enlarge this staged diegesis beyond the stage. Hence, the blitheness of *Blithe Spirit* consists of the revelatory processes through which whatever we imagine to have been offstage was already produced as an effect of what appears on stage. One scene materializes an imaginary other scene. History and memory become the suddenly visible and audible reserve for an ongoing onstage drama, demonstrating how theatre literally emerges from an imaginary called into place by a "medium," in this case theatre itself. The ghost in the theatre is never some realistic reflection of either a past or probable dilemma—there is no "mirror up to nature." Instead the "medium" (both characters and theatre) generates infinite sequels in a temporality that literally pulls aspects of the past into the present. It is "Always."

The Theatre of "Astral Bigamy"

Blithe Spirit demonstrates this scalar capacity of theatre via an encounter with the spirit world conducted by a character who is a literal "medium." Author Charles Condomine, interested in writing a story with occult elements, has invited the neighborhood psychic cyclist, Madame Arcati, to conduct a séance at a dinner party also attended by his wife, Ruth, and the local physician and his wife, Dr. and Mrs. Bradman. Also present in the Condomine household are the Cook (who never appears on stage) and the apparently comic secondary character, the maid Edith, whose primary characteristic in the opening moments is frantic and clumsy haste. After the first scene's dinner with the two couples and Madame Arcati, the second scene stages the séance itself, a process akin to directing a dramatic scene on stage. Madame Arcati lays out the proper sequence of the séance—playing a record, seating the participants, switching off the lights, the medium pacing and perhaps lying on the floor, as she sits at the table between Mr. and Mrs. Condomine, touching their hands, contacting her "control" (the seven-year-old Daphne), and discussing the possibility of an "emanation," or an irritating poltergeistly intruder, an "elemental."[2] She assures everyone not only that she knows how to deal with these intruders, but also that they are not likely to appear "at this time of year."[3] The stage set, Madame Arcati performs the scene for real, enacting the process she had orchestrated: playing "Always" on the gramophone, turning out the lights, pacing, lying on the floor, sitting on the stool between Mr. and Mrs. Condomine, touching their hands, and contacting Daphne, who may have a cold, or, if Daphne doesn't answer, anyone who will answer on the other side.

When the other side finally responds, via raps on the table, Madame Arcati enquires about possible communications between the realms, asking if there might be someone who wants to communicate. Running through a list of possibilities, she ends up with a being who indicates that Mr. Condomine is the intended recipient, though no one can figure out who has recently passed that might want to speak to him. Reluctantly Madame Arcati goes into a trance to discern the communicant, restarts the gramophone with "Always," and begins to moan. When they all hear a child's voice, Madame Arcati screams and falls to the floor. The table begins to bounce and finally falls over, but, as the Bradmans argue about whether they should pick up the table, Charles hears someone command that they "Leave it where it is!"[4] When Charles asks who spoke, it turns out that no one else heard anything. Except, of course, the play's audience. Charles then accuses Ruth of playing a trick on him, when the voice intones, "Good evening, Charles."[5] Accusations of ventriloquism and trickery fly between Charles and Ruth until the voice finally identifies itself to Charles, at which point he suddenly arises, declares the séance over, denies having heard anything, and says he was only playing. Madame Arcati faints.[6]

This séance performance produces a strange version of dramatic irony, a doubled dramatic irony of dramatic irony, in which the audience sees and hears what some of the onstage characters see and hear, but not others. This doubled irony itself draws attention to the staged theatricality of the performance within the staged performance, as those on stage who become the audience to an apparently failed séance are subject to the dramatic irony, having no idea what is going on when Charles, and later Madame Arcati and Ruth, witness the manifestations of another presence. Another layer of irony emerges when the play's audience, like Charles, hears what turns out to be his dead first wife, Elvira's, voice from the start, as the play's audience sees the irony visited upon Charles by a mischievous Elvira whose exclusive manifestation makes it appear as if Charles is hearing things. That the layered ironies of the failed séance produced a real visitation, and that no one but Charles can apprehend it puts the play's audience in the position of a consumer of ironic irony, enjoying the irony engendered by Charles's unconfirmed contact layered over the irony of the stage audience's ignorance. This ironic layering suggests, finally, that the audience to the play, like Charles, may also be the victim of a belief in the appearances conjured by a medium and/or may also be privy to a species of metatheatrics produced by the staged characters' performance of non-apprehension.

A panicked Charles, insisting that they revive Madame Arcati immediately despite Dr. Bradman's advice to leave her alone, finally pours brandy into her mouth (again against Dr. Bradman's advice), which awakens her. Madame Arcati is hale, though she declares she won't be able to sleep, a prospect Charles also embraces. When Ruth asks him why he can't sleep, Charles tells her the episode has "unhinged me."[7] When Madame Arcati asks if the experience worked for them, Ruth assures her that very little occurred after Madame Arcati left. Although Madame Arcati insists that the scene produced an effect, the others deny any of the evidence Madame Arcati asks about from "apparitions" and "protoplasm," in the end claiming the entire event was "only a joke."[8] Worried that she has disturbed the other world, Madame Arcati suggests that if they notice any hints of it, they let her know. In her sensing this other world, Madame Arcati, like the play itself, confirms the layered ironies of disparate knowledge: she both knows and doesn't know.

Protoplasmic Expectations

The ghost, Charles's expired wife, who finally appears in all of her ashen glory shortly after Charles first hears her voice, thus already operates as the return of a past into the staged present, as a marker of irony, and as an embodiment of theatrical self-consciousness. She emerges, "charmingly dressed in a sort of negligee, everything about her is grey: hair, skin, dress, hands, so we must accept the fact that she is not quite of this world."[9] Only Charles on stage and the play's audience, presumably, can see her, taking the dramatic vocal irony of her emergence to a visual realm, in which her performative invisibility to the play's characters becomes even more difficult for the play's audience to affirm. Elvira's ghost both is and is not a ghost. In the terms of the play's framing séance, the ghost is both possible and accounted for, but in terms of the play as a performance, what the characters perform on stage is the open fabrication that they don't see and hear what Charles acknowledges and the audience perceives as present on stage. The ghostly figure, then, operates as the fulcrum of two simultaneous, layered, linked, but ultimately different diegeses: the pragmatic mundanity of the séance as a species of hoax and the realized imaginary of its success.

The differential stage apprehensions and ensuing confusions produced by Elvira's ghost produce a second act that operates like a sitcom, compelling the least likely and most humorously tortuous encounter possible between a dead former wife and the current living spouse. The simple proposition that Charles can hear what the others cannot immediately produces a comedy of misdirection. As the quasi-invisible Elvira joins Charles and Ruth after their dinner guests have departed, Charles drops his drink when he apprehends the grey ghost of Elvira by the fireplace. The ensuing mix of address, as Charles participates in conversations with both wives simultaneously, produces the species of comic misdirection that inevitably results in his both confusing and insulting his current wife, while trying to reason with the one who has passed.

Charles Why are you so anxious for me to sit down—what good will that do?

Ruth I want you to relax—you can't relax standing up.

Elvira African natives can—they can stand on one leg for hours.

Charles I don't happen to be an African native.

Ruth You don't happen to be a *what?*

Charles (*savagely*) An African native.

Ruth What's that got to do with it?

Charles It doesn't matter, Ruth—really it doesn't matter—we'll say no more about it. (*He sits down*) See, I've sat down.[10]

Although Charles in turn both converses with Elvira and asserts her presence while he also attempts to deny that presence by claiming hallucination or insanity, the persistent muddling of addressee occasions what seems to Ruth to be oddly out-of-place statements, such as Charles's evocation of an "African native" or his sudden assertion of his beverage capacity. The audience, who witnesses the production of the two contexts, also witnesses the production of three simultaneous scenarios (Charles and Ruth, Charles and Elvira, Charles and both). The audience, hence, must also actively sort the scenarios while it enjoys their clash and mistaken reference, as this produces continued comic misapprehension. Charles's juggling of addressees continues through the end of the first act and through the second, as his attempts to operate in both diegeses quickly get him into trouble with Ruth and irritate Elvira, who chides him for what she perceives to be his attitude towards her, as he tries to placate Ruth: "You mustn't think me unreasonable," Elvira states, "but I really am a little hurt. You called me back—and at great inconvenience I came—and you've been thoroughly churlish ever since I arrived."[11] Ruth retires at the end of the first act, feeling similarly insulted, leaving Charles with a thankful Elvira.

In the midst of the play's conversational convolutions are disjointed evocations of excessive presence: the characters' persistent declarations of something amiss, complaints about a sick child who claimed that Charles asked for her attendance, Charles's persistent denials that he called anyone, and Madame Arcati's suspicion that there is another co-present entity, even though she cannot perceive anything specific. A continuous reminder that the diegesis is not the diegesis the characters (or even the audience) might think it is, this incessant sense of a presence of something beyond even Elvira haunts the play, like another ghost that neither characters nor audience can see or hear. As a counterpoint to the comic misdirections caused by the clash of staged presumptions, this otherworldly beat expands the stage yet again, hinting at yet another scenario, another world operating beyond consciousness. This otherworldliness itself becomes the ghost of the ghost of the play, both a repetition of the phenomenon that has befallen Ruth, this time on the scale of the play's audience, and another layering of diegetic apprehension that lurks in the vague between-ground of consciousness and knowledge.

The Name Elvira Means All True

The ghostly Elvira increasingly and deliberately incites the second act's series of predicaments, beginning with Ruth's insulted scolding of Charles in Act 2, scene 1. Still incredulous that Charles might be unaware of his unchivalrous behavior, Ruth chalks it up to his being inebriated. But even if a drowsy Charles can recall only that he hallucinated, the audience to the play has seen Elvira's apparitional intervention and unless they, too, have hallucinated, they know more than Charles knows at this point (or think they do). Charles and Ruth's discussion of Charles's behavior, instead, deviates quickly into Ruth's castigations of his "didactic" and "puerile" views about women.[12] Given that Elvira's manipulations play with marital jealousies, the day after's discussion of Charles's boorish ignorance and Ruth's jealousies is expected fall-out from Charles's apparently having even entertained thoughts of his deceased spouse. Their conversation, like many in the play's second act, unwittingly juggles causalities that multiply with the play's layered diegeses, which means that in most of the spousal encounters there is always more than one referent for any evocation and more than one cause for any action. This layering produces persistent misapprehensions on the part of the characters in the play's quotidian diegeses, a certain knowing wisdom on the ghostly plane, and a vision of how these two diegeses interact to constitute the play itself.

Charles's and Ruth's morning discussion, for example, quickly turns to mutual accusations of misbehavior. Charles blames Ruth for not being sufficiently sympathetic, telling her that her lack of comprehension "shocked" him and that she had bossed him around as if she were "a sergeant-major."[13] Ruth, who had been the apparent recipient of Charles's remarks to the invisible Elvira, chastises Charles for calling her "a guttersnipe," telling her to be quiet, and suggesting that an invitation to go to bed was "immoral."[14] As the two argue about the motivation for Charles's behavior—whether he was drunk or really perceiving something supernatural—Elvira enters and the layers of mistaken address commence anew as Ruth mistakes Charles's responses to Elvira's claims that she could hear them arguing as comments Charles is making to her.

The conversational misperceptions multiply to the point that Ruth, taking the initiative, decides that her husband is ill and urges him to go to bed as she calls Dr. Bradman. As she tries to convince Charles to retire, Elvira tells him Ruth is planning something and that her focus on going to bed "is nothing short of erotic,"[15] and that Ruth will have him "straitjacketed."[16] Charles, of course, is already figuratively straitjacketed by the co-presence of his visible and not-so-visible wives.

The verbal misdirection has turned into an open competition that gathers layers instead of changing the characters' assumptions. The presence of the ghostly Elvira multiplies complications produced simultaneously by her invisibility and her active contributions to the exchanges of the living couple. Caught in the middle, Charles finally tries to take charge of the situation and mediate the two scenarios, first by asking Elvira to talk with him only when he is alone, then by trying to prove Elvira's certain presence to Ruth by having the (to Ruth) invisible Elvira transport objects around the room. Elvira reluctantly consents, moving a vase from the mantelpiece and carrying it around the room, but then she takes matters into her own hands (so to speak), banging chairs, slamming windows in Ruth's face, and finally smashing a vase from the mantel. Ruth accuses Charles of trickery, "hypnotism," and "autosuggestion" before she ends the scene in hysterics.[17]

The comedy of dual (and dueling) diegeses turns from matters of circumstantial misunderstanding to more motivated cruelty in the second act's second and third scenes. In self-defense, Ruth invites Madame Arcati to tea in hopes that she will be able to rid the house of Elvira's ghost. Madame Arcati, however, confesses that she cannot accomplish that, conceding that she doesn't know how. Pleased that she has no control over what might happen when she is in a trance, Madame Arcati herself embodies the conflicting dynamics her contact with the spirit world has set loose on the stage. Insofar as Madame Arcati is akin to a stage director as she sets the scene and commences the dramatic encounters, it turns out that she is only the inciter of improvisation, as she is both ignorant of the genre of action she has commenced and powerless to control what ensues. Envisioning the helplessness of her role, Ruth objects to the arrangement and especially to Madame Arcati's "amateur meddling," an insult to which Madame Arcati takes exception, claiming she's a "professional."[18] Ruth continues to try to convince Madame Arcati to act, but like the miscommunications that beset the séance's production of doubled diegeses, Madame Arcati takes Ruth's attempts to persuade her as insults, finally accusing the Condomines of discourtesy, of tampering "with the unseen for paltry motives and in a spirit ribaldry" so that what has happened is their own doing.[19]

The spirit of multiple address having become the inevitability of misconstrual, Madame Arcati leaves just before Charles and Elvira enter. At this point Charles,

Ruth, and Elvira converse, Ruth having apparently accepted the presence of Elvira's ghost, with Charles now transmitting (or, more accurately, censoring) what Elvira says for Ruth's benefit. Although the layers of the diegeses seem for the moment to have collapsed back together, Charles's translations replace the previous layers with yet another doubled scenario, as he attempts to encourage Ruth to embrace Elvira's presence. But when Ruth does address Elvira directly, Elvira (who, of course can hear Ruth without Charles's intervention) uses Ruth's inability to hear her to make snide comments to Charles.

Elvira now uses her clear advantage to cajole Charles as he tries to manage the temporary détente. But Charles loses control when Elvira tries to convey to Ruth that her advent was at Charles's behest. As Ruth asks to what Elvira was aspiring apart from "making Charles into a sort of astral bigamist,"[20] Charles, losing control of the exchange, finally addresses Elvira as "darling," a sobriquet Ruth overhears. When Ruth inquires to whom he was speaking, Charles tells her that he was talking to them both, provoking Ruth to declare the situation "intolerable," in response to which Charles chides Ruth in apparent defense of Elvira. Exasperated, Ruth tells Charles and the phantom Elvira that in the morning she will be going to the Psychical Research Institute in London.

At the end of the scene, after the advent of what appears finally to be a single diegesis in which Elvira attempts to seduce Charles, Charles leaves to dress for dinner, telling Elvira she can play a record. Elvira puts the play's theme song, "Always," on the gramophone. Edith enters the room to retrieve the tea tray, sees the gramophone playing, removes the record and puts it away. As she picks up the tray, Elvira takes the record back out and restarts the gramophone which frightens Edith who runs out of the room while Elvira continues to dance.

The doubled diegesis is back.

The Tragi-comic Wit of Doubled Doubling

The second scene of Act 2 shifts the function of the ghostly Elvira from the comic misunderstandings of misapprehended address to a more self-conscious exploration of the various possibilities created by the inevitable tussle between an invisible, sneaky ex- and an earnest, defensive current spouse. At the same time, the play's entanglement of two distinct diegeses—the corporeal and the incorporeal—also engenders a doubled consciousness: the world of the living and the denizens of a spirit world, each with their own motivations and protocols. Since the directorial Madame Arcati has denied having control of the encounter between these two worlds, the conflict between them continues without interference. The play's various architectures of doubled doubling, now freed from even the imaginary of supervision (as described by Madame Arcati in Act 1), not only encourage a recognition of the play's shifting modes of self-reflexivity, but also bring the question of the offstage and out-of-time onto the stage and into the play's juggled temporalities—a juggling that performs the unambiguous illusion of mixed worlds in a stage world that operates as both the singular diegesis of staged performance and as the mixed diegeses of multiple modes of existence. The departed, historical Elvira is now onstage, so what else can or will happen offstage? Or, given Madame Arcati's denials of responsibility, what might ultimately resolve the complexifying dilemmas?

Several days later, the third scene of Act 2 reveals that bad luck has befallen the Condomine household. Dr. Bradman, accompanied by his wife, has come to treat Charles, who has injured his arm. Dr. Bradman comments that Charles suffers from nerves, causing him to be unable to look at people he addresses as well as having a lack of focus in his discourse. When Ruth asks the doctor for evidence, Bradman replies, "Oh, he suddenly shouted 'What are you doing in the bathroom?' And then, a little later, while I was writing him a prescription, he suddenly said 'For God's sake, behave yourself.'"[21] The doctor's clinical perspective revisits the familiar trope of confusions of address among Charles, Ruth and Elvira, but the doctor's wife adds the offhand hint that all is not well in the Condomine household, noting that Charles and Edith both had a fall.

Onto what initially appears to be more of the same catachrestic address, this time with the unwitting doctor, pile suspicious whiffs of maleficence, of Elvira perhaps engaging in more than taunting access to Charles. Adding a layer of suspicion that hijacks what seemed to be comic misunderstanding into another, perhaps always less obvious but co-existing realm, forces the play's audience into a position similar to Ruth's, once she has accepted Elvira's haunting presence. On the look-out now for potential onslaughts from the spirit world, the play's audience reoccupies a position of dramatic irony in which they suspect what the characters may not yet have surmised, though this time the suspicions veer towards the tragic. For example, when Dr. Bradman suggests to Charles that he might rethink driving into Folkestone, but then concedes that he can drive if he is careful, the scene's ambience, though apparently the innocent aftermath of a group of misfortunes (Ruth has also announced that the Cook gave notice), becomes tainted with skepticism. What might have represented the best wishes of loved ones may now portend the opposite. Ruth urges Charles to stay home and scolds Elvira for selfishness in wanting to go to the movies when Charles is injured. It turns out that Elvira has left the room, as she is, Charles suggests, in an excited mood, which means that she is probably planning to do something.

The Astral Plane

Beginning to take Elvira's side in response to Ruth's warnings that Elvira's presence signals a struggle, Charles's vision of Elvira as someone who simply wants to be around him performs a version of conceited innocence whose naïveté fuels even more suspicion, as the play's layers coat evil onto mischief onto comedy. The extent of the evil becomes manifest when Ruth informs Charles that what caused Edith to fall and almost crack her skull was axle grease coating the top step. When Charles suggests that Ruth is lying, Ruth adds more evidence of malign intentions, including the time when a ladder broke while Charles was trimming a tree. The unwary Charles becomes the center of dramatic ironies when Ruth offers him Elvira's motivation for his demise as Elvira's desire to conquer Ruth so as to have Charles to herself, suggesting Elvira would do anything to that end.

Unwilling to credit Ruth's suspicions, Charles continues to trust Elvira, refusing to believe that she is being duplicitous. Now two apprehensions battle, and which is creditable? Do suspicions of malfeasance or belief in the persistence of love and devotion triumph? Or does the persistence of devotion itself produce the evil that Ruth suspects? Ruth attempts a new tactic to align Charles with her interests, telling Charles not to let Elvira know that they suspect her of plotting to kill Charles—"Don't give yourself away by so much as a flick of an eyelid,"[22] as she leaves the house to fetch Madame Arcati. As Elvira enters and Ruth has finally had enough, Ruth speaks directly to Elvira, telling her what she and Charles had been discussing, assuring her they had no secrets, and telling her that she doesn't approve of their driving to Folkestone. Ruth angrily departs.

The Odor of Protoplasm

The trap has been set, but it will turn out to ensnare the wrong victim. The specter exposes her own layerings: protests of love masking mischievous resentment motivating inhuman cruelties. At the end of the second act, Ruth dies in the crash Elvira had planned for Charles. Ruth had been right. In Act 3, amidst what appears to have been some reduction of the multiple interleaving layers, Madame Arcati reappears to correct her mistake, apologizing for being "remiss" and "untidy."[23] She asks Charles if he was still interested in getting rid of Elvira, but when his response exhibits sympathy for the deceitful ghost, Madame Arcati calls him a "fool."[24] As she tells Charles that she has a formula that can make Elvira disappear without damaging "her feelings in the least," Elvira enters the room, now manifesting bitterness that her plan to

Figure 6.1 *Blithe Spirit* at the Otterbein Theatre, 2015. Courtesy Otterbein Theatre, available under a CC BY-SA 2.0 license.

engineer Charles into the spectral realm had backfired.[25] But as Elvira, who complains about her recent fate, almost bursts into tears, Madame Arcati sniffs and declares that she can "smell protoplasm strongly!"[26]

Happy with the opportunity to commune with the spirit world, Madame Arcati is anxious to delve further into Elvira's state of mind, though Elvira wants Charles to lure Madame Arcati away so that Elvira can confess to Charles the motives for her re-manifestation. But Charles's and Elvira's conversation rapidly turns to alternating objurgation, as Elvira tells Charles she returned because marrying Ruth had "ruined" Charles and that his writing is no longer successful.[27] Insulted, Charles responds by asking about Elvira's affairs during their marriage, while Elvira accuses Charles of self-aggrandizement and frivolity. Because trading these accusations makes Elvira happy that her plan to hijack Charles into the spirit world had failed, she requests divorce from the dieges by asking Charles to have Madame Arcati help her escape the situation.

The so-far inept medium, though until a moment before still unconscious, reluctantly consents, but this time for her own benefit, as she would like to explore Elvira's experiences further. And reassuming her directorial persona, she warns them that she is not sure she can accomplish the task, for which Elvira belittles her efforts—the spirit making fun of the medium. Going through the same protocols as she did in Act 1, Madame Arcati repeats her performance. The diegeses seem finally to be about to merge, and although Elvira does not return, Madame Arcati knows something has happened. Ruth is back, now, like Elvira, a grey ghost, so that now two specters haunt Charles.

Several hours later, with Madame Arcati unconscious on the sofa, the three presences—one mortal and two protoplasmic specters—are quibbling about who brought them back: Charles or Madame Arcati. Focusing at this point on the séances themselves, all three presences resent the process—the stagings—that have either called them forth or forced them into performing such functions as "the damned table tapping."[28] Less acerbic than Elvira, the ghostly Ruth complains about the procedures that she had undergone. Calling Madame Arcati "a muddling old fool," with which Elvira readily agrees, Charles denies having had any part in the debacle. The two wives finally become allies, blaming Charles's lack of ability for their current status.

Agreeing to have Madame Arcati try one more time, they awaken her, though they are no longer convinced of her expertise. Discussing what called both wives back, Madame Arcati declares that "love is a strong psychic force, Mr. Condomine—it can work untold miracles. A true love call can encompass the universe."[29] While granting that, Charles finally confesses that his feelings are not that strong and denies having called them back. Mystified, Madame Arcati informs them that someone had to have wanted them back. Suddenly snapping her fingers, Madame Arcati suddenly recalls a previous séance, her "first smash hit!!" and asks for her crystal ball.[30] Gazing into the crystal, she sees a white bandage, and calls to what she sees, as Elvira declares that she'll scream if it is a "ghost," also hoping it's not someone with whom she is acquainted.[31] Edith appears with her head in a white bandage.

Although Edith first denies any connection to the spirit world, Madame Arcati tests whether or not she can see the two co-present wraiths, and seeing that she can, puts Edith into a trance. Declaring that Edith is a "Natural," Madame Arcati stages the disappearance of the wives, again putting "Always" on the gramophone and turning off the lights. As both ghosts resist one last time, they disappear and Madame Arcati awakens Edith and sends her back to bed. The play and the play of plays all seem to be over, all back where they belong. But Madame Arcati, as she leaves, advises Charles to leave the house as quickly as possible. He reluctantly agrees; she departs and, in a final soliloquy, Charles has the last word, telling his departed spirit wives how glad he is to be free of them. During his speech, the still co-present but now unseen spirits begin to break things and, with Charles's exit, furnishings begin to collapse. But even with the destruction of the set, the play—and its plays within plays—have established the stage as a site of multiple diegeses, at the end, finally, not simply pulling the curtain, but removing its support altogether. Past, present, offstage, onstage, stage/audience are always there, only to be evoked, present in waiting, making a theatre of the theatre. What the ghostly presences reveal is that if all the world is a stage, there is always another world in the wings.

Notes

1 There is not much scholarly criticism of the play *qua* play, as most commentary is presented in accounts of its author. See Robin Roberts, *Subversive Spirits: The Female Ghost in British and American Popular Culture* (Jackson: University of Mississippi Press, 2018); and Jackson F. Ayres, "From Pleasure to Menace: Noël Coward, Harold Pinter, and Critical Narratives," *Journal of Dramatic Theory and Criticism*, 24. 1 (2009): 41–58.

2 Noël Coward, *Blithe Spirit*, in *Three Plays: Blithe Spirit, Hay Fever, Private Lives* (New York: Vintage, 1999), 30.

3 Ibid.

4 Ibid., 33.

5 Ibid.

6 Ibid., 34.

7 Ibid., 35.

8 Ibid., 35–36.

9 Ibid., 38.

10 Ibid., 41.

11 Ibid., 43.

12 Ibid., 49.

13 Ibid., 51.

14 Ibid.

15 Ibid., 56.

16 Ibid.

17 Ibid., 59.

18 Ibid., 64.

19 Ibid., 66.

20 Ibid., 68.

21 Ibid., 74.

22 Ibid., 78.

23 Ibid., 85.

24 Ibid., 86.

25 Ibid.

26 Ibid., 87.

27 Ibid., 89.

28 Ibid., 98.

29 Ibid., 101.

30 Ibid., 102.

31 Ibid., 103.

Works Cited

Ayres, Jackson F. "From Pleasure to Menace: Noël Coward, Harold Pinter, and Critical Narratives." *Journal of Dramatic Theory and Criticism*, 24.1 (2009): 41–58.

Coward, Noël. *Blithe Spirit*, in *Three Plays: Blithe Spirit, Hay Fever, Private Lives*. New York: Vintage, 1999: 7–109.

Roberts, Robin. *Subversive Spirits: The Female Ghost in British and American Popular Culture*. Jackson: University of Mississippi Press, 2018.

7

The Ghost of Unrequited Love Possesses the Modern Heart: Paddy Chayefsky's Dybbuk in *The Tenth Man*

Ben Furnish

Inspired by the classic play of Yiddish theatre, Sh. An-ski's *The Dybbuk*, first produced in 1920, Paddy Chayefsky's 1959 play *The Tenth Man* puts in dialogue two perspectives on the ghostly presence in Jewish tradition.[1] *The Dybbuk* looks back to meanings invested in spirits by the occupants of the mid-nineteenth-century shtetl, a world untouched by the Haskalah or Jewish enlightenment that swept through Eastern Europe in the late nineteenth century. As such, it uses a haunted past to confront Yiddish audiences with a haunting past. *The Tenth Man*, set in mid-twentieth-century New York, evokes the past to confront a world where spirituality has become over-invested in notions of psychological cosmopolitanism. This confrontation was facilitated by the fortuitous confluence of post-World War II assimilation, a general aura of cold war apathy, and Chayefsky's personal fascination with the notions of identity and intimacy in the crucible of spirituality and psychology. The play's prescient critique of society's failure to reconcile scientific understanding of human behavior with traditional reverence for that which transcends reason therefore owes much to Chayefsky's choice of source material. Chayefsky's humorous transposition of *The Dybbuk*, which is neither a translation nor a mere adaptation, enables him to create a serious reconsideration of the Modernist embrace of psychology and of the limitations of science to explain the mystical and the supernatural.

The Dybbuk

The Dybbuk's author, an anthropologist and once-assimilated Russian Jew, wrote the play after participating in a research expedition through a number of Russian Jewish *shtetlekh* (villages) in 1912–1914, in an effort to document the vanishing folkways of these communities.[2] A dybbuk is a form of wandering soul in Jewish folklore and mysticism that occupies the body of a living person. The great poet Chaim Nachman Bialik translated the play into Hebrew for performance as the first full-length production in 1920, staged by Konstantin Stanislavski's Hebrew-language theatre, Habimah, a project of the Moscow Art Theatre.[3] After the great Yiddish-language Vilna Troupe staged the play (also in 1920), it became their signature production and quickly became a global favorite. Harold Bloom called *The Dybbuk* a warhorse of the Jewish stage,[4] and theatre audiences across *The Dybbuk*'s century of performances, in numerous languages, have responded to the play's setting in the culturally insular world of an 1860s shtetl.

The play tells the story of Khonen and his lover, Leah, whose father, Sender, has contracted her to marry another man. Khonen dies, perhaps in despair, and his dybbuk occupies Leah's body so that it can reveal that Sender and Khonen's now-deceased father had betrothed their children to each other before either child was born. After an exorcism removes Khonen's spirit from Leah, she invites the dybbuk to return to her. Confirming a love that predates birth and transcends death, Leah dies, allowing the spirits of the meant-to-be lovers to unite in death.

This was a play without precedent on the Yiddish stage. "[L]ove was a new topic for Jews," as Seth Wolitz notes. "There were no significant Jewish precedents for this topic on the Yiddish stage ... love in the Romantic tradition of the West, deriving from courtly love, remained an 'import' in a society still governed by arranged marriages."[5] The play thus captured a hybrid audience composed of Russians, who appreciated the play's treatment of love, and Jews, who appreciated its depiction of a not-too-distant past. The play's strength, Rachel Elior explains, was its nontraditional perspective:

> An-sky's play cast the dybbuk phenomenon in an entirely new light. Until then, Jewish dybbuk narratives had all been written by authors who had presented events from a traditional point of view—that of the exorcist who had come to reinforce the existing order, to strengthen the normative power relationships within the hierarchical, patriarchal society to assign sacred forces to the norm, and to restore stability.[6]

For Jewish audiences of the 1920s, the An-ski play offered a glimpse into a formerly isolated and largely vanished world, as it grappled with the emerging understanding of an Enlightenment subject whose options and agency were being codified in the first quarter of the twentieth century.

Figure 7.1 Habimah National Theatre's production of Sh. An-ski's *The Dybbuk* in Moscow, 1922.

The Tenth Man

Chayefsky's play, directed by Tyrone Guthrie, opened at the Booth Theatre in New York in 1959 and ran for 623 performances over the course of a year and a half. Its sixtieth anniversary prompted a planned 2020 revival of the play, in Yiddish translation, at New York's Folksbiene National Yiddish Theatre (though the COVID pandemic has delayed this production until a future year). Reviews of the Broadway opening were largely favorable. "Mr. Chayefsky, Mr. Guthrie, and the actors," *Times* critic Brooks Atkinson wrote, "have exorcised a dybbuk that has possessed Broadway since this shabby season began."[7] Although Kenneth Tynan, in the *New Yorker*, had some concerns about ethnic stereotyping, he compared Chayefsky's "meaty" dialogue with that of Clifford Odets.

Chayefsky's career is remarkable for the range of his accomplishments in televised drama, live theatre, and commercial film. Born in the Bronx in 1923 to Jewish parents from Russia and Ukraine, Chayefsky grew up imbibing a love of the arts and culture. He frequently attended Yiddish theatre productions as a child in New York. After graduating from college, he served in WWII (where he was given the name "Paddy" when he asked to be excused from kitchen duty so that he could attend Mass). Although Paddy became his authorial name, many felt the character of pugnacious Irishman better suited the personal persona of this semi-professional football player, while his writerly self came closer to introverted Jew, Sidney Chayefsky, who graduated from high school at sixteen and college at twenty, and who, at age twenty-three, while in the Army, wrote the book and lyrics for a musical comedy that toured Army bases for two years and eventually opened in London's West End. At the same time, his numerous oscillations from Hollywood to Broadway to television and back, again and again, were marked by frequent disputes, feuds, firings, and cancelled contracts. During the course of his career, he rejected, quit, or disowned more projects than many people are offered in a lifetime.

After the war, he earned a five-hundred-dollar writing fellowship which led to a brief stint in Hollywood, after which he returned to New York, where in the 1950s he became a central figure in "The Golden Age" of television drama. His most celebrated script, *Marty* (1953), became a Hollywood feature that won four Oscars. Between 1955 and 1968, Chayefsky wrote five Broadway plays: *The Middle of the Night* (1955), *The Tenth Man*, *Gideon* (1961), *The Passion of Josef D.* (1964), and *The Latent Heterosexual* (1968), and then returned to screenwriting for the rest of his career, producing, among others, screenplays for the Oscar-winning films *The Hospital* (1971) and *Network* (1976).

In the 1950s, Chayefsky became friends with Freudian psychoanalyst Ernst Kris, and, in 1957, shortly after Kris's death, began psychoanalysis. Although a year later he would break angrily with his analyst, Chayefsky biographer Shaun Considine believes Chayefsky remained in some form of analysis for the rest of his life, and it is certain that the poles of his personality could be characterized, at least metaphorically, as his being inhabited by a spirit or demon.

It is not surprising, therefore, that when his mother recommended he adapt the 1920 Yiddish play, *The Dybbuk*, he found it an inspirational vehicle for interrogating the relationship, in the late 1950s, between the spiritual aspects of his upbringing and the haunting qualities of the Freudian unconscious. For this reason, *The Tenth Man*, although clearly inspired by the play *The Dybbuk or Between Two Worlds*, is not an adaptation, a fundamental difference being that *The Dybbuk* asks the audience willingly to suspend its post-Haskalah/Enlightenment disbelief about the supernatural, while *The Tenth Man* asks the audience to question how their fundamentally modernist assumptions, especially Freudian psychology, discredit traditional beliefs in spiritual phenomena and faith-based remedies.

By 1959, the relationship of the psychological to the spiritual and the spiritual to the supernatural had long interested Chayefsky. When, as part of his army training, he became fluent in German, Chayefsky read Freud's *Interpretation of Dreams* in the original, and his 1952 television play, *Holiday Song*, featured an ambiguous collision between Judaism and the supernatural: a cantor in spiritual crisis, on his way to seek counsel from a senior rabbi, getting incorrect directions from a subway platform guard, meets an Auschwitz survivor who tells him how she has lost her husband. Returning to the subway, he meets same guard, who again directs him to the wrong train, where he meets another Auschwitz survivor, one who lost his wife at the same camp. This enables the cantor to reunite the couple, after which he returns to the subway platform, looking for the guard, only to learn that no such guard exists. The television drama ends with the cantor looking up toward heaven, his faith restored.

The Tenth Man, building upon the possibility of supernatural intervention, opens in the poor storefront Congregation Atereth-Tifereth Yisroel (Israel's Crown of Glory, perhaps named with a touch of irony) in Mineola, a Long Island suburb of New York City, where an increasingly frantic search for an adult Jewish male is under way. Jewish congregations conduct three daily services, *shacharit* (morning), *mincha* (afternoon), and *maariv* (evening)—though the latter two are usually compressed together—and each of these services, in order to qualify as public prayer services, not merely private devotions, requires ten adult (over the age of thirteen) Jewish men. As is frequently the case with congregations such as this, a sexton must often cajole members to show up (or even, in exigency, solicit a Jewish adult male from the street). Otherwise, the service, lacking a *minyan*, or quorum, cannot serve those who must attend to recite the mourner's *kaddish*, a prayer (said daily during the year of mourning and annually thereafter) memorializing a departed relative. Much of the play's conflict, as well as its humor, emanates from this need for a religious quorum. The small group of men who provide the core of this congregation's daily minyan are retired. One of them, Schlissel, is even a communist and atheist, who attends, he confesses, because he has nothing better to do.

On this highly unusual day, however, the quorum will also prove necessary to conduct an exorcism. Evelyn, the granddaughter of a congregant named Foreman, is about to be admitted to a mental hospital, but Foreman, fearing that commitment will cost her all chance of a full life, secrets her away to the synagogue. He believes psychiatry has failed to alleviate her schizophrenic symptoms because, he is convinced, she is possessed by a dybbuk, a dybbuk who has spoken to him as the spirit of Hannah Luchinsky, "the whore of Kiev, the companion of sailors," whom Foreman, as a youth in Russia, seduced, impregnated, and abandoned. Subsequently, after being ostracized from her community and forced into a life of prostitution, she met an untimely death at sea. Now, unable to enter heaven, she seeks revenge. Although Alper, Foreman's friend since childhood, remembers Hannah, other congregants remain skeptical until they see Evelyn and hear the dybbuk's voice. In the first act, when the men talk to Evelyn, Hannah, speaking through her, says, "There is one among you who has lain with whores many times, and his wife died of the knowledge."[8]. Zitorsky, a minyan regular, knows she is talking about him. In Act 3, Hannah returns to demand Foreman's soul as her price for releasing Evelyn.

Hirshman, a mystic whose hidden transgressions have led him to embrace piety, contacts his cousin, a famous rabbi, to help exorcise the dybbuk, and two members take off on the subway to see the rabbi while the sexton seeks the tenth man for the minyan. When his phone calls fail, he recruits off the street Arthur Landau, a young lawyer. Arthur, a completely secular Jew, ignorant of Hebrew or of religious practice, responds to the sexton's desperation, in part because he is desperate himself: he is on his way to his psychiatrist, having lost hope in life. Trying to phone his psychiatrist from the synagogue office, Arthur stumbles upon Evelyn and hears Hannah Luchinsky say "I am the whore of Kiev, the companion of sailors."[9]

Then Hannah stops speaking through Evelyn, and she speaks as herself. As they converse, Evelyn and Arthur are immediately intrigued with each other, and they converse with growing seriousness. Arthur delivers a memorable speech explaining that his life is a sham: "Life is utterly meaningless. I have everything a man can get out of life—prestige, money, power, women, children . . . and all I can think of is I want to get out of this as fast as I can."[10] In a turn that pays homage to the Yiddish stage tradition of the sudden arranged-marriage betrothal, Evelyn then suggests that Arthur marry her, an idea that turns out to be as prescient as it appears outlandish. When he rejects the offer as impractical, she counters, "Well, at least we begin with futility. Many marriages take years to arrive there."[11] She shortly becomes convinced that the suicidal Arthur is also possessed: "You are possessed by a dybbuk that does not allow you to love."[12]

In the meantime, Foreman is racing to assemble the minyan and perform the exorcism before the arrival of the police, contacted by Evelyn's father. Near the end of Act 2, the two men who, having gotten lost on the subway, failed to reach the prestigious rabbi, return to the synagogue. Therefore, Hirschman, who, before sinful transgressions in his young adulthood, had been a rabbi, must conduct the exorcism, assisted by the congregation's hapless young rabbi. They remain, however, one man short of a minyan until the policeman who has arrived for Evelyn mentions he is a Jew, and they inveigle him to be the tenth man, even though he does not quite understand what is happening.

In a ceremony on stage, complete with black candles, white shawls, and penitential recitations, the minyan led by Hirschman confronts the dybbuk of Hannah Luchinsky, who says, "I seek vengeance for these forty years of limbo! . . . my spirit has lived in dunghills and ashes, and I demand the soul of David [Foreman] son of Abram be cast . . . for the space of forty years times ten to gasp for air in the sea in which I drowned . . . a soul for a soul! That is my bargain!"[13] Explaining he cannot grant her conditions, Hirschman proceeds with the exorcism, the stage goes black, and the audience hears a body hit the floor. When the lights come up, the body is revealed to be Arthur's, not Evelyn's. Although Evelyn remains mentally ill, Arthur acknowledges his love by promising to marry and care for her, and the play ends with Schlissel, his secular skepticism chastened, saying to Alper, who has also changed his mind about the dybbuk's reality, "An hour ago, [Arthur] didn't believe in God. Now he's exorcising dybbuks," to which Alper replies, "He still doesn't believe in God . . . But now he believes in love, and when you stop and think about it, gentlemen, is there any difference?"[14]

This concluding sentiment has led some critics to fault the play's equivocation as an overly simple evasion of troubling dilemmas. Gore Vidal found "its conclusion pat, sentimental, and familiar,"[15] and Anatole Shub, writing in *Commentary*, an intellectual monthly founded at the end of WWII, expressing conservative views from the perspective of Judaism and Jewish culture, saw Evelyn as "a mere object, a foil, for Chayefsky":

It is Arthur who is saved, and his very character and demeanor announce a serious message—a prescription for all the complex malaises of modern times. The prescription turns out to be a sugar pill. In barely a dozen lines, at 11:10 p.m., we are asked to believe that Arthur's new-found "capacity to love," which allegedly absorbs the essential wisdom of both psychiatry and Judaism, will succeed where education, hard work, his first marriage, bed hopping, drink, power, and the Communist Party have all failed. The switcheroo is too abrupt, the pretension just too overarching.[16]

Chayefsky has taken a plot "that could end only in unhappiness," Abe Laufe argues, "and has foisted upon it a sentimental ending to intrigue audiences that want only a play with a love story, regardless of how contrived it might be."[17]

Robert Brustein, however, recognized the serious implications of Chayefsky's comedy, noting that "Chayefsky makes a comic juxtaposition between Old World simplicity and New World complexity."[18] "In this play," he explains, "simplicity, superstition, and mystical awe are supreme virtues, and one remains pure in heart by turning one's back on the Enlightenment."[19]

Even though Julius Novick finds the redemption of Arthur Landau "perhaps just a little simplistic, a little sentimental, a little too easy," he values the contemporary moral and social crisis that Chayefsky is engaging:

In attacking the spiritual and moral emptiness of American life, Chayefsky takes his place in a tradition that unites Jewish and Gentile playwrights. Unlike most of them, however, Chayefsky has a solution. He shows us a totally secular Jew in totally desperate straits, made whole in a synagogue through an ancient Jewish rite. It is highly unlikely that Chayefsky himself believed literally in dybbuks, or wanted us to; the point seems to be that it does not matter what you believe in— even dybbuks—as long as you believe in something. Of course, real believers tend to believe that it makes a great deal of difference what you believe.[20]

For this reason, as John Clum points out, "What gives *The Tenth Man* its tension is the fact that Chayefsky never lets his audience know whether the dybbuk has indeed possessed Evelyn Foreman."[21] The old Jews, Clum notes, "may be comic, but they are not fools. Moreover, their old-fashioned exorcism proves to be far more successful than the younger generation's psychoanalysis,"[22] in consequence of which, the play "began to dig deeper, to try to lay bare the spiritual malaise that cripples many modern men."[23]

Half a century later, *The Tenth Man* would similarly import the tenets of a lost world, grounded in the spiritual belief and rabbinical judgment that had hermetically preserved the foundations of Judaism in numerous countries, over millennia. In this historical moment, the values and transcendent powers represented by this world must grapple not with human agency driven by romantic love, but by the Freudian unconscious as it navigates the secular values of sex and money. In this context, the play offers a portrait of a struggling Orthodox shul/synagogue in the New York suburbs, where Judaism is not a spiritual center but a marginal allusion. As the atheist communist, Schlissel, says, "Well, look about you, really. Here you have the decline of Orthodox Judaism graphically before your eyes. This is a synagogue? A converted grocery store ... If it wasn't for the Holy Ark there, this place would look like the local headquarters of the American Labor Party."[24]

In this regard, the Mineola shul alludes not only to the state of suburban Judaism but also to the state of Yiddish theatre. The Holocaust destroyed a major portion of the world's Yiddish-speaking population and, with it, the venues and audiences for Yiddish theatre around the world. The thriving Yiddish theatre district of New York City, covering nearly half a square mile of the Lower East Side of Manhattan, shrunk rapidly after the war, and by 1959 only a tiny number of theatres in the city performed plays in Yiddish. Almost in celebration of its long tradition, many of its stars populated the cast of the *Tenth Man*, including David Vardi, one of the founding actors of Habimah, who played the Sexton. Jack Gilford, a vaudevillian comic, played Zitorsky. Jacob Ben-Ami, whose Yiddish- and English-speaking roles spanned half a century, performed his last Broadway show as Foreman, and Risa Schwartz, daughter of Yiddish Art Theatre impresario Maurice Schwartz, as Evelyn. *The Dybbuk*, moreover, was perhaps the most canonical work of the Yiddish theatre.

The Dybbuk, itself, exerts a ghostly presence in *The Tenth Man*. Hannah Luchinsky's voice humorously recalls not only the Old World but also the stage power of the classic play, even if, as the "whore of Kiev, the companion of sailors," she represents a less pure form of love than the chastely contracted romance and profound belief in love shared by Leah and Khonen, a portent of the modern understanding of love. That modern love is not secured for Arthur and Evelyn by psychoanalysis or through Hannah's haunting of Foreman's past. Rather it is resurrected through the ghost of *The Dybbuk*, a play that consolidated a now dead past of Jewish traditions and beliefs, of which Foreman and Hannah are both the diasporic expatriates and the tainted heirs. For this reason, Hannah Luchinsky, like An-ski's dybbuk, does not easily relent, insisting on confronting Foreman and the other minyanaires with a presence not explicable in rational terms, for whether or not Evelyn is psychotic, she still could not know the details of Hannah's life.

Crucially, instead of using the spirits to import the past, Chayefsky employs them to exorcise the postwar world, a world in which the unconscious has replaced the spirit. The ceremony, therefore, does not end up banishing Evelyn's dybbuk, but instead exorcising Arthur's modern ennui. For him, Chayefsky implies, abundant material and scientific advantages inhibit rather than facilitate the ability to love. As Evelyn tells him, "You have some strange dybbuk all of your own, some sad little turnkey, who drifts about inside you, locking up all the little doors."[25] Thus, Arthur and Evelyn's life together, while not promising to be idyllic, has the advantage of starting, as Evelyn has pointed out, where most contemporary marriages end up, and moreover it will do so infused by evidence of a faith not accessible to their contemporary, postwar suburbanites.

The juxtaposition of that superficial world, delimited purely in material terms and reduced to the confines of a suburban storefront shul, with the historically rich, if not exotic, Eastern European setting, from which this latest version of the wandering Jew emanates, contributes to the play's comic tone. The shtetl of old, depicting a time when belief in the supernatural was in some ways the norm, contrasts humorously with 1950s Mineola, where such a belief would be regarded as ridiculous, in the same way as are the intentional anachronisms of Jewish absurdists, such as Mel Brooks and Woody Allen. The absurdity of a storefront shul, practicing a faith devoid of spiritual power, is epitomized by its rabbi, who is conspicuous for his irrelevance in the play's action. Because he is nearly too busy seeking relevance in town to remember to show up at the synagogue, most of what he has to say is said on the phone to a rabbinical colleague: "You are a saintly, scholarly, and pious man, and you have no business being a rabbi. You've got to be a go-getter, Harry, unfortunately . . . let me recommend that you start a little-league baseball team."[26]

Nevertheless, this advantage acquired by Evelyn and Arthur is not limited to them. Rather it extends to the small community haunted by a dybbuk and informed by the traditions of the shtetl that preserved for centuries the practices of Judaism as well as its spirits. The other characters' reactions to the ghost provide a Rorschach test for modern ennui, for honest self-assessment, and for credulous faith in reason's capacity to secure a meaningful life. Those reactions form the work's center of gravity. Appearing in the first and third acts, the "dybbuk is the structural center of the play," John Clum points out, "and every character shows his outlook through his definition of this supernatural power."[27]

The characters' reactions to the dybbuk thus organize the play's action. If Arthur and Evelyn find the power of love in the face of the dybbuk's threat,

Hirschman is redeemed when his spiritual efforts are affirmed. Schlissel and Alper come to re-examine their skepticism, and Zitorsky confronts his own guilt. Even the young rabbi, separated from the telephone, manages to broaden his apprehension of the spiritual world, an apprehension so limited that minyan members realize he lacks enough traditional understanding to advise in the exorcism.

In ironic ways, this same failure of faith is replicated by critics such as Malcolm Goldstein, who took issue with how Chayefsky treated psychological subjects. In particular, Goldstein rejects the ending, "which clearly predicts that a deeply neurotic young man and a psychotic girl can work out their troubles successfully in marriage."[28] In so doing, he is placing a faith in Freudian psychology that affirms its status as a hard science, an idea that by 1959 was on the cusp of superannuation. Yet Freudian psychology, a movement that exerted powerful authority from the end of Freud's life in the 1930s to the early 1960s, would be regarded by the end of that decade as a model of the unconscious based on much more subjective and tenuous suppositions. In other words, it would line up alongside folkways and dybbuks as objects of skeptical scrutiny. Thus, even though Chayefksy called the play, "amusing, nothing more,"[29] it remains haunted by the implication that dybbuks might be real and exorcisms efficacious, not just for the subject possessed by a ghost but for the community performing rituals bereft of their rites, and the audience for whom that community is surrogate.

This very source of incongruous humor, the triumphalism of the modern rationalists, that Chayefsky satirizes, looks in hindsight eerily prescient in comparison with anthropologist Anthony Wallace who, in 1966, reflected a widespread sentiment when he wrote, "Belief in supernatural powers is doomed to die out, all over the world, as a result of the increasing adequacy and diffusion of scientific knowledge."[30] Within American Judaism today, Orthodoxy thrives, and its most strenuously observant branches are growing the fastest. The liberal Reform and Reconstructionist movements, ascendant in 1959, have been outpaced by Orthodox and Haredim, and the middle-ground Conservative movement—in the 1950s the largest trend, especially in the suburbs—is in steep decline. Among Christian denominations, too, evangelical groups, many of which reject science and evolutionary theory for what they believe to be literal interpretations of scripture, have experienced significant growth and exert significant political influence, while so-called mainline denominations (e.g., Episcopalians, Presbyterians, Congregationalists) that do not reject science, are on the decline.[31]

Although Chayefsky had what was in his time a devout Jewish upbringing and remained a proud and practicing Jew until his death, *The Tenth Man* does not merely celebrate Orthodoxy's possible resurgence or the superiority of

Old-Time Religion, nor is it a rejection of the Enlightenment, per se, as Brustein assumes. Rather, the play is a caution against hubris, one of drama's classic subjects. In particular, Chayefsky targets the Modernist hubris of those who, in 1959, were unable to accept that post-Enlightenment reason imposed any limitations on making life meaningful. Sixty years later, Orthodoxy continues to grow on the religious front, mysticism continues to fascinate the popular imagination, and the persuasive power of post-Enlightenment reason continues to encounter debilitating obstacles. For this reason, *The Tenth Man*, with its vexingly ambiguous ghost, speaks to the present moment in perhaps an even more powerful way than when it was first staged.

Notes

1   "Sh. An-ski" was the pseudonym of Shloyme Rapaport.
2   Seth Wolitz discusses the highly contested linguistic origins over this play, perhaps first written in Russian and then translated into Yiddish before the Russian original manuscript was lost. Seth L. Wolitz, "Inscribing An-ski's Dybbuk in Russian and Jewish Letters," in *The Worlds of S. An-sky: A Russian-Jewish Intellectual at the Turn of the Century*, ed. Gabriella Safran and Steven L. Zipperstein (Stanford, CA: Stanford University Press, 2006), 164–202.
3   Habimah eventually split from it and left the Soviet Union for British Mandate Palestine, where it eventually became the national theatre of Israel.
4   In Poland in 1937, it was made into a Yiddish-language feature film by Michal Waszynski.
5   Wolitz, 157.
6   Rachel Elior, *Dybbuks and Jewish Women: In Social History, Mysticism, and Folklore*, trans. Joel Linsider (New York: Urim, 2014), 122–123.
7   John Chapman in the *Daily News*, Richard Watts in the *Post*, Robert Coleman in the *Daily Mirror*, and John MacLain in the *Journal-American* also generally praised the play and the production.
8   Paddy Chayefsky, *The Tenth Man: A New Play* (New York: Random House, 1960), 22.
9   Ibid., 21.
10 Ibid., 69–70.
11 Ibid., 126.
12 Ibid., 129.
13 Ibid., 120–121.
14 Ibid., 154.
15 Gore Vidal, "The Couch in the Shrine: Review of *The Tenth Man*." *The Reporter*, XXI, December 10, 1959, 39.

16 Anatole Shub, "Paddy Chayefsky's Minyan: The Tenth Man on Broadway," *Commentary*, 28 (1959), 526.

17 Abe Laufe, *Anatomy of a Hit: Long Runs on Broadway from 1900 to the Present Day* (New York: Hawthorn, 1966), 250. Allan Lewis similarly sums up the problem: "Boy meets girl in a synagogue and wins her by losing his dybbuk." Allan Lewis, "Man's Relation to God: MacLeish, Chayefsky," in *American Plays and Playwrights of the Contemporary Theatre* (New York: Crown, 1970), 126.

18 Robert Brustein, "Dr. Chayefsky's Panacea: *The Tenth Man*," in *Seasons of Discontent: Dramatic Opinions, 1959-1965* (New York: Simon and Schuster, 1965), 95.

19 Ibid., 96.

20 Julius Novick, *Beyond the Golden Door: Jewish American Drama and Jewish American Experience* (New York: Palgrave Macmillan, 2008), 65–66.

21 John M. Clum, *Paddy Chayefsky* (Boston: Twayne, 1976), 67.

22 Ibid., 68.

23 Ibid., 70. For Ellen Schiff, Arthur was "a paradigm of contemporary cynicism and anomie." Ellen Schiff, "Introduction," in *Awake and Singing!: Seven Classic Plays from the American Jewish Repertoire*, ed. Ellen Schiff (New York: Mentor, 1995).

24 Chayefsky, 40.

25 Ibid., 125.

26 Ibid., 81.

27 Clum, 67.

28 Malcolm Goldstein, "Body and Soul on Broadway." *Modern Drama*, VII (1965): 420–421.

29 Shaun Considine, *Mad as Hell: The Life and Work of Paddy Chayfesky* (New York: Random House, 1994), 192.

30 Anthony Wallace, *Religion: An Anthropological View* (New York: Random House, 1966), 265.

31 Pew Research Center, "Religious Landscape Study," https://www.pewforum. org/religious-landscape-study/. Accessed December 30, 2019.

Works Cited

Astor, Frank. "The 10th Man Opens at Booth," in *New York Theatre Critics Reviews*, ed. Rachel W. Coffin, 20.26 (1960), 232.

Brown, Francie C. "Paddy Chayefsky." *Dictionary of Literary Biography, vol 7: Twentieth Century American Dramatists Part I, A-J*, ed. John MacNicholas. Detroit, MI: Gale, 1981: 111–118.

Brustein, Robert. "Dr. Chayefsky's Panacea: *The Tenth Man*," in *Seasons of Discontent: Dramatic Opinions, 1959–1965*. New York: Simon & Schuster, 1965: 94–97.

Chapman, John. "Paddy Chayefsky: 'Tenth Man' Endearing Play with Great Cast," in *New York Theatre Critics Reviews*, ed. Rachel W. Coffin, 20.26 (1960): 234.

Chayefsky, Paddy. *The Tenth Man: A New Play*. New York: Random House, 1960.

Clum, John M. *Paddy Chayefsky*. Boston: Twayne, 1976.

Coleman, Robert. "Robert Coleman's Theatre: 'Tenth Man' Absorbing," in *New York Theatre Critics Reviews*, ed. Rachel W. Coffin, 20.26 (1960), 235.

Considine, Shaun. *Mad as Hell: The Life and Work of Paddy Chayefsky*. New York: Random House, 1994.

Elior, Rachel. *Dybbuks and Jewish Women: In Social History, Mysticism, and Folklore*, trans. Joel Linsider. New York: Urim, 2014.

Field, Leslie. "Paddy Chayefsky's Jews and Jewish Dialogues," in *From Hester Street to Hollywood: The Jewish-American Stage and Screen*, ed. Sarah Blacher Cohen. Albany, NY: SUNY Press, 1983: 137–151.

Goldstein, Malcolm. "Body and Soul on Broadway" *Modern Drama*, VII (1965), 411–421.

Kerr, Walter. "First Night Report: 'The Tenth Man,'" in *New York Theatre Critics Reviews*, ed. Rachel W. Coffin, 20.26 (1960), 233.

Kerr, Walter. "*The Tenth Man*," in *The Theatre in Spite of Itself*. New York: Simon & Schuster, 1963: 165–168.

Laufe, Abe. *Anatomy of a Hit: Long Runs on Broadway from 1900 to the Present Day*. New York: Hawthorn, 1966.

Lewis, Allan. "Man's Relation to God: MacLeish, Chayefsky," in *American Plays and Playwrights of the Contemporary Theatre*. New York: Crown, 1970: 116–128.

"New Plays on Broadway." *Time*, 74.20 (1959), 59.

Novick, Julius. *Beyond the Golden Door: Jewish American Drama and Jewish American Experience*. New York: Palgrave Macmillan, 2008.

Pew Research Center. "Religious Landscape Study." https://www.pewforum.org/religious-landscape-study/. Accessed December 30, 2019.

Schiff, Ellen. "Introduction," in *Awake and Singing!: Seven Classic Plays from the American Jewish Repertoire*, ed. Ellen Schiff. New York: Mentor, 1995.

Shub, Anatole. "Paddy Chayefsky's Minyan: The Tenth Man on Broadway." *Commentary*, 28 (1959), 526.

Tynan, Kenneth. "The Tenth Man" (rev.), *The New Yorker*, 35 (1959), 21.

Vidal, Gore. "The Couch in the Shrine" (rev. of *The Tenth Man*), *The Reporter*, 21 (1959), 39.

Wallace, Anthony. *Religion: An Anthropological View*. New York: Random House, 1966.

Watts, Richard. "Two on the Aisle: Paddy Chayefsky's Modern Dybbuk," in *New York Theatre Critics Reviews*, ed. Rachel W. Coffin, 20. 26 (1960), 234.

Wolitz, Seth L. "Inscribing An-ski's Dybbuk in Russian and Jewish Letters," in *The Worlds of S. An-sky: A Russian-Jewish Intellectual at the Turn of the Century*, ed. Gabriella Safran and Steven L. Zipperstein. Stanford, CA: Stanford University Press, 2006: 164–202.

8

Of Outlaws and Spirits: Sam Shepard's
Fool for Love (1983) and David Mamet's
Prairie du Chien (1979) and
The Shawl (1985)

Ann C. Hall

Pop culture outlaws made Sam Shepard's and David Mamet's careers. Ne'er-do-well cowboys roam Shepard's Western landscapes, while con men and criminals slither through Mamet's urban environs. Shepard's *Fool for Love* (1983) and David Mamet's *Prairie du Chien* (1979) and *The Shawl* (1985) all introduce another, equally ubiquitous figure in American pop culture—the ghost. These plays, marking the first appearances of ghosts in the work of these major American playwrights, represents a shift in both authors' works, providing a unique way of connecting the audience to the stage. In all three plays, ghosts dramatize the uneasy relationship between fiction and reality and the difficulty of interpretation under such conditions. Characters struggle—how can they draw conclusions on such ethereal ground? Audiences, too, become involved in the interpretive difficulties. Instead of watching characters interact with ghosts, spectators engage with the ghosts, and thus with the play in a more robust way than were those (ironically, often invisible) ghosts absent.

David Mamet argues that art must have a double vision, which presents "problem and artifice."[1] Theatre, therefore, must help the audience resist "the liberal fallacy of assuming that because we can perceive a problem we are, de facto, not part of the problem."[2] Here Mamet reverses or at least revises the Brechtian alienation effect, asserting that to gain insight, audiences must be brought into the action rather than remain at a critical distance from it.

Alice Rayner also highlights the importance of the relationship between the audience and the drama, explicitly linking the experience to dramatic ghosts: "[Ghosts] serve not only to disturb the certainties of empiricism and the confidence of mastery over a field of inquiry but also to complicate distinctions between the scholar and her object, between subjects and objects, personal and political, the past and the presence, the living and dead, materiality and imagination."[3] In other words, stage ghosts make rigid empiricism tremble. But Rayner takes this idea one step further, arguing that stage ghosts not only interrogate easy assumptions and distinctions, but also make the audience experience the interrogation more fully.[4] In some ways, Rayner's argument resembles Martin Esslin's regarding the theatre of the absurd. While philosophy may describe the absurd, theatre creates the experience of it. For Rayner, ghosts trouble certitude in particularly effective ways, moreover, because the separation between spectator and spectacle is also disturbed, blurred, or even dissolved.[5]

Although Shepard's and Mamet's ghosts bridge the audience/stage divide, the playwrights represent their ghosts differently. Shepard's ghost functions in some ways like the return of the repressed. Because unresolved matter haunts the family, the more successful characters exorcise these ghosts, if possible. Mamet's ghosts are more complicated. While they may represent a scandal, something frightful, they also generate an artistic energy: that mysterious force that may or may not comfort but must exist in any world we desire to inhabit.

Fool For Love (1983)

When *Fool for Love* appeared in 1983, Sam Shepard was a celebrity. His good looks, raucous plays, interest in the American West, and personal branding made him the literary equivalent of Clint Eastwood's unnamed and immortal High Plains Drifter. Like the Eastwood character from the 1973 film, Shepard, his press releases claimed, came from nowhere; they asserted he studied with no one and did not revise his work. In other words, he projected himself as embodying the mythic American cowboy and self-made man.[6] He not only wrote about cowboys, he was one—independent, rebellious, hyper-sexual, and violent. While not dismissing his work, Robert Heilman tempered this hype, arguing that Shepard's development was less unusual "almost trite. He starts modestly and then makes it big in the manner of an American folk hero."[7] By 1983, judging from this play and its production process, it seems Shepard was also beginning to question his press releases.

With *Fool*, Shepard wanted to create a more fully developed female character, a departure from his earlier work, which focused primarily on masculine activities and perspectives.[8] And this goal gave him a lot of trouble. Unlike some of his other "one draft" works, *Fool* underwent multiple revisions, with the ghost not appearing until the final draft.[9] The ghost (the Old Man) serves thematic and narrative purposes; it was also a theatrical device that "offered a theatrical [solution], involving the presence of a character who suspends the play between fantasy and reality."[10] In keeping with Rayner's observation, Shepard's ghost not only complicates easy distinctions between fantasy and reality, but also affords the audience the experience. Shepard's ghost, in other words, presents a "real, live" audience with a "real, live" experience of the failure of existential certitude.

Set in a hotel room situated on the sands of the American desert, the play chronicles May and Eddie's turbulent relationship, critiques the powers of patriarchy, and questions the nature of reality. To May and Eddie's apparently "typical" American dysfunctional romantic relationship, Shepard adds a twist: the lovers (and the stage) are haunted by an Old Man who, having led a double life with double wives, is both May and Eddie's father. As "fate" would have it, May and Eddie fall in love only to discover that they are related.

Clearly the Old Man represents the persistence of patriarchy as well as its limits. As Stephen J. Bottoms notes, moreover, he exhibits the stereotypical masculinity that Shepard experienced through 1950s media.[11] At the beginning of the play, for example, even when May attempts to establish a life away from Eddie, the Old Man remains. When Eddie arrives at her new place at the motel, he enters roping and hog-tying everything in sight. It seems that he will win her over like a cowboy wrangling a steer that has escaped his pen. But as quickly as Eddie lassos a chair, May undercuts his machismo by swiftly and deliberately kicking him in the groin. "You can take it, right." May says, "You're a stunt man."[12]

And while Eddie may or may not deserve this swift kick, the moment illustrates that Eddie's "living present," in the words of Fredric Jameson, his macho assumption of power "is scarcely as self-sufficient as it claims to be."[13] Despite this assault on Eddie's masculinity, in the following scene, his machismo reanimates itself because, despite having been kicked by May, Eddie can construct any kind of reality he wants if he follows the lead of his Old Man. Immediately following the attack, the Old Man, uttering his first words in the play, supplies a masculine, existential balm: "I thought you were supposed to be a fantasist, right? ... You dream things up."[14] Because Eddie, confused and disoriented, does not concur, the Old Man offers an example: "Would you believe me," he asks Eddie, about a picture of Barbara Mandrell on the wall, "if I told ya I was married to her?" When Eddie responds negatively, the Old Man reveals the secret of his patriarchal power: "Well, see, now that's the difference right there. That's realism. I am actually married to Barbara Mandrell in my mind."[15] Through this speech, to which Eddie accedes understanding, the Old Man articulating a tenet of mythic American masculinity, has made Eddie "right" again, after May's attempted unmanning.

As David Derose notes, the Old Man's function is not just thematic. While the Old Man is "like some eccentric visiting dignitary who has been offered the best seat in the house, or a ghostly witness to a ceremonial family rite, the old man's unintegrated onstage presence takes the play out of the realm of realism, placing the reunion of Eddie and May, two incestuous half siblings, within a meta- theatrical framework."[16] The scene, in other words, not only foregrounds unusual family relationships and macho behavior grounded in illusion, but also highlights the act of interpretation. What is reality? And what is its relationship to truth? How do we draw conclusions or make interpretations, given this situation?

Such questions are not new to Shepard. His earlier play, *True West* (1980), illustrated the high stakes of interpretation. In it, two brothers compete to write a script for a Hollywood producer on the "true west." One brother creates his script using clichéd fictional images, such as cowboys, wild horses, and unbelievable chase scenes. The other brother wants to write a more "realistic" fictional tale. Instead of asking us to determine the best script, the play presents, in the battle between the two men, the violent nature of artistic creation.

Fool for Love, on the other hand, asks us, as well as an outsider, Martin, to evaluate Eddie and the Old Man's versions of the family's history versus May and the mothers' versions. Although Martin, like the audience, is just looking for an innocent night out—he has arrived to take May to the movies—he, too, must draw conclusions about the evening's events and entertain questions regarding reality and illusion. Because Martin, an outsider, is not a macho man, he needs instructions on the rules of this patriarchal game. While May is out of the room, Eddie explains them to him:

> **Eddie** I mean after a while you probably wouldn't have to take her out at all. You could just hang around here.
>
> **Martin** What would we do here?
>
> **Eddie** Well, you could uh—tell each other stories.
>
> **Martin** Stories?
>
> **Eddie** Yeah.
>
> **Martin** I don't know any stories.
>
> **Eddie** Make 'em up.
>
> **Martin** That'd be lying wouldn't it?
>
> **Eddie** No, no. Lying's when you believe it's true. If you already know it's a lie, then it's not lying.[17]

Following Martin's instruction, Eddie begins his story. He reveals that the Old Man fell in love twice, once with Eddie's mother and once with May's mother. He lived separate lives. One evening, when Eddie accompanied his father on one of the walks, he sees May for the first time: "the second we saw each other that very second, we knew we'd never stop being in love."[18] That ends Eddie's story. Like the Old Man, having found the woman of his dreams he has nothing to add. He has learned how to interpret his life and his legacy from the Old Man. According to the Old Man and Eddie, this tumultuous story is a love story.

May, however, has a different version. The "romance" was painful to the women, and Eddie's mother committed suicide as a result. When the women discovered the Old Man's "double life," they tried to keep Eddie and May apart, but it was too late. As David Derose argues, "May's subsequent story does not contradict Eddie's so much as broadens the perspective, continuing past the romantic conclusion Eddie has reached for the old man's sake."[19] But because May for the first in the story time is revealing the truth about the mothers, the stakes are much higher.

Shepard wanted to create a play with new gender representations, particularly a strong female character. It is important that May's response to Eddie's version of the story indicates that she no longer upholds the male "side of things." Even though she is initially tempted to deny Eddie's story and just silence it, she instead incorporates her mother's story into her own, speaking their truths about this "romance" between the Old Man and the two mothers. May's story reveals the dark underside of the romantic fiction that Eddie and the Old Man tell. It shows what must be silenced for the fiction to exist. To be "cowboys," in other words, the men must define as love what the women experienced as abuse. May's speech changes her status, so the Old Man, resists, claiming that this version cannot "hold water . . . That's the dumbest version I ever heard in my whole life. She never blew her brains out. No one ever told me that."[20] The play's representation of storytelling tempts us to believe the Old Man and treat May's story as just an alternative "version" that the Old Man dislikes. But when Eddie verifies May's version, even adding a supporting detail by telling the Old Man, "It was your shotgun,"[21] the Old Man pleads with Eddie, not by asserting his veracity, but on the basis of their "pact" to uphold the story as the Old Man told it, omitting the mother. Even if May's requiring Eddie's verification may not be the most feminist aspect of the play, it nevertheless valorizes Eddie's opting to oppose the Old Man by honoring the women's truth.

But the play does not end here. Eddie's momentary transformation ends when the appearance of another women, "the Countess," revives his allegiance to the Old Man. Like his father, Eddie juggles two women and two lives, and as in his father's situation, the women's discovery of one another has incendiary results. At the moment Eddie and May come together, ignoring the comments of the Old Man, the Countess sets fire to his horse trailer and Eddie runs out of the motel. Chasing a woman who thinks he's a Marlboro man, he heads out into the desert, never to return. May leaves, too, in a different direction. Her story having exorcised her past and her submission, she is no longer haunted by the ghost of her father.

The Old Man, left alone with Martin, ends as he begins, telling Martin the same story he had told Eddie, that Barbara Mandrell is not his wife, but the "woman of my dreams. That's who that is. And she's mine. She's mine forever."[22] Although Martin may not hear or see him, the audience does, giving the play its cautionary conclusion—imposing our will, our thematic interpretation, a meaning, is like being married to Barbara Mandrell in our minds.

The Old Man's ghostly presence highlights the influence of patriarchy and the perpetuation of stereotypical masculine behavior. Even if Eddie leaves the motel, he still repeats the sins of his father. May departs and finds her own voice, but the Old Man remains, haunting the stage and our lives. Although he remains perpetually ready to distort, obfuscate, and influence, the play exposes his perspective, his conclusions, his interpretations as only half of the story, the "male side of things." Shepard reminds us of alternative versions, to be considered as we draw conclusions about life and art.

Prairie du Chien (1979)

Frequently dismissed as a minor Mamet work or atmospheric piece, *Prairie du Chien* (1979) originated as a radio play for National Public Radio's "Earplay." Like Shepard, Mamet had experienced success and was at the time more fully branding himself as a member of the con artist and card sharp culture. This early piece, which was produced singly and contains elements of his later, longer works, such as *Glengarry Glen Ross* (1984) and the film *House of Games* (1987), was revived and linked with *The Shawl* in 1985, when Gregory Mosher took over the Lincoln Center Theatre. Although the radio play and the 1985 combination production received lackluster reviews, the later production led to the more successful Mamet-Mosher collaboration, *Speed-the-Plow* (1988). The pieces also indicate a shift in Mamet's artistic direction. *Prairie Du Chien*, for example, is set in Shepard country, "a railroad parlor car heading west through Wisconsin in 1910," as opposed to Chicago, the usual setting for Mamet's earlier works. *The Shawl* also contains the first homosexual couple in the Mamet canon. And both plays have a calmer pace. As Ben Brantley said of a recent revival, the plays make clear "that in a world ruled by the hustle, a whisper often trumps a scream."

In the Mamet canon, cons, cards, theatre, and religion occupy the same shelf. As Ira Nadel points out, Mamet's "ultimate confidence man is the writer who builds a world of illusion from actual experience."[23] Cards, moreover, connect with divinity: "when we are betting on the cards, we love their combinations. Their beautiful unfolding means that God Loves Us, their malevolent conjunction means that Someone is Trying to Teach Us a Lesson."[24] Both of these sentiments are present in *Prairie du Chien*, a short play featuring a storyteller whose ghost story seems to take on a life of its own during a card game that goes wild.

The play, which opens with a gin rummy player and a card dealer playing cards while another man is about to tell a story, immediately establishes a metatheatrical structure by including a listener and his sleeping son. Although the card players are merely playing, the storyteller is performing, and we, like the listener and his son, are his audience. While Deborah Geis correctly notes that Mamet frequently challenges us to rethink metadramatic conventions, choosing to throw "into relief the ability of the theatrical work to 'con' or persuade its audience,"[25] here the tale is told "straight." It is not a con, so the metadramatic techniques engage the audience, rather than expose the artistic production's scaffolding. As the play progresses, the audience becomes part of the play's action as much as the listener and his son become part of the story, such that the ghost story unites the characters and the audience.

With the gin rummy game continuing, the storyteller begins his tale, making the interruptions of the game seem almost incantatory. As the story intensifies and the game escalates, they feed off of the other's energy. The ghost tale is about a man and woman who fall in love, marry, and then fall out of love. The husband abuses the wife, and the wife is having an affair with their hired hand. One day, the storyteller, who visits the family during his occasional visits to town, runs into the husband, who says he's on his way to kill his wife because she is pregnant with a child he knows is not his. When the storyteller attempts to stop him, the man knocks him down, so the storyteller notifies the sheriff and the two go to the man's farm, only to find he has committed suicide and his barn is on fire. A woman's voice then directs them to the barn, where they find the woman, dressed in a beautiful red dress, dead along with her deceased lover. The confused men wonder whether another woman on the premises called them.

At this moment, the card dealer interrupts the story, asking, "You want it? Do you want the card?" To which the player responds, "yes,"[26] implicitly seeming to comment on the mystery of the woman's disembodied voice. We want that card, the play implies, or we want to know the truth. Do we want the riddle solved by seeing that connection to the otherworld, afforded, Mamet says by cards, cons, and fiction? Like the player, we, of course, answer yes, and the story continues: The storyteller and the sheriff find no woman in the house, but as the sheriff claims he saw the wife running through one of the rooms, the card game again interrupts the story: "You deal," he says. The player says, "*High* card deals,"[27] making it clear that, for both the story and the card game, the stakes are getting higher.

Pursuing the sheriff's claim, the two men go into a bedroom. The townsmen who have arrived plead with them to leave the house, now in flames, but the sheriff refuses. Suddenly they hear crying from a closet and, opening it, they find burning from the hem the red dress the wife was wearing in the barn, "as if it had just been lit."[28] Although the storyteller and the sheriff both survive, the sheriff never recovers. He sleeps all the time, loses his job, and tries to kidnap a ten-year-old girl he thinks is his daughter. The last heard of him, he was found in a rocking chair, in a red dress, sending visitors to the barn to help "him."[29] The storyteller, also affected by the tale, repeatedly mentions his inability to sleep and, as he tells the tale, seems to enter an altered state or trance. Ignoring questions from his listener about the story's details, he reflects, "They think they can talk to you, 'cause they see you so seldom,"[30] suggesting that this story has connected him to the townspeople in a disturbing way, a point underscored by the fact that the gin rummy game becomes violent as the story reaches its conclusion: the player, accusing the dealer of cheating, pulls out his gun, and fires. At first it appears that no one has been hit, but then boy wakes up and calls for his father, who tells him to go to sleep, but the boy is never heard from again, implying that the stray bullet killed him.

The story and the card game have exposed something evil, violent, otherworldly. The story, along with cards, which were frequently used in spiritualist practices, have conjured a presence in the railroad car, one that cost the boy his life. Clearly the ghost story affected both the sheriff and the storyteller. The father has heard the tale, and his young boy is dead. We have heard the tale and, in true ghost-story fashion, we have to ask what our haunting will bring or reveal. One answer, unlike Shepard's, is, if nothing else, a great story.

The Shawl (1985)

With its focus on a medium and a séance, *The Shawl* (1985) has roots in the American spiritualist movement that spread very quickly in nineteenth-century America, sparked by the Fox sisters' claims, in 1848, that they could contact the dead. By 1867, it was considered a religion, with one-third of the American population believing communication between the living and the dead was possible.[31] Although there is disagreement about the size of its following, the movement merited attention from important writers, thinkers, and religious leaders of the day.[32] Its popularity had many causes, including the new technologies of the telegraph and telephone: if people could now talk across time and space, they reasoned, why not to the dead? Spiritualism not only persists, Barbara Weisberg argues, but it also "dramatically influenced our ideas about immortality,"[33] an issue that, like a shawl, figuratively envelopes this play.

Although *The Shawl* resembles Mamet's film, *House of Games*, a long con with a female "mark," in this play an actual ghost appears, undermining the commitment to realistic cause and effect upon which the cleverness of a con game relies. As did *Fool for Love* for Shepard, *The Shawl* represents a departure for Mamet. Alain Piette notes that 1985 "was a turning point for David Mamet. His theatre, which had been criticized for its violence, its obscenity, its machismo, its misogyny, and its homophobia, seemed to open up to another range of characters, such as homosexuals and women."[34] Later Mamet would explore both in greater detail in his full length, *Boston Marriage* (1999). But unlike Shepard's work and even the earlier *Prairie*, *The Shawl*, uses its ghost to express the power of art.

The play opens with John, a medium, discussing supernatural forces. Since there are rhythms at work in our lives, he reasons, there must be connections to the otherworld.[35] He tells his customer, Miss A, that she, too, has psychic abilities: "For what brought you here? That knowledge. That there is a hidden order in the world."[36] Like *Prairie du Chien*, the play contains metatheatrical components, in this case expressed through John's interactions with his homosexual lover, Charles.

During the second act, John reveals his conning techniques to Charles, explaining that he received fifty dollars from Miss A, as part of the reading, which, he explains is "confidence money," money he is holding to see how far he can con Miss A. He even has Miss A sign the bill as proof of his integrity. Charles, astounded, asks "How will this money *come* to us?"[37] "It will come to us. *At the end.*" John replies, "When she asks, 'How can I pay you?' We say, 'Leave something. To help us with our work. Leave what you will' ... 'They will ask and they will reward.'"[38] Unconvinced and greedy, Charles wants more money quickly. John counters by telling Charles that he knows that he has pawned something. Shocked, Charles asks how he knew, and John reveals he discovered it accidentally but used the knowledge to prove his "psychic powers," just as he used powers of observation to "read" Miss A and her reason for coming to him. As he explains to Charles:

> I show you the trick "from the back" and you're disappointed. Of course you are. If you view it as a "member of the audience." One of the, you will see, the most painful sides of the profession is this: you do your work well, and who will see it? No one, really.[39]

Figure 8.1 David Mamet's *The Shawl* at the Atlantic Theatre Company, 2015. Courtesy of Ahron R. Foster, Stills & Motion Photography.

At the same time, of course, Mamet reveals the "backside" of the theatrical con, that we are manipulated by craft, not magic. And this revelation includes us in the con.

Pressured by Charles, John accelerates the con, which causes the séance to fail by exposing John's trick. When John misidentifies a fake picture of Miss A's mother, she threatens to leave and expose him as a charlatan, at which point he has another vision: "Oh, God Help Me. I see your Sainted Mother. Wrapped you in a Shawl. . . . And she thinks of you still. And calls to you. And she calls to you now. And I saw her by your bed. She Wore the Shawl."[40]

By appearing to have contacted Miss A's mother, John averts a scandal, impresses Miss A, and, most importantly, John convinces Charles he is a genuine medium worth Charles's time and effort. But it also reveals Charles's true character, leading John to break off their relationship by lying. He did not really see Miss A's mother; he merely did some research and deduced that her mother would have worn a shawl. Significantly, John tells Charles he is "now equipped to live in a world without mystery."[41] But since John is lying about having seen the vision, he is indicating how worthless he considers a world without mystery, lying, and fiction.

But the play preserves the sense of mystery Charles loses. When Miss A returns, John reveals that she burned her mother's shawl "in a rage. Standing somewhere by the water, five years ago,"[42] something that no one but she would know, thus affirming ghosts and clairvoyance while allowing us to choose between believing in money and cons or in mystery. "*The Shawl* tells a story, then, which Mamet feels can be seen 'from the back' without losing the simultaneous acknowledgement of the unseeable, the intangible—in effect, it insists upon a recognition of theatrical narrative's power to 'conjure' images."[43] And the ghosts enable a double vision that reveals the knowable while conjuring the unknowable.

All three of these short plays make the audience reflect upon mystery, afterlife, and spirits, thereby unavoidably engaging the importance of theatre. As Mamet writes, "the purpose of the theatre is not to fix the social fabric, not to incite the less perceptive to wake up and smell the coffee, not to preach to the converted about the delights (or burdens) of middle-class life. The purpose of theatre, like magic, like religion—those three harness mates—is to inspire cleansing awe."[44] In *The Shawl*, moreover, Mamet extends the spectral to its existential conclusions. Unlike Shepard's ghost, or even Mamet's in *Prairie*, the ghost in *The Shawl* represents the uncanny that makes theatre necessary and possible by luring the audience into an otherworld that mysteriously makes possible a "cleansing awe."

Notes

1   Christophe Collard, "Power of Description: Mamet's Matters of Confidence." *Pivot*.1.1 (2011). Available from https://doi.org/10.25071/2369-7326.32158.
2   David Mamet, "Decay: Some Thoughts for Actors," in *Writing in Restaurants* (New York: Viking, 1986), 114.
3   Alice Rayner, *Ghosts: Death's Double and the Phenomena of Theatre* (Minneaoplis: University of Minnesota Press, 2006), xxv.
4   Ibid., xxvi.
5   In "Boxing with Brecht," Ira Nadel, while examining Mamet's connection to Brecht, notes that Brecht encouraged people to smoke in theatres as a way of enhancing the alienation effect. The activity would prevent them from completely identifying or engaging with the action. But smoking could also connect audience and stage action and serve as an apt metaphor for the way in which the ghosts in plays unite spectators to spectacle. Just as characters smoking on stage would not be able to contain the smoke, so, too, the ghosts in these plays. Spectators and characters smell the smoke. Spectators and

characters experience the ghosts. What Brecht thought of as a means of distancing, could also unite. Ira Nadel, *David Mamet* (New York: Palgrave, 2008).

6   David Derose notes that when *Fool* came out on film, Shepard already had celebrity status: he was a "ruggedly handsome movie star and icon of American popular culture whose film presence has been compared to that of Gary Cooper. David J. Derose, *Sam Shepard* (New York: Twayne, 1992), 114.

7   Robert B. Heilman, "Shepard's Plays: Stylistic and Thematic Ties." *The Sewanee Review* 100.4 (1992): 631.

8   He says, "I was determined to write some kind of confrontation between a man and a woman, as opposed to just men. I wanted to try and take this leap into a female character, which I had never really done. I felt obliged to, somehow. But it's hard for a man to say he can speak from the point of view of a woman. But you can make an attempt." James A. Crank, *Understanding Sam Shepard* (Columbia: University of South Carolina Press, 2012), 14.

9   Derose, 122.

10   Ibid.

11   Stephen J. Bottoms, *The Theatre of Sam Shepard: States of Crisis* (Cambridge: Cambridge University Press, 1998), 16–17.

12   Sam Shepard, "Fool for Love," in *Fool for Love and Other Plays* (New York: Bantam, 1984), 26.

13   Mary Luckhurst and Emilie Morin, eds. *Theatre and Ghosts: Materiality, Performance, and Modernity* (London: Palgrave Macmillan, 2014), 9.

14   Shepard, 27.

15   Ibid.

16   Derose, 115.

17   Shepard, 45.

18   Ibid., 50.

19   Derose, 119.

20   Shepard, 54.

21   Ibid.

22   Ibid., 57.

23   Nadel, 6.

24   David Mamet, "Black as the Ace of Spades," in *Some Freaks* (New York: Viking, 1989), 173.

25   Deborah Geis, "The Melodramatic Tradition," in *David Mamet: A Casebook*, ed. Leslie Kane (New York: Garland, 1992), 50.

26   Mamet, *Prairie*, 67.

27   Ibid., 70.

28   Ibid., 71.

29   Ibid., 75.

30   Ibid., 81.

31   Robert S. Cox, *Body and Soul: A Sympathetic History of American Spiritualism* (Charlottesville: University of Virginia Press, 2003), 237.

32 See, for example, Howard Kerr's *Mediums, and Spirit Rappers, and Roaring Radicals: Spiritualism in American Literature, 1850-1900* (Urbana: University of Illinois Press, 1972), 3–22.

33 Barbara Weisberg, *Talking to the Dead: Kate and Maggie Fox and the Rise of Spiritualism* (New York: Harper Collins, 2004), 4.

34 Alain Piette, "The 1980s," in *The Cambridge Companion to David Mamet*, ed. Christopher Bigsby (Cambridge: Cambridge University Press, 2004), 83.

35 Mamet, *Shawl* 3–5.

36 Ibid., 6.

37 Ibid., 19.

38 Ibid., 20.

39 Ibid., 26.

40 Ibid., 45.

41 Ibid., 48.

42 Ibid., 53.

43 Deborah Geis, "The Metadramatic Tradition," in *David Mamet: A Casebook*, ed. Leslie Kane (New York: Garland, 1992), 65.

44 David Mamet, *3 Uses of the Knife: On the Nature and Purpose of Drama* (New York: Columbia University Press, 1998), 69.

Works Cited

Bottoms, Stephen J. *The Theatre of Sam Shepard: States of Crisis.* Cambridge: Cambridge University Press, 1998.

Brantley, Ben. "David Mamet's 'Ghost Stories,' Bedtime Tales With a Gunshot." *New York Times.* June 16, 2015.

Collard, Christophe. "Power of Description: Mamet's Matters of Confidence." *Pivot.*1.1 (2011). Available from https://doi.org/10.25071/2369-7326.32158.

Cox, Robert S. *Body and Soul: A Sympathetic History of American Spiritualism.* Charlottesville: University of Virginia Press, 2003.

Crank, James A. *Understanding Sam Shepard.* Columbia: University of South Carolina, 2012.

Derose, David J. *Sam Shepard.* New York: Twayne, 1992.

Geis, Deborah. "The Metadramatic Tradition," in *David Mamet: A Casebook*, ed. Leslie Kane. New York: Garland, 1992: 49–68.

Heilman, Robert B. "Shepard's Plays: Stylistic and Thematic Ties." *The Sewanee Review*, 100.4 (1992): 630–644. JSTOR, www.jstor.org/stable/27546616. Accessed January 19, 2020.

Kerr, Howard. *Mediums, and Spirit Rappers, and Roaring Radicals: Spiritualism in American Literature, 1850-1900.* Urbana: University of Illinois Press, 1972.

Luckhurst, Mary and Emilie Morin, eds. *Theatre and Ghosts: Materiality, Performance, and Modernity.* London: Palgrave Macmillan, 2014.

Mamet, David. *3 Uses of the Knife: On the Nature and Purpose of Drama*. New York: Columbia University Press, 1998.

Mamet, David. "Black as the Ace of Spades," in *Some Freaks*. New York: Viking, 1989: 172–174.

Mamet, David. "Decay: Some Thoughts for Actors," in *Writing in Restaurants*. New York: Viking, 1986: 110–117.

Mamet, David. *The Shawl* and *Prairie du Chien*. New York: Grove, 1985.

Nadel, Ira. *David Mamet*. New York: Palgrave, 2008.

Piette, Alain. "The 1980s," in *The Cambridge Companion to David Mamet*, ed. Christopher Bigsby. Cambridge: Cambridge University Press, 2004: 74–88.

Rayner, Alice. *Ghosts: Death's Double and the Phenomena of Theatre*. Minneapolis: University of Minnesota Press, 2006.

Shepard, Sam. "Fool for Love," in *Fool for Love and Other Plays*. New York: Bantam, 1984: 17–58.

Weisberg, Barbara. T*alking to the Dead: Katie and Maggie Fox and the Rise of Spiritualism*. New York: Harper Collins, 2004.

9

Literal Ghosts, Figurative Humanity and the Specter of Capitalism in August Wilson's Pittsburgh Cycle

Alan Nadel

In just over twenty years, August Wilson established himself as one of America's greatest playwrights, completing a ten-play cycle, each play focusing on African American life in a different decade of the twentieth century. Although some characters appear in more than one play, and all but one of the plays takes place in the same racially mixed Pittsburgh neighborhood, only one play can be genuinely considered a "sequel."[1] Rather, the cycle functions more like a CD compilation from a century of black blues compositions, no play qualifying as an historical drama, but each providing renditions of African American life, circumscribed by historically specific conditions. Instead of doing historical research on each decade, Wilson listened to as many blues records from that decade as he could acquire. That music, he felt, told him all he needed to know about African American life.

In terms of compositional trajectory and artistic development, the plays, not having been composed in the same order as the century unfolds, offer several distinct temporal prisms for interpreting Wilson's work. Three of the plays, *Ma Rainey's Black Bottom* (set in 1927), *Jitney* (set in 1977), and the earliest version of *Joe Turner's Come and Gone* (set in 1911), were conceived before Wilson developed the idea of a ten-decade dramatic cycle, and the last two plays, *Gem of the Ocean* (set in 1904) and *Radio Golf* (set in 1997), were composed as bookends to a cycle whose entire shape and contents were known to Wilson in the way that was not the case in writing the previous plays. That makes possible the appearance in *Gem* of Aunt Ester, alleged to be over three hundred years old,[2] who in two previous plays is an unseen presence of great wisdom and spiritual power, but whose existence was not known to Wilson until he had completed half of the cycle.

Thus, if we read the plays according to historical chronology, we start with the penultimate composition, *Gem*, and then move on to two of the very earliest, *Joe Turner's Come and Gone*, and *Ma Rainey's Black Bottom*. *Joe*

Turner, which marks Wilson's transition from writing individual plays to dramatically sculpting a century, also introduces his movement away from naturalistic compositions to plays that include uncanny, supernatural, and shamanistic qualities. One could posit, in this regard, that spirits haunt his plays and characters until the last play, *Radio Golf*, which leaves ambiguous the role of the uncanny, or, perhaps, the degree to which the uncanny may actually be the Muse of History in disguise. Wilson's opus, in other words, is haunted in many ways, equally by uncanny phenomena and by all-too-canny historical practices, economic institutions, and racial biases whose ghostly qualities reside in the invisible transparency with which the historical record has treated them as natural.

Ghosts of one sort or another, therefore, haunt his entire cycle, in some cases, as in *Ma Rainey's Black Bottom*, only as the figurative specter of the blues. Other plays specify ghostly features, as in *Fences*, where Troy Maxson battles with the figure of Death, or in *King Hedley II*, when, at the end, the cat belonging to the shamanistic Aunt Ester is resurrected. In *Seven Guitars*, which begins immediately after the funeral of the play's central character, Floyd Barton, the characters talk about the six spirits—those who saw them believe them to be angels—that ascended from his coffin. Even in *Radio Golf*, among Wilson's most "realistic" dramas, Aunt Ester's house exudes a spiritual power over Harmond Wilks that impacts the Pittsburgh politician and wealthy realtor, from the first time he enters it. Haunted by its aura, he abandons political aspirations in favor of community action.

This chapter, however, will focus more narrowly on the plays where the power of history manifests explicitly ghostly incarnations. In my book, *The Theatre of August Wilson*, I have discussed extensively the ghosts abounding in *The Piano Lesson* (set in 1936), several embodied by their onstage and offstage effects, and others, even more potent, as memories that haunt the Charles family. The play ostensibly focuses on the dispute between two siblings, Berniece and Boy Willie, about the disposition of a piano that, during the antebellum period, their great-grandfather at the instruction of his owner, Sutter, engraved with images of the enslaved family's history, such that a series of family tragedies haunts the piano. To acquire the piano, Sutter had swapped Berniece and Boy Willie's great-grandmother and their grandfather (at the time nine years old) with another slaveholder. If the piano, because it was acquired in exchange for chattel, signifies the family's commodification, it nonetheless displays the extraordinary woodcraft that turned that tragedy into art, which in turn transformed the piano into the only material history of the family. Because it was also purchased with the value of the family's labor, Berniece and Boy Willie's father, Boy Charles, felt the piano rightfully belonged to the Charles family, rather than to the Sutter family; so long as

Sutter owned the piano, he felt, Sutter still owned them. This led to his stealing the piano from Sutter, which cost Boy Charles his life; he died in a railroad car where he had tried to escape the sheriff, immolated by a fire that also killed four hobos. Local legend has held that those hobos (called the Ghosts of the Yellow Dog after the train line they were riding) had hunted down the sheriff's mob, for, in the period since the boxcar fire, each of the men who killed Boy Charles and the hobos died by mysteriously falling down a well.

The demise of the last of these, Sutter's grandson, has made it possible for Boy Willie to purchase the farm on which his ancestors had been slaves. To acquire the down payment, Boy Willie has traveled to Pittsburgh to ask Berniece to sell the piano, which they co-own, but she refuses, in part because she feels the spirits of her ancestors inhabit the piano, both materially as artistic representations and supernaturally as revenants. Adamant that they not sell the piano, Berniece threatens to shoot Boy Willie if he tries to take it, and he, comparably adamant that they sell it, is willing to risk dying. The piano, in other words, haunts Berniece's Pittsburgh residence with the violence and family rupture endemic to slavery, that violence re-enacting *within* the Charles family the conflict that slavery and its aftermath had imposed upon it.[3]

The destruction of yet one more Charles family generation is averted, however, by the intervention of the recently deceased Sutter, whose ghost has invaded Berniece's home so that he can play the piano his grandfather purchased with her grandfather (and her great-grandmother). In the play's climax, the attempt to exorcise Sutter's ghost instead provokes the ghost to reassert his claim on the piano and, implicitly, on the family, two commodities that the Sutters had possessed since "slavery time" (as Berniece and Boy Willie's uncle, Doaker, calls it). The Ghosts of the Yellow Dog miraculously appear to assist Boy Willie's fight with Sutter's ghost, but only when Berniece, who had previously refused to play the piano, does so to summon her family's ancestral spirits can Boy Willie manage to expel Sutter's ghost.

The Piano Lesson, in other words, empowers numerous ghosts to fight physically over the piano. Their dispute over legitimate ownership—how the haunted piano should be possessed and by whom—turns on a conflict between human rights and property rights of the sort that informed a body of nineteenth-century American jurisprudence. The principle of "comity"— mutually acknowledged consideration—informed significant instruments of legal precedent, including the *Dred Scott* decision's affirmation of property rights. This is not surprising since comity was crucial to the construction of transcontinental capitalism. Comity, American judicial precedent asserted, made equally binding ownership of the piano and ownership of human beings exchanged for it. The legitimacy of one, in fact, depended on the legitimacy of the other: Sutter could only assert his right to the piano *because* the slaves with which he purchased it were legally his. This is exactly why Boy Charles felt enslaved so long as Sutter owned the piano and why Sutter's ghost, nearly four score years after Emancipation, continues to assert his property rights. *The Piano Lesson* thus represents Jim Crow America as so possessed by the specter of slavery, empowered by its inherent violence, and bedeviled by its unrevenged victims, that the battle for history impels the living to grapple with slavery's specter or otherwise remain in its grips, forever inhabiting possessed property.

Outside of *The Piano Lesson*, however, Wilson most explicitly employs ghosts in *Gem of the Ocean*. That play, set in Aunt Ester's house in 1904, is initiated by the death of Garret Brown, who jumped into the river because he was wrongfully accused of stealing a bucket of nails. The play starts when Citizen Barlow, new to Pittsburgh, comes to Aunt Ester seeking redemption because he was the person who actually stole the nails. This implicates Barlow in the spiritually charged world of Aunt Ester, Eli, and Aunt Ester's other assistant, Black Mary. In Aunt Ester's house, we also see enacted the conflict between two antagonists, Black Mary's semi-estranged brother, Caesar, and Solly Two Kings, an independent man, who collects dog shit—or "pure," as he calls it—and sells it to leather tanners.[4] Solly, who lives in the world of artisans not dependent on the accumulation of capital or subject to the control of the factory or mill, will not subject himself to Caesar's authority as the constable who, in order to facilitate the regular flow of labor and production at the local steel mill, oversees the black population in his Pittsburgh neighborhood. Their antagonism, therefore, implicitly, and sometimes directly, concerns the power of the capitalist state to subjugate would-be citizens on the basis of race.

But, as the play understands (and much recent scholarship has affirmed), slavery and capitalism are not discrete historical phenomena.[5] The rise of capitalism was not only concurrent with the institution of slavery but dependent upon it, because the lifeblood of the industrial revolution, which made the accumulation of modern capital possible, was the textile industry, whose cheap cotton was only available because of slave labor. That labor, moreover, produced capital gains that multiplied by virtue of investment in numerous enterprises, such as banks, railroads, shipping companies, fur trading, and retail stores, not directly implicated in slave commerce or its ancillary enterprises. Thus, abundantly cheap labor—translated, via state-endorsed human subjugation, into comparably inexpensive cotton—enabled the rise of capitalism.

Mercantile capitalism—or what Sven Beckert, has called "war capitalism"— was a system "based not on free labor but on slavery."[6] Although cotton, from roughly the year 1000 until the moment of *Gem*'s action, was the world's most important manufacturing industry, only when global networks created systems of circulation and exchange capable of harnessing and reproducing cheap labor could eighteenth- and nineteenth-century technological developments coalesce into an encompassing economic system. If modern capitalism, Beckert makes clear, privileges property rights, its precursor, "[war capitalism] was characterized just as much by massive expropriations:"

> [C]apitalism's early phase ... was frequently based on unrestrained actions of private individuals—the domination of masters over slaves and of frontier capitalists over indigenous inhabitants ... [As a result] Europeans came to dominate the centuries-old worlds of cotton, merge them into a single empire... and invent the global economy we take for granted today.[7]

For this reason, the specter of slavery haunts Wilson's opus, for a haunting requires, as Derrida points out, the situation Hamlet was forced to recognize after encountering his father's ghost: "The Time is out of joint." The reason for this, Derrida makes clear, is that a ghost's first appearance is always also necessarily its reappearance—the making present of someone whose time is past. Thus, if historical research "unearths" the past, haunting negates the possibility of that unearthing by making the past present. Even more vexing than spectral evidence that what was buried is not dead, a ghost reconfigures the future as much as it does the present, for haunting requires we presume the ghost's continuous capacity to reappear. In order to haunt, in other words, it must retain the ability to be present, for if it is not to be present, the haunting has been exorcised—to be and not to be: time is out of joint.

The specific disjointure made present in the failed exorcism that concludes *The Piano Lesson* emanates from the fact that although the final battle may hold Sutter's ghost at bay, the collaborating community of ancestral spirits, murdered hobos, a living warrior, and a blues shaman cannot completely not expel him.[8] Such remains the enduring power of one dead slave owner in Jim Crow America. The play concludes, therefore, with the shared recognition that staving off Sutter's ghost is an ongoing process. Berniece must continue to play the piano, evoking ancestral power with ritualistic vigilance, because the ghost's potential reappearance remains constant: when Berniece stops playing the haunted piano, Sutter will start. To put it another way, time continues to be out of joint because the specter of slavery remains enthroned as the revenant father of capitalism, the fallen King Hamlet, always seeking revenge for the loss of the realm.

As Nicholas Lemann points out in his review of Harvard historian Walter Johnson's extensive work on the Mississippi River, as the western artery of "racial capitalism": "Once slavery is positioned as the foundational institution of American capitalism, the country's subsequent history can be depicted as an extension of this basic dynamic."[9] "Johnson's guiding concept is [that] racism [is a] technique for exploiting black people and for fomenting the hostility of working-class whites toward blacks, so as to enable white capitalists to extract value from everyone else."[10] Consistent with the perspective of his recent book, *The Broken Heart of America: St. Louis and the Violent History of the United States,* Johnson's earlier work, *River of Dark Dreams: Slavery and Empire in the Cotton Kingdom*, establishes the Mississippi as geographical and economic bookend to what, in 1993, Paul Gilroy identified as the "Black Atlantic," a matrix of cultural production delimited by the circulatory system created to nurture and sustain the capitalist body, stitched together, Frankenstein style by, as Beckert has shown, innumerable cotton threads. If textiles were the fabric of capitalism, slave labor was the raw material from which that fabric was made, and cotton was its cash crop. But capital, like the rivers and oceans that kept it afloat, is a fluid phenomenon or a phenomenon made fluid by money, the concept that Derrida accurately identifies as property's ghost.

In capitalism's tidal currents, *Gem of the Ocean*'s Caesar, as both constable and entrepreneur, is the avatar of that ghost. As the spokesman heralding money as the abstraction haunting all property relations, Caesar extols free enterprise in terms of money's capacity to haunt the properties from which it is derived, even though, as Caesar, himself, understands, capitalist enterprise is foundationally corrupt. At the same time that Caesar proclaims repeatedly the supremacy of the law—"People don't understand the law is everything"[11]— he praises his own entrepreneurial success, achieved by flaunting the law. Caesar had first earned money by selling hoecakes and beans off the back of wagon, but the police ran him off the corner because he needed a license. "Took me a while, but I got a license. I had to pay six or seven people. . ."[12] In order to get collateral to buy property, he explains, he opened a gambling joint in the back of a barber shop:

> Sold whiskey. The police closed it down. I had to put some bullet holes in a couple of niggers and the police arrested me. Put me on the county farm. I had to bust a couple of niggers upside the head for trying to steal my food. A couple tried to escape. I caught them.[13]

Caesar now owns a bakery that sells magic bread: "Got a big sign that say you have to eat half as much to get twice as full. And I charge them one and a half times for it."[14] "I give the people hope when they ain't got nothing else," he explains, perfectly exemplifying the Marxist concept of false consciousness.

"They take that loaf of bread and make it last twice as long. They wouldn't do that if they didn't pay one and a half times for it."[15] Caesar's flexible interpretations of the law might seem hard to reconcile with his draconian praise for it until we understand that Caesar has compartmentalized the law into two discrete realms, property rights and human rights, under a system of segregation that makes property absolute and humanity contingent. For that reason, he can swindle people into buying magic bread and, with impunity, kill a boy for stealing a loaf of it. Justifying his killing of the boy, Caesar explains that "the law is everything."[16]

Caesar's interpretation of the law thus replicates antebellum court decisions and postbellum practices that, on the basis of race, similarly prioritized property over humanity. Because Caesar implicitly makes property the foundation of universal law, so long as people can be treated as property or, more specifically, as far back as this was possible, the law was, as Caesar asserts, "everything," and humanity, consequently, was nothing. Even in prison, Caesar could therefore beat other prisoners for stealing his food.

By equating this hierarchical distinction between human rights and property rights with "the law," Caesar has, without explicitly saying so—in fact, because for him it goes without saying—racialized the distinction. As Wining Boy says in *The Piano Lesson*, the difference between the white man and the colored man is that "the colored man can't fix nothing with the law."[17] The reduction of black humanity to white property, entailed in Caesar's distinctions, therefore, makes those who perished in the Middle Passage— the millions who died on the slave ships during voyages from Africa to the New World—ghosts haunting the conception of property rights. They are, in other words, the specters of capitalism. When Caesar says, "You got to respect the law. Unless you dead,"[18] he is inadvertently identifying the ghosts of the Middle Passage as the resistance to the legal sanctity of capital, for those who died in transit to the New World in effect prevented their humanity from being converted into the legal tender of capitalist transactions.

Thus, when Garret Brown drowned to prove, as Aunt Ester explained, that his life was worth more than a bucket of nails, he became the spiritual heir of those lost in the Middle Passage. As a result, his death haunts the Pittsburgh steel mill and the black labor there processed into capital, in part because his death incarnated the exploitation, which drained the lifeblood from a steady flow of black migrants out of the Jim Crow South at the beginning of the twentieth century. Although Barlow's theft of the nails initiates the events by which Brown died, his act and Brown's action share a common motivation. In order to avoid forced labor, Barlow had to "sneak out"[19] of the South: "Say they didn't want anybody to leave. Say we had to stay there and work."[20] When Barlow goes to Pittsburgh, however, instead of escaping indenture he

Figure 9.1 August Wilson's *Gem of the Ocean* at the Huntington Theatre Company, 2012. Courtesy of Huntington Theatre Company, available under a CC BY 2.0 license.

discovers its universality. He cannot leave the mill where he works or the house where he boards because, as he discovers, in both cases his debt, like that of southern tenant farmers, exceeds his income. "The mill wouldn't pay me," Barlow confesses to Aunt Ester, "so I stole the bucket of nails."[21] Barlow allowed Brown to drown because he thought Brown was going to come out of the water, "but he never did. I looked up and he had drowned. It's like I got a hole inside of me. If I ain't careful seem like everything would leak out that hole."[22] In order to address Barlow's pain and fear, Aunt Ester decides, he needs to visit the City of Bones, the residence beneath the ocean constructed by the refugees of the Middle Passage. To prepare him for that journey, she instructs him to wander along the Monongahela River until he finds two shiny new pennies.

As he sets off on that search, Aunt Ester, Black Mary, and Eli discover that the riots at the mill following Brown's death have culminated in the mill's being set on fire. The fire, it turns out, was set by Solly Two Kings, who, defying the mill and the law, aligns himself with Citizen Barlow, who stole the nails, and Brown, who refused to come out of the water (and thus fomented the strike and riots at the mill). Starting with the petty insurrection of taking nails and culminating with major arson, these three men, with escalating intensity, assert the value of human life, which has been subordinated by law and economy to the pre-eminence of property. Consider how Aunt Ester frames Barlow's mission:

> He think there power in them two pennies. He think when he find them all his trouble will be over. But he need to think that before he can come face to face with himself. Ain't nothing special about the two pennies. Only thing special about them is he think they special. He find them two pennies then he think he done something. But, he ain't done nothing but find two pennies.[23]

Aunt Ester is teaching Barlow a lesson in worth by making him seek something worth even less than a bucket of nails. This is the first step in enabling him to reorganize the privileged values of the world in which he lives. In so doing, he can begin to invert the hierarchical pyramid of capital, which places money and the law at its pinnacle. Remembering that Black Mary's semi-estrangement from Caesar followed his killing a boy for stealing a loaf of bread, we see how Brown's making his life more valuable than a bucket of nails directly refutes Caesar's treating the boy's life as worth less than a loaf of bread.

This is why Brown, after drowning, appropriately joins his lost ancestors in the City of Bones, which is not a watery graveyard but the gem of the ocean. The stage directions make this clear, identifying the City of Bones as the most beautiful sight Barlow has ever seen. Additional stage directions tell us that, "*Overwhelmed by the sheer beauty of the city and the people with their tongues on fire, Citizen Barlow, now reborn as a man of the people, sits down and begins to cry.*"[24]

The City of Bones, that undersea community constructed out of the bones of those who perished in transit and inhabited by their spirits, thus represents a direct inversion of the America John Winthrop projected as the proto-capitalist, Puritan "City *on the Hill*" [emphasis added], three centuries later proclaimed by Ronald Reagan, a "shining" city, implying that what Winthrop had identified as God's challenge to the settlers of the New World had materialized into God's affirmation that they had met the challenge. By locating the shining city in the watery depths rather than on Winthrop's (and Reagan's) summit, Wilson challenges not only the economic seeds of the New World empire but also its theological mandate, because the City of Bones, especially when connected to the spirit of Garret Brown, who died for the sins of property rights, suggests an alternative to Protestant capitalism. Unlike Jesus, the sacrificial figure who walks on water, Brown, a black sacrificial figure, is resurrected underneath it, on the ocean floor, which signifies the Middle Passage's repository of lost capital and dead investments, even though the law of 1904 Pittsburgh sees only what is floating on the surface, that is, what is literally superficial. Caesar indicates as much when he says, "Money ain't got nobody's name on it. It's floating out there."[25] Caesar's perspective also underscores the relationship between Brown's life and capital. For as long as Brown can stay afloat, his body equals capital, but as soon as he sinks, he changes from material flesh to the ghostly reminder of human worth, which Caesar deems worthless.

The spiritual conflict between the God of property and the God of humanity takes place, as well, between Caesar and Solly, in Pittsburgh, at the beginning of the twentieth century. Solly's name, after all, is meant to call attention to the fact that one cannot serve two kings, that one must render unto Caesar what is Caesar's and unto God what is God's. Like Brown, Solly—echoing Aunt Ester's assertion that Brown's life cannot be reduced to material value—attacks Caesar by inverting his water imagery, in the same way that the ghosts in the City of Bone's invert the spirit informing Winthrop's hill:

> They wave the law on one end and hit you with a billy club with the other. . . . I can't just . . . collect dog shit while the people drowning. The people drowning in sorrow and grief. That's a mighty big ocean. They got the law tied to their toe. Every time they try to swim the law pull them under.[26]

Solly also explains to Barlow that it's hard to be a citizen. "You gonna have to fight to get that. And time you get it, you gonna be surprised how heavy it is."[27] Thus, Barlow's first task in earning the name of Citizen is visiting the City of Bones, where he must find the ghost of Garret Brown, because Barlow needs to comprehend the heritage that connects Brown's ghost with their spiritual ancestors, the slaves whose resistance makes the City of Bones shine. It does so because the City of Bones literalizes the process wherein humanity was capitalized to build cities. This city, however, is built from the bones of those who denied their labor, their bodies, their identities to commodification, industrialization, and the construction of a civilization that denied them the name "citizen." In confessing he stole the nails, Barlow thus allies himself with Brown. He stole the nails for the same reason that Brown refused to come out of the water: to subordinate the mill's right to own nails to their right to own their labor, possess their bodies, control their lives.

Barlow's meeting with Brown as kindred spirits admits Barlow to the City of Bones while he is still battling to earn and retain the name of Citizen. In visiting this city under the ocean, moreover, Barlow turns upside down the model that kept capitalism afloat by making white property literal and black humanity figurative.[28] Wilson underscores this by inverting the procedure of the séance, wherein the living call forth ghosts. Instead of summoning ghosts into the material world, Barlow must ask the ghosts to admit him to their city, thereby acknowledging the reality of their jurisdiction.

Barlow makes his journey, moreover, on a paper boat made out of Aunt Ester's bill-of-sale, a bill-of-sale she subsequently demands that Caesar acknowledge as worthless, even though it is based on the same principles that Caesar continues to extol: that black lives matter less than a bucket of nails. If her bill-of-sale has no worth, Aunt Ester reasons, isn't Caesar's arrest warrant, based on the same principles, equally worthless? In contradistinction to the bill-of-sale's legal value, the play asserts its performative value as the vehicle that transports Citizen Barlow from the discredited world of property rights to the real world of resistance to human commodification.

If the City of Bones is built of human matter and inhabited by the ghosts of the humans to which that matter belonged, it constitutes the site where the enslaved cold inhabit their own bodies rather than live as the chattel property of slave owners, that is, of capitalism. Thus, the play ends with Barlow's initiating Wilson's century by assuming Solly's role in the fight for equality, a fight made possible by Barlow's journey to the City of Bones, in the name of the citizen, in the ship of the citizen—the citizenship—of the nation whose democracy he could not yet capitalize in his own name.

Notes

1 *King Hedley II*, set in 1985, takes place in the backyard of the same small house as did *Seven Guitars*, set in 1948 and the plot concerns several of the same characters. August Wilson, *King Hedley II* (New York: Theatre Communications Group, 2007). August Wilson, *Seven Guitars* (New York: Plume, 1997).

2 Because characters interact with Aunt Ester in 1968, we learn about her death in 1985, and we see her in 1904, she has different ages in each play. The important thing to know, however, is that the year of her birth coincides with the advent of slavery in America.

3 This is a theme of many Wilson plays, including *Ma Rainey's Black Bottom, Seven Guitars, Fences, King Hedley II, Jitney, Radio Golf* and *Gem of the Ocean*.

4 Animal feces, especially dog dung, was essential in the leather-tanning of that period.

5 Gene Dattel details the definitive role cotton played in constructing American economy, society, and political composition, inextricably linking the manipulation of hostility and the suffering of African Americans. Edward Baptist, elaborating on this symbiosis, details the instrumental relationship

between slavery and American capitalism. Sven Beckert, in a major work, shows with global scope the bond between slavery, capitalism, and cotton, which he sees as tentacles of the same system, rather than discrete historical phenomena; Walter Johnson, makes clear the elaborate networks that continued to expropriate the West as Europe expropriated the global south in perpetuation of slavery. Importantly, Beckert makes clear, the shift from what has been called mercantile capitalism to industrial capitalism was the paradigmatic structure—especially in regard to human exploitation—that the former provided the latter. Sven Beckert, *Empire of Cotton: A Global History* (New York: Alfred A. Knopf, 2015).

6   Beckert, xvi.

7   Ibid.

8   Wining Boy, in this play acts as the shamanistic figure, a figure instrumental in more than half of Wilson's dramatic arrangements. His crucial intervention at the moment when Berneice is about to shoot Boy Willie averts the potential tragedy long enough for the attempted exorcism to evoke Sutter's ghost and thereby unite the family in repelling him. See Alan Nadel, *The Theatre of August Wilson* (London: Metheun Drama, 2018), 87–108.

9   Nicholas Lehman, "Is Capitalism Racist?" *The New Yorker*, May 18, 2020.

10 Ibid.

11 August Wilson, *Gem of the Ocean* (New York: Theatre Communications Group, 2007), 36.

12 Ibid., 37.

13 Ibid.

14 Ibid., 35.

15 Ibid., 35–36.

16 Ibid., 36.

17 To "fix" can mean an array of things, including to repair, to rig, to prevent from changing, and to get even; similarly, "with the law" can mean using the law in an instrumental way, or it can mean entering into a legal (or extra-legal) agreement, such as getting the legal authorities to look the other way. Thus, one can fix something with the law to obtain legitimate recompense for a wrong or injury. This is the basis for such areas as tort law, libel law, and contract law, at the same time as one can rig the legal system to preclude redress for injury or swindle. Similarly, one can pass legislation to address an injustice or curb an abuse, or pass legislation to make specific injustices legal. The myriad ways that the possibilities of fixing things with the law have supported racial caste are important in all of Wilson's plays, but they are most extensively engaged in *The Piano Lesson, Two Trains Running*, and *Radio Golf.* See Nadel, chapters 6, 7 and 9.

18 Wilson, *Gem*, 36.

19 Ibid., 22.

20 Ibid.

21 Ibid., 44

22 Ibid.

23 Ibid., 47.
24 Ibid., 69–70.
25 Ibid., 33.
26 Ibid., 60.
27 Ibid., 27.
28 For an extended analysis of the role of the figurative and the literal in African American history and literature, see Nadel, chapter 5.

Works Cited

Beckert, Sven. *Empire of Cotton: A Global History*. New York: Alfred A. Knopf, 2015.

Derrida, Jacques. *Specters of Marx*. New York: Routledge, 1994.

Johnson, Walter. *The Broken Heart of America: St. Louis and the Violent History of the United States*. New York: Basic Books, 2020.

Johnson, Walter. *River of Dark Dreams: Slavery and Empire in the Cotton Kingdom*. Cambridge, MA: Harvard University Press, 2017.

Lehman, Nicholas. "Is Capitalism Racist?" *The New Yorker*, May 18, 2020.

Nadel, Alan. *The Theatre of August Wilson*. London: Methuen Drama, 2018.

Wilson, August. *Gem of the Ocean*. New York: Theatre Communications Group, 2007.

Wilson, August. *King Hedley II*. New York: Theatre Communications Group, 2007.

Wilson, August. *Radio Golf*. New York: Theatre Communications Group, 2007.

Wilson, August. *Jitney*. New York: Overlook Press, 2001.

Wilson, August. *Seven Guitars*. New York: Plume, 1997.

Wilson, August. *The Piano Lesson*. New York: Plume, 1990.

Wilson, August. *Joe Turner's Come and Gone*. New York: Plume, 1988.

Wilson, August. *Fences*. New York: Plume, 1986.

Wilson, August. *Ma Rainey's Black Bottom*. New York: Plume, 1985.

10

"All Spooked Out":
Topdog/Underdog's Ghosts

Jennifer Larson

Suzan-Lori Parks makes no secret of the vital role that the dead, disappeared, and forgotten play in her writing. In her essay "Possession," she explains that "because so much of African-American history has been unrecorded, disremembered, washed out, one of [her] tasks as a playwright is to—through literature and the special strange relationship between theatre and real-life—locate the ancestral burial ground, dig for bones, find bones, hear the bones sing, write it down."[1] The work makes Parks both an archeologist and "a medium."[2] The process also reads like a ghost story, the narrative of a quest to discover who haunts whom and why.

Lincoln and Booth, the volatile brothers and only two characters in Parks's Pulitzer Prize-winning play *Topdog/Underdog*, are haunted by multiple "ghosts": certainly by their eponyms—Abraham Lincoln and John Wilkes Booth—but also by their estranged mother and Booth's probably-dead (and metaphorically named) girlfriend Grace. Each haunting represents some element of the brothers' lives that ultimately drives them to their mutual destruction. These ghosts' particular insidiousness comes from their connections to the myriad forces that pose specific threats to individual identity and accurate historical representation. At the same time, *Topdog/Underdog* also posits that productively communing with ghosts and their hauntings can foster healing, create opportunities for agency, and/or lead to a more inclusive understanding of history—both personal and communal. Applying Parks's "Rep & Rev," her unique model of literary repetition and revision, from her earlier Lincoln-focused work *The America Play*, to *Topdog/Underdog*, also demonstrates this potential.

Thus, *Topdog/Underdog*'s ghosts and hauntings have seemingly paradoxical functions: the potential to destroy and the potential to create. This paradox is not necessarily surprising given that, in her essay "from Elements of Style," Parks provides an enigmatic definition of "ghost":

> A person from, say, time immemorial, from, say, PastLand, from
> somewhere back there, say, walked into my house. She or he is always
> alone and will almost always take up residence in a corner. Why they're
> alone I don't know. Perhaps they're coming missionary style—there are
> always more to follow. Why they choose a corner to stand in I don't know
> either—maybe it's the intersection of 2 directions—maybe because it's
> safe.
>
> They are not characters. To call them so could be an injustice. They
> are *figures, figments, ghosts, roles, lovers* maybe, *speakers* maybe, *shadows,*
> *slips, players* maybe, maybe someone else's pulse.[3]

This definition leaves open the possibility that sundry ghosts—nefarious,
benign, or some combination thereof—might inhabit her work. And the
ghosts' preference for the "corner," that is "the intersection of 2 directions"
also insinuates their tendency toward, or even comfort with, liminal and
paradoxical spaces.

Arthur Redding offers a compatible examination of ghosts' role in
American literature. What "haunts us," Redding argues, are "the ghosts of
potential, of alternative."[4] Redding asserts that ghosts are "that which survives,
singular, jealous, persistent, and beckoning—specters, absences that refuse to
absent themselves, which would rise from the graves to which a national
history has hastily consigned them."[5] In Toni Morrison's and Louise Erdrich's
works, ghosts can therefore manifest as "threatening, dangerous, greedy, and
divisive."[6] At the same time, "the ghost is a figure by which we might imagine
bridges across difference, but also recognize—and honor—that which is lost
or sacrificed in any act of exchange or translation or history—that which is
abandoned, left behind."[7] In other words, ghosts persistently assert themselves
in the lives of the haunted, and inevitably, this interference can cause harm.
Or it can push the haunted toward knowledge, acceptance, and/or healing.

Parks's ghosts—and *Topdog/Underdog*'s ghosts especially—are also
capable of interference that becomes possession rather than mere haunting.
Parks's non-fiction prose articulates this possibility. To open the essay
"Possession," she provides another definition: "possession. 1. the action or fact
of possessing, or the condition of being possessed. 2. the holding or having of
something as one's own, or being inhabited and controlled by a demon
spirit."[8] The fact that a demon "spirit," rather than a demon itself, possesses
creates space for other types of possession beyond pop culture and religious
traditions. Even a "spirit" alone has the power to possess.

Also, the definition equates "being inhabited and controlled by a demon
spirit" with "the holding or having of something as one's own" by placing the
ideas together in the second option. Even just perceived ownership, therefore,

can lead someone to be/feel possessed. This potential opens up myriad possibilities for possession, especially in a play directly engaging economics and slavery. Yet, this potential is paradoxical because, as Parks notes, "The definition of possession cancels itself out. The relationship between possessor and possessed is, like ownership is, multidirectional."⁹

This multidirectional relationship between possessor and possessed, ghost and haunted, shows up most notably in Lincoln's obsession with and seeming dependence upon the Lincoln costume and his job as a Lincoln impersonator. The costume and job signify the complicated, incomplete history that Lincoln represents as well as past and present racialized economic oppressions. These concepts become "ghosts" because they haunt Lincoln, so aggressively asserting themselves in his life that they obscure his ability to be and to see his true self. This "haunting," then, consistently blurs the lines between Lincoln's identity and the identities the ghosts project onto him. Lincoln is thus also possessed by these spirits as they essentially attempt to claim some ownership—literal or figurative—over him.

Early in the play, Booth calls Lincoln—who is wearing the whiteface and Lincoln costume that is his job's uniform—"all spooked out and shit."¹⁰ Booth tells his brother, "you make me nervous standing there looking like a spook …."¹¹ When Booth labels Lincoln a "spook," he evokes the term's multifarious meanings—spy (channeling Greenlee's *The Spook Who Say by the Door*), racialized insult, and ghost. Notably, Booth uses both "a spook," the noun that defines Lincoln's state or identity, and "spooked," the past participle that implies not only action, but action inspiring fear. In this moment, Booth says Lincoln is "a shadow of himself who has given up his chosen profession as a card dealer and become reduced to the haunting image of a dead president and a dark era in American history."¹² Lincoln, therefore, "is completely stripped of his identity" such that he is "unrecognizable and undesirable even to his own brother" or is merely "a spy, a white man's pawn," disconnected from his racial heritage and his own/his people's needs; either option "foreshadows the merging of Lincoln and Lincoln-the-President later in the play as well as Lincoln's death at Booth's hand."¹³

As the play progresses, Lincoln becomes less and less able to define himself outside of his relationship to the Lincoln costume/his job and the history it evokes. He struggles, John Dietrick explains, with the "tangle of self and role" in that he "is clearly ill at ease regarding the difficulty of drawing a line between who he is and who he appears to be, and a confusion between his role and his 'real' self repeatedly breaks through to the surface."¹⁴ Although Lincoln claims in Scene 2 that he never feels like the arcade patrons are shooting him instead of a fake President Lincoln, in the same sentence he clearly struggles with the division between actor and character. He describes how his costume has residue from "where they shoot him, where they shoot me I should say . . . ."[15] So, despite his vehement denials, Lincoln clearly feels his job's duality creates serious identity confusion.

By Scene 3, when he describes his daily assassinations, all distancing is gone. Lincoln says of the shooter, ". . . for a minute, with him hanging back there behind me, its real. Me looking at him upside down and him looking at me looking like Lincoln."[16] Lincoln eventually acknowledges the emotional toll playing President Lincoln has on him when he explains, "That shit is hard. But it works. Cause I work it."[17] Lincoln understands that "in '[leaving his] own shit at the door'" to put on the Lincoln costume, part of his own identity is being usurped by Lincoln-the-President's; that is, "he must leave himself behind in order to put it on, thereby rendering himself invisible."[18] He also realizes "the assassins cannot logically believe that they are killing Lincoln-the-President; they are there to kill him" and, with this realization, he "identifies the role he plays in his own assassination" and that he "has willingly accepted the superficiality that defines his invisibility—a superficiality that only 'works' because he works it."[19] Yet, when the arcade fires Lincoln, he does not leave the costume behind, as the previous performer did and as he insisted he would. Rather, he brings it home, puts it on, and eventually dies in it.

This "tangle of self" and role parallels Lincoln's struggle to understand and reconcile with the recorded histories about President Lincoln and the inherently interconnected history/legacy of slavery. Parks's ghosts, after all, don't typically travel alone, and "there are always more to follow."[20] Lincoln, haunted by this idealized and sanitized vision of President Lincoln, "The Great Emancipator," essentially believes that "he cannot leave the Lincoln suit empty because to do so has social as well as personal implications—it leaves America without an emancipator, and more immediately it leaves him and Booth without the money to survive and liberate themselves from poverty," if even just in theory.[21] This need for "emancipation" also evokes the history of slavery, as Booth reminds Lincoln when he tells him that by impersonating Lincoln, "You aint going back but you going all the way back. Back to way back then when folks was slaves and shit."[22] This history also haunts Lincoln by highlighting his ongoing enslavement by his job and the economic realities it signifies. The play confirms this when Lincoln considers begging the arcade to take him back, but Booth counters: "Link. Yr free. Dont go crawling back. Yr free at last!"[23] Booth's words invite more ghosts—Dr. King and the long struggle for civil rights—to the room.

These nods to slavery are also important because the enslaved were legally owned, (possessed) by slaveholders and because slavery's enduring social and economic legacies (ghosts) still very much inform (or haunt) contemporary civil rights efforts. Soyica Diggs Colbert notes, for example, that both "the history of black enslavement and the subsequent brutality enacted in practices like lynching clarify how blackness functions as a state of being possessed even as the drive for freedom essential to blackness often results in individual seeking redress through possessions."[24] Lincoln wants to keep working at the arcade because he sees it as a good job: "Its a sit down job. With benefits."[25] But this work has turned his life into a commodity. In the play, Dietrick explains, "Lincoln not only spends money but also, in an important sense, *is* money," not only because he is the family's breadwinner, but also because he is literally dressed as "a dead president," the living embodiment of paper currency.[26] Although Lincoln wants the potential stability and cachet of a non-manual-labor job, even this labor dehumanizes him, because he is only a drone, a commodity, in an oppressive, racist economy.

The most relevant element of Lincoln's costume, though, is his whiteface. The whiteface nods not only to the reality, which both brothers acknowledge, that the arcade pays Lincoln "less than theyd pay a white guy,"[27] but also to the legacy of blackface minstrelsy, which commodified and degraded black culture. Since the arcade assassins shoot Lincoln from behind, the whiteface isn't actually necessary; rather, the makeup serves only to remind Lincoln of his social and economic roles. The direct impact of this haunting by the ghosts of minstrels past is that it allows Booth to question Lincoln's masculinity vis-à-vis his sexuality and virility. In Scene3, Booth tells Lincoln, "Yr dick, if it aint falled off yet, is hanging there between yr legs, little whitefaced shriveled-up blank shooting grub worm. As goes the man so goes the man's dick."[28] Just as blackface minstrelsy rendered its black performers impotent, powerless to control or change the stereotypical roles that often provided their only opportunities for professional success, so too, Lincoln's role as a whiteface President Lincoln impersonator emasculates him.

Yet, it's Booth who encourages Lincoln to put the costume on one last time so they can take a photograph of him in it.[29] This need to capture and preserve the Lincoln costume and its impact demonstrates that Booth can see and name the ghosts that possess his brother, but he is not immune to their influence. In the photo scene, for example, he tells Lincoln, "Im gonna miss you—coming home in that get up."[30] Booth is startled, however, by Lincoln's entrance early in Scene1. "The presence of Lincoln doesn't surprise him," the stage directions explain, "the Lincoln costume does."[31] This note implies that the costume is much more than a costume to Booth; he feels its historical and even personal significance. Similarly, one of the ghosts that chooses "to follow" the ghost of President Lincoln on to the stage is the ghost of John Wilkes Booth. As Booth and Lincoln practice adding "spicy shit" to Lincoln's performance, Booth eventually screams, "I am the assassin! *I am Booth!!* Come on man this is life and death! Go all out!"[32] Lincoln complies, and both men are disturbed because, as Booth states, "It was looking too real or something."[33] This awareness during the "rehearsal" of Lincoln's death, though, doesn't carry through to the end of the play, where Booth again becomes "the assassin" and—just like the ghost he's named for—actually kills Lincoln.

But the seeming inevitability of this ending does not preclude the possibility of a more redemptive reading of ghosts, haunting, and possession in these events. Even "if Lincoln and Booth are possessed, controlled by their names," Fraden argues, this need not be completely destructive because "they also turn the historical Lincoln and Booth upside down and inside out."[34] Fraden explains, "I suppose one can try to disown one's name or change it or ignore its history, just as one could try with a word to pull it up by its roots and wrestle a new meaning into it. But Parks portrays encounters that refuse such disentanglement."[35] The goal is not to forget or completely dissociate from the historical Lincoln and Booth; neglect is not typically salvific. Rather, a "new meaning" (or meaning*s*) can exist alongside the existing meanings. The ghosts could help Lincoln—and the play's audiences—accept that history is not neat, as dominant historical narratives suggest, but rather inherently "raggedy and bloody and screaming."[36] This acceptance, in turn, creates opportunities for reckoning and recovery.

Realizing the need to challenge dominant historical narratives echoes Lincoln's lesson about three-card Monty; it's the beginning of being able to see what "separates thuh Player from the Played," understanding the hustle, and thus defeating "thuh man."[37] Colbert explains that, historically, "while the structure of slavery sought to enact the complete materialization of black people as property, enslaved Africans created modes of resistance that not only reclaimed their alienated parts but also addressed the ostensibly benign regulatory forces that enabled their possession."[38] We see such resistance in *Topdog/Underdog* when Lincoln hustles the boy on the bus out of twenty dollars. Lincoln explains, "Theyd just done Lincoln in history class and he knew all about him, he'd been to the arcade but, I dunno, for some reason he was tripping cause there was Honest Abe right beside him on the bus."[39] Lincoln initially considers charging five dollars for the autograph "cause of the Lincoln connection," but instead, "something in me made me ask for 10" and then take twenty dollars, promising that "Honest Abe would give him back the change tomorrow" on the bus.[40] That "something in me" is not the ghost of "Honest Abe," but rather his deliberate rejection of that figure. In this rejection, Lincoln finds agency as his struggle with President Lincoln's ghost pushes him to resist "the ostensibly benign regulatory forces" Colbert describes, forces symbolized by government-issued currency as well as by a public education system that produces children who cannot distinguish between historical accuracy and its twisted "facsimile."

Lincoln's character, then, shows the greatest potential for ghosts to foster a transformative understanding of communal history. Because Booth's ghosts are more personal, however, he is also more profoundly impacted by the play's other major ghosts: his estranged mother and his probably-murdered girlfriend, Grace. It is worth mentioning here that the play does not confirm the fates of either the parents or Grace. But Parks's definition specifies that ghosts come from "time immemorial," not that they need to be dead, "PastLand," or "somewhere back there." Both Lincoln and Booth reflect on their parents' disappearances, and the circumstances surrounding them. Despite definitive indication that either parent has died, the play treats both as deceased, because each has bequeathed an "inheritance" to the brothers when they left. Booth has also "inherited" his father's love of clothing, which manifests in the younger brother's obsession with stealing clothes and accessories. Lincoln's obsession with the Lincoln costume, arguably, has the same paternal roots.[41] Similarly, Booth talks about his present-tense interactions with Grace throughout the play; yet, at the end of the play, when he confesses to having killed her, he doesn't say when, so it's possible that she's been dead for most, or all, of the play.[42] And since neither the parents nor Grace appear on stage, they are not characters—as they can't be, per Parks's definition of "ghost." Their rejection and subsequent absence, nevertheless, haunts the brothers as a constant presence in the men's lives, a persistent reminder that they are unworthy of unconditional love and that their relationships can be reduced to money.

The brothers' parents in general—and their reasons for leaving specifically—rank with the Lincoln costume and three-card Monty as the play's most important conversation topics. After Lincoln recklessly spends all his arcade severance, he returns home drunk and abruptly asks Booth why he thinks their parents left. Lincoln suggests, "I think there was something out there they liked more than they liked us and for years they was struggling against moving toward that more liked something"[43] Lincoln's theory implies that his parents were haunted by their own ghosts and/or they were possessed by something that compelled them to leave. He wonders if they hoped that moving into a nicer house and having the illusion of a nuclear family and financial/professional success meant that their ghosts "would just leave them be" and let the whole family be "just regular people living in a house."[44] Here again, the play offers an example of African Americans so profoundly possessed by the past and/or its legacies that they end up, ironically, "seeking redress through possessions."[45] This possession also sets up the family's ultimate commodification: as Dietrick describes, "the boys' real family was essentially replaced by money when the mother and father paid each brother and left."[46] Lincoln and Booth have inherited their parents' material possessions—money and clothes (and money wrapped in clothes)—but, more importantly, they have also inherited the predisposition for economically-driven haunting and possession.

Since the parents left separately, Booth offers the alternate theory that they "had some agreement between them."[47] More importantly, a few lines later he suggests that his parents may have reunited elsewhere and started a new family, to which Lincoln adds, "Maybe they got 2 new kids. 2 boys. Different than us, though. Better."[48] This exchange underscores how the circumstances of their parents' departure also continue to influence the men's self-evaluations and their understanding of family as indistinct from economics. They are haunted by "maybes" that suggest some idea or someone whom their parents—who were supposed to love them unconditionally—valued more than their children.

Booth, especially haunted by his mother's abandonment, claims to have felt a connection with her that neither Lincoln nor their father shared, particularly since her parting words to him were so enigmatic and disturbing. Booth reminds Lincoln that the day their mother left, "Dad read the sports section" and Lincoln ate his "dick toast" while Booth was "feeling something changing."[49] Insinuating his father and brother's stereotypically masculinist preoccupations—sports and not just food, but "dick toast"—rendered them oblivious to the mother's needs, Booth feels a responsibility to her that they do not. The mother reads Booth's empathy as emotional maturity, because, as Booth recounts to Lincoln, the mother said "that I should look out for you. Yeah. So who gonna look out for me."[50] Because Booth, in the mother's estimations, was the topdog in the sibling relationship, he again feels obligated to fulfill her mandate. However, his "underdog" label in the play's dramatis personae, indicates that Booth is not fit for the role. This frustrating mandate becomes the vehicle through which the mother's spirit continues to possess Booth, his ongoing power struggle with Lincoln underscoring his need to overshadow his brother by assuming the topdog role his mother assigned him.

The unopened money-filled stocking, then, becomes a constant reminder of the mother's charge. Booth's hesitation to destroy the stocking and spend the "inheritance" shows he fears that doing so will negate the mother's favoritism, force him to acknowledge Lincoln as the actual topdog. Booth criticizes Lincoln for spending the money his father gave him and brags about still having the mother's gift. He sees possession of the stocking not only as proof that he is as economically viable as Lincoln, but more importantly, that he is emotionally superior. Lincoln counters, "Thats like saying you don't got no money cause you aint never gonna do nothing with it ...."[51] And since Booth admits he never opened the stocking, neither brother knows if it actually contains money.[52] Lincoln understands, though, that the monetary value of Booth's inheritance doesn't matter nearly as much as its symbolic value. By spending his inheritance and burning the clothes the father left behind, Lincoln "has at least started the process of dissociating himself from his father's legacy."[53] Booth, alas, cannot or will not do the same for the mother's.

Thus, when Booth puts the money stocking down as a wager in the brothers' final, deadly game of three-card Monty, Lincoln, instinctively, wants to stop playing.[54] But Booth insists, eventually losing the game and the stocking. No longer possessing the stocking, Booth is no longer possessed by the mother's ghost. Lincoln's claiming of Booth's inheritance "simultaneously invalidates and destroys the mother's mandate to Booth to watch over Lincoln" and to thus be the topdog.[55] Rather than accept—or be liberated by—this dispossession and reversal, Booth simply becomes possessed by a new ghost and takes on a new role: the assassin.

As Lincoln raises his knife to cut the stocking, Booth confesses to killing Grace.[56] Grace, like the mother, haunts Booth throughout the play. Booth, who spends much of the play waiting for Grace to arrive and/or explain her tardiness that her absence, combined with the absences of all the other women in the play, she comes to represent "the brothers' failed attempts to achieve a stable masculinity" since "once women have to be accounted for, black men confront not only issues of racial oppression but the impact their success or failure has on black women."[57] Grace works as an omnipresent force pushing Booth to re-evaluate his masculinity and overall self-worth. Grace, for example, purportedly affirms Booth's desire to re-invent himself as "3-Card." He says, "Grace likes 3-Card better than Booth" and he puts so much value on her evaluation that he prophesizes, "Anybody not calling me 3-Card gets a bullet."[58] Yet, like a ghost, Patricia Stuelke posits, Grace is "flickering in and out of life" throughout the play.[59] Accordingly, she transcends time and space, as Lincoln acknowledges when he observes, "I'll meet her. I met her years ago. I'll meet her again."[60] Also, like the circumstances of the mother absence and of her fate, Grace's are ambiguous. Booth's description of her murder is jumbled and confused. Unable to remember how many times he shot her, Booth at first insists he didn't kill her, but then waivers "She alive not to worry, she aint going out that easy, shes alive shes shes..." Lincoln finishes Booth's sentence: "Dead. She's—", and Booth then finishes his: "Dead."[61]

Despite this ambiguity, the play emphasizes that Grace's ghost has redemptive potential: she could have saved Booth (and thus probably Lincoln) and helped him to come to terms with the mother's legacy, if only Booth had embraced the possibility. Booth describes Grace's seemingly supernatural power over memory when he tells Lincoln that Grace simply "wiped her hand" over all the time she and Booth were apart to make it disappear.[62] And Verna Foster highlights the play's emphasis on how "[Booth] could have spent his inheritance on his girlfriend Grace, whom the brothers refer to repeatedly as 'Amazing Grace'—Booth's saving grace, as she might have been—but he chose not to."[63] But Booth is unwilling to exorcise his mother's ghost, embodied in the money stocking, and have a future with Grace and Lincoln, because that would mean relinquishing his perceived, matrilineal power over his brother.

Booth also realizes that Grace is sensitive to how memories of the past affect the brothers, and anticipating this sensitivity makes Booth himself more aware of the complexity of personal history and its enduring impact. When Lincoln starts reminiscing about the brothers' childhood home, Booth criticizes the "raggedy recollections."[64] Memories and "raggedy recollections" conjure ghosts who in turn haunt or "jinx up the joint." In considering Grace's reaction to these ghosts/haunts and their effects, Booth also becomes aware that personal histories—like the shared/communal history of President Lincoln—are "raggedy" (as well as soon to be to be bloody and screaming). Thus, while he doesn't productively reconcile himself with the realities of this personal history, the play shows that the ghosts offered him the chance to do so.

The most promising ghost in the play, though, is extratextual: since Parks's earlier Lincoln-impersonator-focused work, *The America Play*, addresses many of the same issues and themes as *Topdog/Underdog*, the former play in effect "haunts" the latter. Reading the two plays together, therefore, reveals a profound literary and artistic conversation. In her author's note for *Topdog/Underdog*, Parks explains:

> In January 1999 I was thinking about a play I'd written seven years earlier called *The America Play*. In that play's first act we watch a black man who has fashioned a career for himself: he sits in an arcade impersonating Abraham Lincoln and letting people come and play at shooting him dead—like John Wilkes Booth shot our sixteenth president in 1865 during a performance at Ford's Theatre. So I was thinking about my old play when another black Lincoln impersonator, unrelated to the first guy, came to mind: a new character for a new play. This time I would just focus on his home life.[65]

Although Parks dismisses any deliberate connections between the two plays, insisting that Lincoln is "unrelated" to *The America Play*'s Lincoln impersonator, The Foundling Father, critics such as Foster have successfully shown that "the historical themes of the later play can best be understood in light of their more explicit articulation in the earlier one."[66] Foster argues that "*The America Play* and *Topdog/Underdog* illuminate one another"[67] and calls *Topdog/Underdog* an "echo" of *The America Play*.[68] The echoes, specifically, are "some of the themes of the earlier play, but what is metaphorical in *The America Play* has to be made literal in the realistic context of *Topdog/Underdog* and then, if we like, we can read the literal symbolically."[69] Given this interpretation, we can also read Parks's note literally and then symbolically: although the Foundling Father and Lincoln aren't blood kin, their connection, despite being "unrelated," posits a more liberal reading of personal and communal history, extending beyond family trees and recorded narratives, even beyond page and stage.

Near the end of her definition of "repetition and revision"—Rep & Rev—in "from Elements of Style," Parks writes, "Through reading lots I've realized how much the idea of Repetition and Revision is an integral part of the African and African-American literary and oral traditions," and she ends the section with a question: "How does Rep & Rev—a literal incorporation of the past—impact on the creation of a theatrical experience?"[70] Through this observation and question, Parks aligns her efforts with a shared literary and cultural tradition and nods to the tangible effects of that alignment. In sum, she summons the ghosts and then invites them to haunt both her written plays and their performances. Such efforts have unparalleled healing potential, Redding claims, because "it is by excavating the suppressed possibilities of the past that has been erased, by conversing with those ancestral ghosts that lay claim on us, that we can begin, again, to participate in the process of ethnic self-determination," and through those conversations, "the past, which has been either denied or utilized as a means of imprisoning us, can begin to function in a haunted place, a place through which we begin to imagine a future."[71] A liberated future, therefore, requires listening to, reconciling with, and responding to the past's ghosts.

Parks's Rep & Rev is the quintessential implementation of this process—the best way to tell a good ghost story. It's "key in examining something large than one moment" and it aims to "create space for metaphor & c."[72] Rep & Rev in general, then, and its specific manifestation in the move from *The America Play* to *TopDog/Underdog* demonstrates that although ghosts—like the histories they represent—may frighten, even terrorize, those that they haunt or possess, ghostly interactions ultimately help the haunted see history more clearly and thus create more inclusive sites for personal and communal healing.

Notes

1   Suzan-Lori Parks, "Possession," in *The America Play and Other Works* (New York: Theatre Communications Group, 1995), 4.
2   Rena Fraden, "A Mid-Life Critical Crisis: Chiastic Criticism and Encounters with the Theatrical Work of Suzan-Lori Parks," *The Journal of American Drama and Theatre*, 17.3 (2005): 39.
3   Suzan-Lori Parks, "from Elements of Style," in *The America Play and Other Works* (New York: Theatre Communications Group, 1995), 12.
4   Arthur Redding, "'Haints': American Ghosts, Ethnic Memory, and Contemporary Fiction," *Mosaic: An Interdisciplinary Critical Journal*, 34.4 (2001), 180.
5   Ibid., 176.
6   Ibid., 175.
7   Ibid., 180.
8   Parks, "Possession," 3.
9   Ibid.
10 Suzan-Lori Parks, *TopDog/Underdog* (New York: Theatre Communications Group, 2002), 9.
11 Ibid., 11
12 Jennifer Larson, *Understanding Suzan-Lori Parks* (Columbia: University of South Carolina Press, 2012), 64.
13 Ibid., 64–65.
14 Jon Dietrick, "Making it 'Real': Money and Mimesis in Suzan-Lori Parks's *TopDog/Underdog*," *Modern Drama* 27.1 (2007), 58.
15 Parks, *TopDog*, 58.
16 Ibid., 50.
17 Ibid., 52.
18 Larson, 72.
19 Ibid.
20 Parks, "Elements," 12.
21 Larson, 75.
22 Parks, *TopDog*, 22.
23 Ibid., 62.
24 Soyica Diggs Colbert, "'When I Die, I Won't Stay Dead': The Future of the Human in Suzan-Lori Parks's *The Death of the Last Black Man in the Whole Entire World.*" *boundary 2* 39.3 (2012), 203.
25 Parks, *TopDog*, 53.
26 Dietrick, 55.
27 Parks, *TopDog*, 29.
28 Ibid., 45.
29 Ibid., 90.
30 Ibid.
31 Ibid., 9.

32 Ibid., 52.
33 Ibid.
34 Fraden, 55.
35 Ibid.
36 Ibid., 52.
37 Parks, *TopDog*, 106.
38 Colbert, 198.
39 Parks, *TopDog*, 11.
40 Ibid.
41 Larson, 74.
42 Parks, *TopDog*, 107.
43 Ibid., 67.
44 Ibid., 67–68.
45 Colbert, 203.
46 Dietrick, 61.
47 Parks, *Topdog*, 69.
48 Ibid., 70.
49 Ibid., 21.
50 Ibid.
51 Ibid., 17.
52 Ibid., 105.
53 Larson, 79.
54 Parks, *TopDog*, 101.
55 Larson, 80.
56 Parks, *TopDog*, 107.
57 Myka Tucker-Abramson, "The Money Shot: Economics of Sex, Guns, and Language in *TopDog/Underdog*," *Modern Drama*, 50.1 (2007): 90.
58 Parks, *TopDog*, 17.
59 Patricia Stuelke, "Trayvon Martin, *TopDog/Underdog*, and the Tragedy Trap," *American Literary History*, 29.4 (2017): 772.
60 Parks, *TopDog*, 62.
61 Ibid., 108.
62 Ibid., 38–39.
63 Verna Foster, "Suzan-Lori Parks's Staging of The Lincoln Myth in *The America Play* and *TopDog/Underdog*," *The Journal of American Drama and Theatre*, 17.3 (2005): 34.
64 Parks, *TopDog*, 65.
65 Ibid., iii.
66 Foster, 25.
67 Ibid.
68 Ibid., 29.
69 Foster, 33.
70 Parks, "Elements," 10.
71 Redding, 174–175.
72 Parks, "Elements," 9.

Works Cited

Colbert, Soyica Diggs. "'When I Die, I Won't Stay Dead': The Future of the Human in Suzan-Lori Parks's *The Death of the Last Black Man in the Whole Entire World.*" *boundary 2* 39.3 (2012): 191–220.

Dietrick, Jon. "Making it 'Real': Money and Mimesis in Suzan-Lori Parks's *TopDog/Underdog*," *Modern Drama* 27.1 (2007): 47–74.

Foster, Verna. "Suzan-Lori Parks's Staging of The Lincoln Myth in *The America Play* and *TopDog/Underdog*," *The Journal of American Drama and Theatre* 17.3 (2005): 24–35.

Fraden, Rena. "A Mid-Life Critical Crisis: Chiastic Criticism and Encounters with the Theatrical Work of Suzan-Lori Parks." *The Journal of American Drama and Theatre* 17.3 (2005): 36–56.

Larson, Jennifer. *Understanding Suzan-Lori Parks*. Columbia: University of South Carolina Press, 2012.

Parks, Suzan-Lori. "from Elements of Style," in *The America Play and Other Works*. New York: Theatre Communications Group, 1995: 6–18.

Parks, Suzan-Lori. "Possession," in *The America Play and Other Works*. New York: Theatre Communications Group, 1995: 3–5.

Parks, Suzan-Lori. *TopDog/Underdog*. New York: Theatre Communications Group, 2002.

Redding, Arthur. "'Haints': American Ghosts, Ethnic Memory, and Contemporary Fiction." *Mosaic: An Interdisciplinary Critical Journal*, 34.4 (2001): 163–182.

Stuelke, Patricia. "Trayvon Martin, *TopDog/Underdog*, and the Tragedy Trap." *American Literary History*, 29.4 (2017): 753–778

Tucker-Abramson, Myka. "The Money Shot: Economies of Sex, Guns, and Language in *TopDog/Underdog*." *Modern Drama*, 50.1 (2007): 77–97.

11

Deficient Visitations: Staging Ghostliness and Irishness in Martin McDonagh's Comedy

Craig N. Owens

By the last minutes of Martin McDonagh's comedy *Hangmen* (2015), Shirley, the fifteen-year-old daughter of Harry, a hangman and local pub owner, is missing and presumed dead, probably strangled in a garage near the seaside town of Oldham, in the north of England, in 1964. Morose, lonely, unpretty, and unloved by any but her parents, she has, it appears, been seduced and abducted by Mooney, a creep who, only the day before, turned up in her father's bar. Her disappearance and death, we are given to understand, are the unintended consequences of an otherwise straightforward blackmail-cum-revenge scheme against Harry. But, moments after Harry and his pals have interrogated and—accidentally—hanged Mooney, the front door flies open, and with a crack of thunder and flash of lightning, Shirley appears. Dressed for a date and drenched from the rain, she has returned from where she had expected to meet Mooney hours earlier. She is angry and disappointed at having been stood up, and she is repentant and defensive about having not phoned her parents when she went off on her own.

"Alright, I *know!*" Shirley screams from the doorway, in an attempt to forestall her parents' wrath:

> I *know* you're going to be bloody mad and I *know* it's been hours and I
> *know* I should've bloody rung, but I don't bloody care, do I?! I were
> waiting for me new fella, Peter, yes, Peter, and I don't care that you don't
> like him cos I *do* like him, or I *did* like him until he never came back, so
> more the fool me for falling for somebody in one stupid day ...[1]

In this scene, Shirley recalls Banquo. Her repeated use of "bloody" recalls the wounds and "gory locks" Shakespeare's ghost revealed to Macbeth, and her presence exposes her father and the audience to the horrible fact that she had not been abducted and killed. Mooney, the man they "accidentally" hanged, was innocent. Harry, in this formulation, thus becomes a poor man's Macbeth, defeated by hubris (believing himself the best hangman in England), leaving his witless wife, Alice, who, throughout the play, exchanges the "perfumes of Araby" for a steady drip of gin, to restore order. Instead of chiding, Alice extends tea, sympathy, and *blancmange* to her no-longer-wayward daughter, and she dismisses Harry's anger that his underage daughter had gone off on her own accord.[2]

But unlike Banquo, Shirley's claim to "know" is hollow: she, in fact, has no idea what has taken place in her absence. She cannot possibly imagine the convolution of plots, counterplots, errors, and miscalculations during her day out, nor can she conceive that her father and his friends have strangled the first man to show her affection, a man whom she subsequently believes, because he had failed to meet her, was only leading her on. Even what she claims to know—that her parents will upbraid her—is wrong. If *Macbeth*'s Banquo represents the return of occluded history and buried knowledge— the return of Macbeth's repressed—Shirley's appearance signals only the return of the depressed: a shallow, taciturn adolescent whose ken extends no further than her immediate experience.

My chief aim is to make some sense of this dynamic, developed over a century of Irish drama, that typifies McDonagh's work: characters returned from the dead fail to haunt properly. As ghosts, McDonagh's undead consistently fall short of all but minimal expectations for ghostliness. In comparison to the portentous, minatory, and menacing appearances of Shakespeare's revenants, as well as those of Yeats, Beckett, and Marina Carr, McDonagh's "ghosts" always seem to bollix their return. They mislead, misunderstand, or misinterpret; they impede discovery and resolution; they foment confusion and doubt. In nearly every way, they are not harbingers of truth, revealing long kept secrets or dimly foretold futures but, rather, ignorant and perplexed figures. If ghosts in serious drama represent memory and history, in McDonagh's dark comedies they are amnesiac bearers of ambiguity and unknowability.

Isolated in a northern region, *Hangmen* invites broad comparisons to *Macbeth*, in that it too features a hubristic and fame-addled main character on a corpse-strewn path to a small amount of fame, which he can only imperfectly enjoy. Most significantly, however, in McDonagh's nearly-Scottish play, as in Shakespeare's Scottish play, supernatural prediction and ghostly return compound disorder, rather than resolve it, even though Banquo is Shakespeare's most discreet specter. Visible only to Macbeth, he appears at a royal banquet, first sitting in the seat reserved for Macbeth and then driving him to distraction by continually disappearing and reappearing. Macbeth's "most admired disorder" shakes the nobles' faith in his reason and embarrasses Lady Macbeth, who tries to draw attention away from her husband's raving.

Although Banquo's appearance at Macbeth's table indicates that Macbeth's men have assassinated him, the ghost's presence does not set Macbeth at ease. Instead, Banquo throws it into "disorder" because Macbeth interprets the ghost both as the accusation he has committed murder and a warning that the act will not safeguard his throne. The apparition thus makes the banquet a fulcrum between a fraught past and a fraught future.

Banquo's silent presence causes Macbeth's temporary madness because Macbeth has interpreted the ghost's meaning as both accusatory and portentous, accurate interpretations that contrast sharply with Macbeth's misinterpretations of the weird sisters, upon whom he has depended. The effect of Banquo's ghost's warning-*cum*-accusation, moreover, is immediate but temporary, as the weird sisters have already foretold, however cryptically, the major plot points that will follow Banquo's appearance. Thus, like Shirley's return from her presumptive death, Banquo's visit is primarily stage spectacle and only secondarily a plot mechanism.

In *Hangmen*'s opening scene, two years prior to the main action, Harry arrives at the prison cell of James Hennessy, a man convicted, despite a lack of material evidence and his protestations of innocence, of abducting and killing a young woman. Hennessey is disgusted that Harry, rather than the more professionally accomplished Pierrepont, will carry out the execution, a disgust in part justified by the way Harry ineptly inflicts violence on Hennessey to force compliance. After complaining about Harry and his assistant Syd's treatment, Hennessey, a Londoner, lamenting that he is to be "hung by a rubbish hangman," threatens Harry and Syd:[3] "I'm holding *you* and *you* personally responsible. Not you two—(*The Guards.*) You were nice. *You* two. I will come back to whatever northern shithole you live in and I will fucking haunt you."[4] Two years to the day after Hennessey's execution, amid persistent rumors of his innocence, Mooney, another young Londoner, arrives in Harry's bar. Using innuendo and evasive small talk, Mooney engages Harry's friends and, in an aside to a reporter, also insinuates that he knows something about Harry, which leads Harry to suspect that Mooney may be Hennessy's supernatural embodiment returned to exact his promised revenge.

Mooney, we learn later, is there to avenge not Hennessey but Syd, whose reputation and career Harry has ruined. Mooney's "*vaguely* menacing" demeanor, however, rattles Harry and his cronies, and when Shirley disappears for a day, they suspect Mooney has re-enacted the crime for which Hennessey was hanged. Syd encourages their suspicions by overplaying his role in this revenge tragedy *manqué* by telling Harry that Mooney has "shown [him] photos" of a more recently murdered girl "on the beach, there."[5] This (mis)information drives Harry to make Mooney reveal what he has done to—and with—Shirley. Harry, to safeguard his reputation against rumors that he hanged an innocent man, also wants to keep Mooney quiet about the recent kidnapping and murder, which closely resemble the murder for which Hennessey was hanged. Although Mooney, like Shirley, is credited with special information, they are both actually ignorant. And to the extent that either serves as a ghost, they are both insufficiently ghostly.

Derrida's meditation on King Hamlet's ghost in *Specters of Marx* (1997) helps articulate how ghostliness can be fruitfully construed, because Derrida conceives of the ghost in terms of what it does or signifies. King Hamlet, he argues, is a figure that points to the "anachrony" of any present moment,[6] revealing the "non-contemporaneity with itself of the living present."[7] The ghost, despite having arrived to represent a past manqué, also "is the future." Because the ghost offers a threat or a promise presenting itself "as that which could come or come back,"[8] it returns from the past in order to guarantee futurity itself.

Importantly, Derrida eschews the term "ghost" in favor of "revenant," from the French verb *revenir*: to come back or return. Because what a ghost is derives mainly from what it does, Derrida wants to consider how the revenant functions as a sign and as an agent of change:

> It does not belong to ontology, to the discourse on the Being of beings, or to the essence of life or death. It requires, then, what we call, to save time and space rather than just to make up a word, *hauntology*. We will take this category to be irreducible, and first of all to everything that makes it possible: ontology, theology, positive or negative onto-theology.[9]

Sarah West, in considering how voice often structures and textures Beckett's later plays, uses *revenant* similarly, to characterize the voices that "visit" Beckett's characters.[10] West's deployment of the term thus helps make sense of visitations in more recent Irish drama by allowing us to view any ghostly effect—memory, reverie, haunting, hallucination—as hauntological, that is, as a remainder capable of unhinging the present by standing for a past that threatens temporal linearity forward into the future, even as it makes that future possible. In twentieth-century Irish drama, in particular, the memories and reveries represented and recounted by the revenant—the dreamer, the ghost, the old man alone in his room or in his skull—are almost always deficient. Repeatedly the historical and expository certainties that traditionally anchor plots fail, forcing us to accept, instead, ignorance and indirection.

An early twentieth-century exception, Yeats's short play *Purgatory* (1939) helps nuance our approach to McDonagh. Its plot is simple: the Old Man is the son of an Irish noblewoman and a stable groom, poorly matched, who were the last inhabitants of the ruined house in front of which the play's dialogues (there is hardly any action) take place. The Old Man has intentionally brought his son, the Boy—the only other live human in the play—to this house because it is his parents' wedding anniversary, the night he was conceived. As the conversation progresses between the Old Man and the Boy, who at first won't listen and then believes his father is raving, we learn that the groom whom the Boy's grandmother had married was a spendthrift drunkard who, after his wife's death in childbirth, ruined the family's fortune and honor. Having grown into young adulthood witnessing the precipitous decline of the family, the Old Man, then an adolescent, avenged his mother and her noble ancestors by stabbing his drunken father, setting fire to the house, and running off to live as a tinker. The Boy is the issue of what we are told was a brief relationship between the Old Man and the daughter of an itinerant.

As the Old Man recounts this story, he hears hoof-beats, and the silhouette appears of the dead woman standing in an eerily lit upstairs window, waiting for her ghostly husband to arrive from the pub, where he has been celebrating their betrothal. Later, the husband, too, appears in the window, pouring himself a *post-coitu* glass of whiskey. According to the Old Man, his mother's spirit is doomed to "re-live" her night of nuptial passion and to suffer the guilt of this shameful and, in effect, morganatic match, until she has expiated her sins. As the play draws to a close, The Old Man, attempting to quiet his mother's spirit by ending the tainted bloodline, stabs the Boy four times. Shortly after the Boy dies, however, the Old Man hears hoof-beats anew, signaling that the ghostly pantomime has begun again. His attempt to end the continual posthumous coupling has failed.

In *Purgatory*, the knowledge of the past is perfect, the history complete. Although nothing suggests The Old Man's account is false, his action to quell the trauma represented by the re-enactment of his mother's coupling nevertheless fails. While *Hangmen*'s plot hinges on its characters' possessing incomplete or incorrect information, *Purgatory*'s tragedy, which hinges on misinterpretation, suggests that a repressed past, however transparent and complete, cannot make itself legible and actionable in the present.

The suggestion in Carr's *Portia Coughlan* (1996) that a ghostly return demands drastic action to pacify a restless past provides a thematic bridge between *Purgatory* and McDonagh's plays. On the eve of her thirtieth birthday, Portia struggles with a deep sense of emptiness. Isolated from her husband, Raphael, from her friends, and from family, she prefers her brother Gabriel's ghostly voice (which she alone can hear), singing near the place where he drowned himself fifteen years earlier. As the play unfolds, those who knew them make cryptic remarks suggesting that if their relationship was not incestuous, it was unusually strange and strong, even for twins. Their father, Sly, explicitly condemns their attachment and, particularly, Gabriel's part in it. He tells Portia to "forget … that unnatural child who shamed me and your mother so."[11]

Portia's response, however, raises questions about whether Gabriel is a ghost or a manifestation of Portia's memories and desires:

> Forget Gabriel! He's everywhere, Daddy. Everywhere. There's not a corner of any of your forty fields that don't remind me of Gabriel. His name is on the mouths of the starlin's that swoops over Belmont hill, the cows bellow for him from the barn on frosty winter nights. The very river tells me that once he was here and now he's gone. And you ask me to forget him.[12]

Although the *dramatis personae* lists Gabriel as "a ghost," in performance, he appears to be more hauntological. Because only Portia hears Gabriel's voice and it fades when she is distracted, it is impossible to know whether Gabriel is ghostly or imagined. And since Gabriel's ghost sings only an eerily wordless song, the audience never learns with certainty why he continually returns to the Belmont valley. Nor does Portia attempt to "translate" the singing into natural language; instead, remaining a force that takes her more deeply into herself, it draws her to the place where Gabriel drowned himself. Whatever his nature, Gabriel's apparent return is certainly meaningful to Portia, who has been increasingly unable to find fulfillment or happiness in the rural Irish midlands. But Gabriel's ontological ambiguity makes Portia's motivation unclear: is she driven by an otherworldly imperative or a deranged mind?

When the first scene of Act 2 reveals Portia also drowned in the river, the discovery suggests her suicide fulfilled the ghost's imperative. Interpreting Portia's suicide in this way, however, misinterprets the ghost. After all, Portia is the one who feels she has the right to demand justice, the one who has been betrayed: "Oh, Gabriel, ya had no right to discard me so, to float me on the world as if I were a ball of flotsam. Ya had no right. (*Begins to weep uncontrollably*)."[13] More importantly, Gabriel expresses success not when Portia's body is discovered but, rather, the night before, when she acknowledges, in the play's final speech, that she cannot love Raphael as she loved Gabriel:

> I thought, how can anyone with a name like [Raphael Coughlan] be so real, and I says to meself, if Raphael Coughlan notices me I will have a chance to enter the world and stay in it, which has always been the battle for me. And you say you want me to talk about ya the way I talk about

Gabriel—I cannot, Raphael, I cannot. And though everyone and everythin' tells me I have to forget him, I cannot, Raphael, I cannot.[14]

At this point, the play's analeptic concluding scene ends with a stage direction telling us Raphael exits and we hear the "[s]ound of Gabriel's voice, triumphant."[15]

Although Carr does not go so far as Yeats in denying certain understanding, her ghost resembles Yeats's because it invites misinterpretation. In McDonagh's *Leenane Trilogy*, this invitation to misinterpret combines the tragic revelations with the comic, and this combination, over two decades, facilitates a key feature of McDonagh's stage and screen work: the playing out of an irrepressible past as it returns to catalyze comic misinterpretations by reconfiguring otherwise indecipherable meanings and unknowable truths.

Judith Roof has described the dynamic whereby plays such as Harold Pinter's *Betrayal* position audiences to construct spectatorial desire around the flow of information, rather than its revelation. The "lure of knowledge," according to Judith Roof, "divulges" not knowledge itself, but "the desire for knowledge and the means by which knowledge is conveyed."[16] In contrast to the "lure of knowledge," McDonagh's plays exploit a lure of ignorance that makes the desire not to know, the *sine qua non* of narrative pleasure. In the *Leenane Trilogy*, as in *Hangmen*, the imperative for revelation constantly competes with the desire to distort, occlude, or bury the past.

In the first play, *The Beauty Queen of Leenane*, Mag ultimately dies because she burned a letter from Pato Dooley, professing his love to Maureen, Mag's emotionally troubled, middle-aged daughter. Mag did so to prevent Maureen from marrying Pato and leaving home. For much of the play, Mag and Maureen's squabbling generates verbal and physical comedy. But Maureen's violent tendencies emerge, first when she intentionally scalds her disabled mother's hand and, finally, when she crushes Mag's head with a fire poker in revenge for her having destroyed Pato's letter. These developments validate Mag's repeated accusations and fears, which the play had invited us earlier to dismiss as a sour woman's paranoid ravings. Maureen's violence thus invokes an incompletely repressed past that turns verbal comedy into savage revenge. The connection established here between violent death and the return of repressed history is more extensively developed in the trilogy's second and third plays, *A Skull in Connemara* (1997) and *Lonesome West* (1997). In those plays, the dead who return, like the revenants in *Purgatory* and *Portia Coughlan*, acting in ways that are accidental, ill-timed, or short-lived, prove unable to send clear messages.

A Skull in Connemara centers on the mysterious death, seven years earlier, of Mick Dowd's wife, Oona, attributed to Mick's drunk driving. Midway through the play, Mick and Mairtin Hanlon, a half-witted teenager, must exhume bodies in the local churchyard—including Oona's—to make room for the coming year's newly dead. Mick, however, does not know that Mairtin's brother, Tom, had secretly exhumed Oona's body. A bungling local policeman thirsty for recognition, Tom hopes to prove that Mick murdered Oona or, failing that, to frame him for her murder, and so he has inflicted new wounds on her skull and hidden the corpse away until he can get the case re-opened. But Mairtin, who witnessed Tom's evidence-tampering, reveals his brother's plot. So, Oona, literally returned from the grave—although not by her own volition—unable to shed light on past events, helps to perpetuate the status quo in her unchanging village. The pervasive rumors that Mick murdered Oona remain only rumors.

The failure of the dead to reveal the truth is comically underscored by Mick's failed attempt to bludgeon Mairtin to death with a sledgehammer and to stage an automobile accident when he suspects that Mairtin, not Tom, has exhumed Oona (to steal her jewelry). Near the end of the play, moments after Mick confesses to having just murdered Mairtin, Mairtin enters, quite alive—a literal revenant—staunchly claiming the bloody wound on his forehead came not from Mick's assault but from drunken driving. Bent on arresting Mick for attempted murder, Tom becomes so infuriated by Mairtin's refusal to admit he was assaulted that he, too, attacks Mairtin with the sledgehammer. Life in Connemara, however, is so stagnant that even Mairtin's grandmother, Maryjohnny, who has witnessed Mick's confession to assaulting Mairtin and is certain Mick killed Oona, continues to drop in on Mick to share gossip and a glass of poteen with him.

A Skull in Connemara, thus connects the ineffectual return of the dead to Irish history and culture. Whereas Yeats's play suggests that tortured repetitions and empty enactments characterize the lives of particular individuals and families, McDonagh treats them as broadly cultural phenomena: neither the insufficiently dead Mairtin nor Oona's exhumed skull can change anyone's lives. Because life in Connemara tenaciously resists change, Oona's and Mairtin's cranial damage is of a piece with that life.

The final scene of *The Lonesome West* (1997), which concludes *The Leenane Trilogy*, is the closest the trilogy comes to representing a true voice from the grave. Two brothers, Valene and Coleman, begin admitting their faults to one another, apologizing for past wrongs, and accepting each other's apologies. A local priest's heartfelt imprecations have inspired their attempts to end their feud, conveyed in a letter they received the morning after the priest's suicide. A proxy revenant, delivering the Priest's warning from beyond the grave, the letter makes clear that Father Welsh's immortal soul may depend on whether the brothers redeem his sacrifice. When Coleman admits, however, to having stolen money from Valene, Valene chases him from the house with a shotgun.

The dead priest's living words have been ineffectual, and the brothers' continuing squabble testifies to the incorrigibility of Connemara natives. Alone on stage, Valene complains about the priest's posthumous interference, using words that make his letter starkly hauntological:

> And you, you whiny fecking priest. Do I need your soul hovering o'er me the rest of me fecking life? How could anybody be getting on with that feck? . . . Well I won't be buying the fecker a pint anyways. I'll tell you that for nothing Father Welsh . . . .[17]

The single ray of hope at the end of the play is literal: before the stage darkens, a stage light briefly lingers on the crucifix to which Father Welsh's letter was attached.

All three plays in the trilogy feature murderers who are unprosecuted or acquitted. Lamenting the "three slaughterings and one suicide amongst [his] congregation,"[18] Father Welsh, concludes:

> I don't fit into this town. Although I'd have to have killed half me fecking relatives to fit into this town. Jeez. I thought Leenane was a nice place when first I turned up here, but no. Turns out it's the murder capital of fecking Europe.[19]

Irish theatrical revenants are ineffective and misleading, therefore, not because they are ghostly (often, they're not), but because they epitomize Irish marginalization and inaction. What these deficient revenants say on stage is frequently irrelevant or ineffective, sometimes because they aren't listened to (Father Welsh), sometimes because the listeners cannot understand (Gabriel and The Old Man's Mother), sometimes because they aren't taken seriously (Mairtin), and sometimes because they aren't saying anything at all (Oona). But if they prove deficient in their inability to convey clear, actionable information about the past of the fictional world they inhabit, McDonagh's revenants, especially, speak clearly about a much deeper extra-theatrical history. For they attest to the persistence of a pernicious notion of Irishness— pugilistic, drunken, unserious, and self-defeating—stretching back centuries, which found its most salient theatrical representation in the nineteenth-century "stage Irishman," made famous by actor-manager-playwright Dion Boucicault. While George Bernard Shaw argued, in the first decade of the twentieth century, that the "mendacity and mendicity" stereotypical of the unfortunate Irish underclass were effects of British colonization internalized by the Irish themselves, this stage conception of Irishness has remained a recognizable comic figure.[20] Its repeated return in McDonagh's plays speaks, then, to the effect of centuries-long British violence and cultural repression, indicating how nearly impossible it has been to neutralize and disempower the stage-Irish notion of Irishness despite decades of scholarly and creative production meant to exorcise this ghost of Ireland's colonial past.

Notes

1 Martin McDonagh, *Hangmen*, Rev. edn (London: Faber and Faber, 2015), 102.
2 Ibid., 103.
3 Ibid., 12.
4 Ibid., 13.
5 Ibid., 69.
6 Jacques Derrida, *Specters of Marx: The State of the Debt, the Work of Mourning, and the New International*, trans. Peggy Kamuf (New York: Routledge, 1997), 7.
7 Ibid., xix.
8 Ibid., 39.
9 Ibid., 51.
10 Sarah West, *Say It: The Performative Voice in the Dramatic Works of Samuel Beckett* (Amsterdam: Rodopi, 2010), 70.
11 Marina Carr, *Portia Coughlan. Plays I* (London: Faber and Faber, 1999), 213.
12 Ibid., 213–214.
13 Ibid., 211.
14 Ibid., 255.
15 Ibid.
16 Judith Roof, "Betrayal of Facts: Pinter and Duras Beyond Adaptation," in *Pinter at Sixty*, ed. Katherine H. Burkman and John L. Kundert-Gibbs (Bloomington: Indiana University Press, 1993), 80.
17 Martin McDonagh, *A Skull in Connemara*, in *Beauty Queen of Leenane and Other Plays* (New York: Random House, 1998), 258–259.
18 Martin McDonagh, *Lonesome West*, in *Beauty Queen of Leenane and Other Plays* (New York: Random House, 1998), 213.
19 Ibid., 212.
20 George Bernard Shaw, *Our Theatres in the Nineties*, 3 Vols (London: Constable and Company, 1932), 2:29.

Works Cited

Carr, Marina. *Portia Coughlan. Plays I*. London: Faber and Faber, 1999.
Derrida, Jacques. *Specters of Marx: The State of the Debt, the Work of Mourning, and the New International*, trans. Peggy Kamuf. New York: Routledge, 1997.

McDonagh, Martin. *The Beauty Queen of Leenane and Other Plays.* New York: Random House, 1998.

McDonagh, Martin. *The Beauty Queen of Leenane,* in *Beauty Queen of Leenane and Other Plays.* New York: Random House, 1998.

McDonagh, Martin. *Hangmen.* Rev. edn. London: Faber and Faber, 2015.

McDonagh, Martin. *Lonesome West,* in *Beauty Queen of Leenane and Other Plays.* New York: Random House, 1998.

McDonagh, Martin. *A Skull in Connemara,* in *Beauty Queen of Leenane and Other Plays.* New York: Random House, 1998.

Roof, Judith. "Betrayal of Facts: Pinter and Duras Beyond Adaptation," in *Pinter at Sixty,* ed. Katherine H. Burkman and John L. Kundert-Gibbs. Bloomington: Indiana University Press, 1993. 79–89.

Shakespeare, William. *The Tragedy of Macbeth.* In Greenblatt et al., eds. *The Norton Shakespeare: Based on the Oxford Edition.* New York: W.W. Norton and Company, 1997.

Shaw, George Bernard. *Our Theatres in the Nineties.* 3 Vols. London: Constable and Company, 1932.

Spenser, Edmund. *A View of the Present State of Ireland,* ed. Marianne McDonald et al. Cork: Corpus of Electronic Texts (CELT), 2010. Online. www.ucc.ie/celt/published/E500000-001/index.html. July 27, 2012.

West, Sarah. *Say It: The Performative Voice in the Dramatic Works of Samuel Beckett.* Amsterdam: Rodopi, 2010.

Yeats, William Butler. *Purgatory. Modern Irish Drama,* ed. John P. Harrington. New York: Norton, 1991.

12

Holding the Dead Close: The Comfort of Ghosts in the Plays of Sarah Ruhl

Amy Muse

In the theatre, ghosts are a given. We believe in them; we take them for granted; we leave lights on for them. As Alice Rayner writes, "theatre, in all of its aspects, uniquely insists on the reality of ghosts" because "theatre itself is a ghostly place in which the living and the dead come together in a productive encounter."[1] Ghosts in the plays of Sarah Ruhl are not traditional "secret-bearers," ghosts of illusion of the modern theatre; they are, instead, the ghosts of the earliest ritual theatre, in which there's "no dichotomy between reality and artifice."[2] The form of theatre Ruhl writes refuses to "consent to the idea that invisible, immaterial, or abstract forces are illusions, that the spirits of the dead are imaginary, or that the division between spirit and matter is absolute."[3] For Ruhl, the theatre becomes a place where her father, who died from cancer when she was twenty, can continue to live. Her plays reveal the stubborn hope of a grieving daughter. Throughout her career, Ruhl has summoned her father onstage, calling him back from time to time to reassure her that his passage was successful and that he is comfortably settled, and to reassure him that he is remembered and loved. In return, this ghost doesn't haunt. He has no agenda to wreak havoc or urge revenge; his presence does not dredge up regret for past wrongs or things not said. Instead, he comforts. When the ghost of Ruhl's father visits, it is to bless. Onstage these visitations feel like instances of what theologian Mark McInroy calls the "radiant invisible," in which we see the invisible radiating through the visible and have the experience of two shimmering worlds co-existing, accompanying one another.[4]

Ruhl has always been interested in the "more invisible terrains" of drama—in theatre's affinity with ritual and the metaphysical, theatre as a "place where you can actually look at the invisible"[5]—than in the drama of drawing room or kitchen sink. While that can be attributed, in part, to her childhood fascination with the Catholic mass, her father's death gave her a lasting experience of perceiving the "fabric between death and life as a little bit porous."[6] As she told poet Elizabeth Metzger, "I think dreams and art create a boundary-crossing between the two—little punctures in the fabric that separates us."[7] Using the stage to explore the liminal realm between the worlds of the living and the dead has allowed Ruhl to keep crossing those boundaries and connecting with her father. Her early plays are suffused with grief and longing, "characterized by a strong desire to reunite with the lost loved one," which gets "lightened through mechanisms of fantasy and magic realism"[8] to create Ruhl's signature move, her "habitual tightrope act," as Celia Wren put it in *American Theatre*, of "joining humor to sadness."[9] The passage of time sees that raw grief soften into memory. In *Dog Play* (1994) and *Eurydice* (2001), written soon after her father's death, the acute anguish exists on the surface of the plays, which feature fathers who have died and daughters who mourn them. Writing these fathers helps bring her own back from the dead. The characters not only closely resemble her father—words he spoke in real life are woven into the plays. As the grief subsides in Ruhl's body and mind and she goes on to write about other subjects (though always "death, love, and how we should treat each other in this lifetime"),[10] she resurrects her father more indirectly. *The Oldest Boy* (2014) reveals the father reincarnated as a son; in *For Peter Pan on Her 70th Birthday* (2016), the dead father walks among the living, accompanying them in their everyday lives. In all of these plays, the ghosts are soothing rather than scary.

All of Ruhl's plays have permeable boundaries between life and death, the visible and invisible. All have their own ghostly demarcations. I am ignoring, therefore, plays with onstage dead characters (notably, *Dead Man's Cell Phone*, in which Gordon, the dead man of the title, comes back to get his cell phone, and *The Clean House*, in which cleaning lady Matilde's dead parents are resurrected in moments of memory), and am not addressing haunted characters such as *Passion Play*'s character P, who plays Pontius Pilate and bears the moral burden of his character and, eventually, his nation. "I suppose I hold my dead close," Ruhl has said.[11] To do this, she creates a ritual space of remembrance where dead and living can enjoy moments of being together. To explore that aspect of Ruhl's work, what follows will focus only on personal ghosts, in the four plays where Ruhl reconnects with her father through a character either explicitly or implicitly modeled on him: *Dog Play*, *Eurydice*, *The Oldest Boy* and *For Peter Pan on Her 70th Birthday*.

Raw Grief: Calling Back the Newly Dead

Dog Play and *Eurydice*, two of Ruhl's earliest plays, were written soon after her father's death, while her grief was still fresh. Both present a father who has just died and a daughter who misses him; both allow the father and daughter moments of reconnection. *Dog Play*, a one-act play written for Paula Vogel's playwriting class at Brown just months after Ruhl's father died in 1994, had a reading at the Chicago Dramatists Ten-Minute Play Festival in 1998 but remains unpublished. Only a sophomore at the time, Ruhl was grieving and struggling to write. Vogel assigned an exercise: to write a short play with a dog as protagonist. As Vogel describes it, Ruhl approached her father's death from a

> unique angle: a dog is waiting by the door, waiting for the family to come home, unaware that the family is at his master's funeral, unaware of the concept of death. And, oh yes, the play was written with Kabuki stage techniques, in gorgeous, emotionally vivid language. I sat with this short play in my lap in my study, and sobbed.[12]

Dog Play was inspired by Vogel's *The Baltimore Waltz*, which Ruhl had seen at Brown the year before. *The Baltimore Waltz* was written as a tribute for Vogel's brother Carl, and Ruhl admired how Vogel "created a modern architecture for grief," how she "transmuted personal loss into something formal, and how she both stepped back from the grief formally, but laid the grief bare in an extraordinary, transparent way at the end."[13] In *Dog Play*, Ruhl created "a remarkable anthropomorphic portrait of the no man's land we occupy when a loved one falls ill. You wait and wait, hoping for a recovery, yet sensing, and at some level knowing, there won't be one."[14] In it, the father of a family (named just Father) has died. While the daughter (named just Daughter) and the rest of the family tend to end-of-life preparations, the father enters scenes and watches over them quietly, leaning against the moon (a giant puppet) when his daughter leaves the hospital after his death, or against a tree when the family stands around the gravesite. Only the family dog (named just Dog, played by an actor in a dog mask) can see him. While humans think there's an impenetrable barrier between the living and the dead, dogs see no barrier at all. Dog tells the audience, "I dreamed last night that I could speak and everyone could understand. I was telling them that he is not dead, that I can see him. No one believed me."[15] When Father enters the scene right after his death, Daughter has just removed her hospital mask and sits outside with Dog, who sees Father enter and, wagging his tail, walks over to lick Father's hand:

> **Dog** I've missed you. You don't know how I've missed you. I never got to say good-bye. You look good, you look fine—are you happy?
>
> **Father** You're smart enough to know there's no heaven or hell. I'm still angry and I'm still sad. I live on the moon, mostly.[16]

Although there's no further exploration of this—Daughter, puzzled by Dog's behavior, calls him away from the (to her) invisible Father—it feels like a moment of Ruhl wishing her father a pleasant afterlife on the moon. (In another scene we see him sitting on top of the moon drinking tea with an English queen.) This way he will always be in her sky.

Daughter longs to connect physically with Father. She attempts to join him on the moon: when "*a rope falls from the ceiling*," Daughter "*climbs the rope higher and higher until the audience can't see her anymore.*"[17] In a later scene, she's in Father's room, touches his now-empty chair, and starts singing "Blue Moon" ("Blue moon, you saw me standing alone. Without a dream in my heart, without a love of my own") but then notices the audience and stops singing.[18] At the end of the play, Ruhl gives the audience (and herself) a much-needed moment of reconnection between Father and Daughter. Daughter walks into a room in which a radio is playing and "*seems startled to hear music on the radio—she's the only one home. The father and dog look on sympathetically.*"[19] She asks Dog, "Who turned on the radio? Who turned on the radio?" The stage directions tell us "*She can't see anyone. She sits down and puts her head in her hands.*"[20] Then Father says:

Father   Don't be sad.

Daughter (*Looking for him*)   Where? Where? Oh! Oh! Oh.

He goes to her. She becomes quiet.[21]

This concludes the play. She is not agitated or frightened by the awareness that her father's spirit is in the room with her. Feeling his presence allows her to calm down. He is there to soothe her. He is, after all, her father.

In *Eurydice*, Ruhl extends this final moment from *Dog Play*, allowing direct and sustained connection between a grieving daughter and a comforting father. Ruhl has called *Eurydice* a "transparently personal" play: "I wanted to write something where I would be allowed to have a few more conversations with him." Again inspired by Vogel's model of formally stepping back from grief, yet laying it bare, Ruhl explained that "a myth exploring the underworld and the connection between the dead and the living was a way to negotiate that terrain."[22] Within the world of *Eurydice*, the father himself is not a ghost; he dwells in the land of the dead and does not cross the threshold back to the living. He is, however, the ghost of Ruhl's own father, restored to life on the stage. He speaks lines spoken by her father in real life, most memorably in the letter that Father writes to Eurydice on her wedding day, offering advice: "Continue to give yourself to others because that's the ultimate satisfaction in life—to love, accept, honor and help others."[23] When they reunite in the Underworld, he teaches Eurydice the words "ostracize," "peripatetic," and "defunct," words Ruhl's father introduced to her and her sister during Saturday morning breakfasts when they were children. Eurydice also listens to her father tell a story about going duck hunting with his father (a story also included in *Dog Play*).

Ruhl complicates and personalizes the tale of Orpheus and Eurydice by making her father the primary and lasting love of Eurydice's life. On her wedding day she and her father imagine being together. When the wedding music plays, the Father hears it from the Underworld, and, as though he were walking his daughter down the aisle, he "*looks at his imaginary daughter; he looks straight ahead; he acknowledges the guests at the wedding; he gets choked-up; he looks at his daughter and smiles an embarrassed smile for getting choked-up.*"[24] Eurydice tells the audience "a wedding is for a father and a daughter. They stop being married to each other on that day."[25] Eurydice does not seem ready to marry yet. Ruhl tells us that she and Orpheus should seem "a little too young and a little too in love,"[26] which tilts our affection, like Ruhl's, toward the father-daughter relationship. When Eurydice finds herself bored on her wedding day, she is lured away by a Nasty Interesting Man because he tells her he has a letter from her dead father. Eurydice: "I knew he'd send something!"[27] Hungry for connection to her father, she follows the Nasty Interesting Man to his high-rise apartment to get the letter, but when he tries to seduce her there, she grabs the letter and runs out, tripping and falling down his six hundred steps, into the Underworld.

As in *Dog Play*, the father, in the realm of the dead, knows his daughter but she cannot recognize him because, having had to swim through the River of Lethe, Eurydice has forgotten everything. (Until the end of the play her father has somehow escaped that fate.) What gives the play its "gripping and sustained potency"[28] is the father's tender care for Eurydice; this is Ruhl's grateful acknowledgment, or fervent hope, that her father remains present and cares for her, even when she is unaware of it. When Eurydice is fussy because there are no rooms in the Underworld in which to set down her suitcase and rest, her father painstakingly builds her a room out of string. They sit together in the string-room while he reads her the reunion passage from *King Lear*, where Lear tells Cordelia, hoping beyond hope, "We two alone will sing like birds in the cage. / When thou dost ask my blessing, I'll kneel down / And ask of thee forgiveness; so we'll live, / And pray and sing."[29]

Eventually, even though he misses his daughter terribly, he instructs her to return to Orpheus in the world of the living. "You should go to your husband," he tells her; "you should love your family until the grapes grow dust on their purple faces."[30] He then immerses himself in the river so that he can finally forget. In this deeply personal moment, the playwright releases her father from the emotional labor of always watching over her life and from the pain of feeling distant from her. Within the play, Eurydice, after reuniting with Orpheus long enough to urge him to go on and to write a letter to his next wife, instructing her how to love him, returns to the Underworld, dips herself in the river of forgetfulness, and lies down next to her father. This last image can look darker than is probably intended: Eurydice and her father (Ruhl and her father), dipped in forgetfulness, physically together but no longer conscious of one another, dead. Visible through the radiant invisible layers of world and of play, we see a daughter decide to hold her father close.

Grief Metabolized into Memory

Over the years, as Ruhl ages, marries, and becomes a mother, she resurrects her father in her plays from the perspective of caregiver—that is, instead of expecting him to comfort her, she checks in on him to let him know he is remembered and loved, which comforts her as well. In a letter to Max Ritvo, included in *Letters from Max*, Ruhl writes that she used to imagine her father "growing up in death": she imagined him at the moment of death starting over, as it were, "as a baby," then as the years went on, mirroring the years since his death, she would imagine him at different stages of growth. For instance, she explains, "three years after his death I imagined that he was in preschool, and I was his mother, having to drop him off at the door, having to let go. I was suffering as he happily went to explore counting beads." Now, though, she is able to remember him, to listen to music he loved and feel happy in her memory, which, she says, "makes me think he is happy."[31]

In another letter, Ruhl reveals that her oldest daughter, Anna, "thinks she might be a reincarnation of my father." Anna says to Ruhl, "Mom, promise me that you'll come back and be my child and I'll be able to recognize you."[32] The desire for this cycle, and for recognition and awareness of it, is present in *The Oldest Boy*, where Ruhl reincarnates her father. Although most of Ruhl's ghosts do not fit Alice Rayner's argument that "a ghost, particularly in the theatre, ought to startle an audience into attention with a shiver,"[33] this one does. *The Oldest Boy* is a story of a mother whose three-year-old son is the reincarnation of a Tibetan Buddhist lama and her struggle to let him live out his dharma. At the end of the play, after the son (the Oldest Boy of the title) has been installed as lama in his temple in India, the mother gives birth to a second child, a daughter. The final line of the play induces that shivery chill we tend to associate with a ghost's visitation. The son holds his newborn sister; when his mother cautions him to hold the baby's head gently, he responds, "I've done this before. I used to be your father, remember? . . . Many lifetimes ago I held you in my arms, like this."[34]

Although the father character in this play does not seem to be a stand-in for Ruhl's father, his spirit imbues this play about reincarnation with autobiographical details sprinkled throughout, and with the themes of attachment and letting go. In a conversation about religious beliefs, the mother character tells a visiting lama about a dream she had when her father died:

> and in the dream these huge letters in silver spelled out "There is no God," written across the heavens, and I turned to my father in the dream, and I said, "But who could have written that in the heavens?" and he said, "Exactly." And since then I have been looking for God—.[35]

This was a dream Ruhl herself had, a dream that comforted her.[36]

The Oldest Boy asks whether the attachment we have to others is the same as loving them. In the conversation between the mother and the lama, she has described to him the concept of "attachment parenting" ("you wear your child around, you breast-feed for a long time, you sleep in the same bed as

Figure 12.1 Christina Baldwin (Mother), Tenzin the puppet, and Masanari Kawahara (puppeteer) in Sarah Ruhl's *The Oldest Boy*. Directed by Sarah Rasmussen, Jungle Theatre, Minneapolis, November 2018. Photo courtesy Dan Norman.

your child"),[37] which he finds fascinating, and funny since the mother, as someone interested in becoming Buddhist, practices nonattachment. "Well, yes," she answers, "but I guess not as a mother."[38] "Do you think attachment is the same as love?" the lama asks her. "No Yes No," she answers. "Do you?"[39] "I can tell you it is not the same," the lama says; "attachment is grasping, clinging, it is not comfortable."[40] This feels like a question Ruhl is asking herself. In a letter to Max Ritvo she describes seeing a Korean acupuncture master who

> took one look at my face and said, "Father, father, father, I get nothing from you but your father. What does your father do?" "He's dead," I said. "Ah," he said, "lie down. You have to let your father go." And I thought, "No no no no! I Won't Let Him Go."[41]

The acupuncturist was concerned that if she didn't let him go, Ruhl's father wouldn't have a good reincarnation but would stay attached to this world. Ruhl has the husband/father of *The Oldest Boy* articulate this thought, explaining why he allows his recently deceased mother in Tibet to go instead of mourning her excessively. Although the acupuncturist doesn't use this word, it seems as though he's suggesting Ruhl exorcise the ghost of her father. Instead, we might say she exercises him, bringing him onstage. Whether or not one believes that she keeps her father attached to this world by resurrecting him in her plays, she is able to stay attached to him this way, and to reassure him that he is remembered.

For Peter Pan on Her 70th Birthday feels as though Ruhl, from her position as a now middle-aged woman, conjures her father again, imagining him as an old man. Ruhl calls this play, which of her works is most explicitly a ghost play, "a contemporary Midwestern Noh drama": "the protagonist meets the ghost, then recognizes the ghost, then dances with or embraces the ghost."[42] That genre description, John Lahr writes, gives us "a clue to the paradoxical game of loss and reparation" that Ruhl is playing;[43] "*For Peter Pan* moves between the diurnal and the spiritual, lightly contending with death in order to befriend it."[44] She wrote the play for her mother, Kathleen Kehoe Ruhl; its protagonist, clearly based on Kathleen Ruhl, is the oldest daughter in a family of five opinionated siblings, who have come together to be with their father (Sarah Ruhl's grandfather) as he dies. Yet because of the echoes with *Dog Play*, the shared kindness of the fathers in *Eurydice* and *For Peter Pan*, and the attachment of the daughter, the father figure feels like Ruhl's own father.

The play is structured in three movements. At the end of the first movement, "Waiting," which takes place in the hospital room, the father, George, dies. After his children, the five siblings, who are gathered around his bed, recite the Lord's Prayer, we hear a sound effect, "*A small sound: ping*," and "*George very simply gets up from his hospital bed*" and leaves the room.[45] The other characters continue looking at the hospital bed as though he's still there. They are seeing his body; we are seeing his spirit. In the second movement, "Remembering," we see George re-enter as a ghost. The siblings are now at their family home, holding a small wake for their father. They sit around the breakfast table drinking Jameson and eating Chex party mix and sharing memories. As they toast the father, the stage directions indicate "*A slight pause—a hole in time*" and George enters. "*He is an ordinary ghost,*"[46] Ruhl tells us. "*He wears glasses. He has a kind face.*"[47] He sits at the table with his children, reading the newspaper. They don't see him and, perhaps, more curiously, he "*doesn't pay much attention to them*" either.[48] The scene is not sentimental; it is resolutely mundane. George uses the bathroom; when the others hear the toilet flush, they don't feel haunted, just assume that the old toilet is running. They continue their conversation about religious beliefs, theories about what happens to us after death, and (one of Ruhl's longstanding questions) whether consciousness persists. To try to prove that consciousness persists, sibling four says, "Dad—if you're here, give us a sign."[49] After "*A silence,*" George "*drops the bowl of Chex party mix on the floor*"; this causes a "*hubbub*" and they all "*react with surprise*" overlapping one another with exclamations of "Oh my god—" "Holy shit!" and "I told you!"[50] A similar moment happens later in the scene when George, stirring Metamucil into a glass of orange juice, creates a tinkling sound. They've just been talking about Tinker Bell and belief in fairies and "*they look up for a moment, registering the sound,*" but "*then dismiss it.*"[51] Even though they've received two signs, they don't pursue the reality of their father as a ghost dwelling in the room with them.

The funniest and most delightful ghost moment occurs when the siblings talk about the death of their old family dog, Capp. Immediately afterward, George re-enters the room with Capp, who walks about them and eats the spilled Chex party mix off the floor. "*George pats the dog,*" which shows us that the dog exists in *his* world; they are both ordinary ghosts. Ruhl gives George no lines to indicate his awareness of his children or his thoughts about them or about his life. This seems true to the depiction we get of George when he was alive; he was a father of his era, leading his own life, not always centered on his children. But it leads me to wonder: are we witnessing *his* consciousness persisting, or is the significance here onstage the *memory* of him, the presence of him, which is important to the living, not the dead?

In the third movement, "Neverland," the worlds of living and dead finally connect. The stage turns into a community-theatre-style *Peter Pan* set with siblings one through five playing characters from that story. At the end of their flying about—which they can't do as well as they used to—siblings two through five realize they have outgrown their nursery games and must leave to attend to their adult responsibilities. They are grown up: they no longer need a father to build rooms of string for them. But character one, Ann, the Peter Pan character, does not want to grow up. Here Ruhl echoes a concern that she introduced in *Eurydice*: does growing up mean leaving your father behind? Does growing up mean forgetting him? If you stay young, maybe he stays young, and therefore stays alive. At this moment Ann experiences a layered moment of time "in the theatre's disconcerting liminal space between ordinary and extraordinary worlds,"[52] in which she is simultaneously the seventy-year-old Ann mourning the death of her father, and seventeen-year-old Annie, whose father has come to her premiere of *Peter Pan* at the Davenport Children's Theatre. George enters the stage again, carrying a bouquet of flowers. As George, in the past, comes to take Annie home to the family celebration, for which her mother has made Chex party mix, Ann talks to him in the present, asking, "Did you die? / What was it like? / Your breathing was terrible. / It seemed like you didn't want to go. / Was it awful?"[53] George answers, "Come on now, change your costume."[54] As John Lahr writes, "the pulse of Ruhl's melancholy heart is powerfully felt beneath the understatement of this stage-managed resurrection."[55] At the end of the scene "*They embrace. He exits*" and "*She watches him go.*"[56] Ann turns to the audience and tells us she stayed in the theatre just a little while longer, because in the theatre "you don't have to grow up."[57] In the theatre you also never really die.

Moments of Being

Ruhl, our "poet laureate of grief," has a "unique ability to depict the bereaved as they struggle to find a balance between going on and remembering."[58] Her plays often express a longing for rituals to assist us in our loss and remembrance. One of the things she admired most about *The Baltimore Waltz* was how Vogel "creates sites" for an audience "to be given a place to mourn" because "this is at the root of why we make theatre, in an ancient, ancient way."[59] In her own plays, these sites are intimate moments of communion or wonder, a shift out of regular time, which Ruhl calls, inspired by Virginia Woolf, "moments of being." Woolf, in her autobiographical portrait *A Sketch of the Past*, writes that most of life is taken up with moments of "non-being"—all the unmemorable tasks of the day—but that occasionally she is graced with "moments of being" when she becomes attuned, connected, aware of a "token of some real thing behind appearances,"[60] in which she can see the radiance of the invisible in the visible. All of Ruhl's plays give us such moments. As John Lahr writes about *For Peter Pan on Her 70th Birthday*, these plays are "at once a mourning and a celebration," both "ghost story" and "love story," a "meditation on death and an assertion of the triumph of imagination over time."[61] In Ruhl's moments of being with her father, her resurrections of his ghost, there are no rattling chains, no angels bursting through the ceiling. Instead, these are quiet, gentle moments in which the boundaries between the living and the dead become permeable and a daughter can savor one more moment with her dad.

Notes

1   Alice Rayner, *Ghosts: Death's Double and the Phenomena of Theatre* (Minneapolis: University of Minnesota Press, 2006), xii.

2   Ibid., xi.

3   Ibid.

4   Mark McInroy, "Beholding the Radiant Invisible: The Incarnate Image in Maurice Merleau-Ponty, Hans Urs von Balthasar, and Jean-Luc Marion," in *Image as Theology: The Power of Art in Shaping Christian Thought, Devotion, and Imagination*, ed. C.A. Strine, Mark McInroy, and Alexis Torrance. Turnhout: Brepols, 2022.

5   Wendy Weckwirth, "More Invisible Terrains," *Theatre*, 34.2 (2004): 31.

6   Elizabeth Metzger, "The Porous Fabric Between Life and Death: Sarah Ruhl," *BOMB*, September 24, 2018, https://bombmagazine.org/articles/sarah-ruhl-max-ritvo/.

7   Ibid.

8   James Al-Shamma, *Sarah Ruhl: A Critical Study of the Plays* (Jefferson, NC: McFarland and Company, 2011), 7.

9   Celia Wren, "The Golden Ruhl," *American Theatre*, 22.8 (2005), 30.

10 Sarah Ruhl, *The Oldest Boy* (New York: Farrar, Straus, and Giroux, 2016), 145.

11 Metzger, "The Porous Fabric."

12 Paula Vogel, "Sarah Ruhl." *BOMB*, April 1, 2007. https://bombmagazine.org/articles/sarah-ruhl/.

13 Sarah Ruhl, "*The Baltimore Waltz* and the Plays of my Childhood," in *The Play That Changed My Life*, ed. Ben Hodges (New York: Applause Books, 2009), 121.

14 Lawrence Goodman, "Poet Laureate of Grief." *Brown Alumni Magazine*, March/April 2007. https://www.brownalumnimagazine.com/articles/2007-03-20/playwright-laureate-of-grief.

15 Sarah Ruhl, *Dog Play*. Unpublished manuscript, courtesy of the author (1998), 15.

16 Ibid., 11.

17 Ibid., 18.

18 Ibid., 20.

19 Ibid., 21.

20 Ibid.

21 Ibid.

22 Weckwirth, 30.

23 Sarah Ruhl, "*Eurydice*," in *The Clean House and Other Plays* (New York: Theatre Communications Group, 2006), 344.

24 Ibid., 344.

25 Ibid., 345.

26 Ibid., 332.

27 Ibid., 350.

28 Charles Isherwood, "A Comic Impudence Softens a Tale of Loss." *New York Times* (October 3, 2006). https://www.nytimes.com/2006/10/03/theatre/reviews/a-comic-impudence-softens-a-tale-of-loss.html.

29 Ruhl, *Eurydice*, 377.

30 Ibid., 392.

31 Sarah Ruhl and Max Ritvo, *Letters from Max: A Book of Friendship* (Minneapolis: Milkweed Press, 2018), 274.

32 Ibid., 264.

33 Rayner, xiii.

34 Ruhl, *Oldest Boy*, 131.

35 Ibid., 23.

36 Ruhl and Ritvo, 135.

37 Ruhl, *Oldest Boy*, 27.

38 Ibid., 28.

39 Ibid.

40 Ibid., 28–29.

41 Ruhl and Ritvo, 273.

42 Sarah Ruhl, *For Peter Pan on Her 70th Birthday* (New York: Theatre Communications Group, 2018), xvii.

43 John Lahr, "Foreword," in *For Peter Pan on Her 70th Birthday* (New York: Theatre Communications Group, 2018), x.

44 Ibid., xi.

45 Ruhl, *For Peter Pan*, 34.

46 Ibid., 40.

47 Ibid.

48 Ibid.

49 Ibid., 52.

50 Ibid., 52–53.

51 Ibid., 61.

52 Ibid., x.

53 Ibid., 99.

54 Ibid., 99.

55 Ibid., xi.

56 Ibid., 100.

57 Ibid., 101.

58 Goodman.

59 Ruhl, "*The Baltimore Waltz*," 123.

60 Virginia Woolf, *Moments of Being: Unpublished Autobiographical Writings*, ed. Jeanne Schulkind (New York: Harcourt Brace Jovanovich, 1976), 72.
61 Ruhl, *Peter Pan*, x.

Works Cited

Al-Shamma, James. *Sarah Ruhl: A Critical Study of the Plays*. Jefferson, NC: McFarland & Company, 2011.

Goodman, Lawrence. "Poet Laureate of Grief." *Brown Alumni Magazine*, March/April 2007. https://www.brownalumnimagazine.com/articles/2007-03-20/playwright-laureate-of-grief.

Isherwood, Charles. "A Comic Impudence Softens a Tale of Loss." *New York Times*, October 3, 2006. https://www.nytimes.com/2006/10/03/theatre/reviews/a-comic-impudence-softens-a-tale-of-loss.html

McInroy, Mark. "Beholding the Radiant Invisible: The Incarnate Image in Maurice Merleau-Ponty, Hans Urs von Balthasar, and Jean-Luc Marion," in *Image as Theology: The Power of Art in Shaping Christian Thought, Devotion, and Imagination*, ed. C.A. Strine, Mark McInroy, and Alexis Torrance. Turnhout: Brepols, 2022.

Metzger, Elizabeth. "The Porous Fabric Between Life and Death: Sarah Ruhl." *BOMB*, September 24, 2018. https://bombmagazine.org/articles/sarah-ruhl-max-ritvo/

Rayner, Alice. *Ghosts: Death's Double and the Phenomena of Theatre*. Minneapolis: University of Minnesota Press, 2006.

Ruhl, Sarah. *100 Essays I Don't Have Time to Write*. New York: Faber & Faber, 2014.

Ruhl, Sarah. "*The Baltimore Waltz* and the Plays of my Childhood," in *The Play that Changed My Life*, ed. Ben Hodges. New York: Applause Books, 2009: 119–127.

Ruhl, Sarah. *Dog Play*. Unpublished manuscript, courtesy of the author. 1998.

Ruhl, Sarah. "*Eurydice*," in *The Clean House and Other Plays*. New York: Theatre Communications Group, 2006.

Ruhl, Sarah. *For Peter Pan on Her 70th Birthday*. New York: Theatre Communications Group, 2018.

Ruhl, Sarah. *The Oldest Boy*. New York: Farrar, Straus and Giroux, 2016.

Ruhl, Sarah and Max Ritvo. *Letters from Max: A Book of Friendship*. Minneapolis: Milkweed Press, 2018.

Vogel, Paula. "Sarah Ruhl." *BOMB*, April 1, 2007. https://bombmagazine.org/articles/sarah-ruhl/

Weckwirth, Wendy. "More Invisible Terrains," *Theatre*, 34.2 (2004): 28–35.

Woolf, Virginia. *Moments of Being: Unpublished Autobiographical Writings*, ed. Jeanne Schulkind. New York: Harcourt Brace Jovanovich, 1976.

Wren, Celia. "The Golden Ruhl." *American Theatre*, 22.8 (2005): 30–32.

13

Anishinaabe, Dakhòta, and Nimiipuu Hauntings in the Indigenous Drama of Alanis King, LeAnne Howe, and Beth Piatote

Margaret Noodin

A shadow, a shimmer, an extra unexplained sound, something slightly offstage and yet the center of attention: theatrical ghosts invoke a visceral thrill. By hearing, seeing, fearing, and facing what is not of our own world, we enter parallel planes of experience where Jesus travels with Nanabush, Mary Todd Lincoln is mad, and museum directors are schooled by a chorus of aunties. In these worlds, ghosts guide the story, shifting shapes, sometimes singing, sometimes stealing the scene with silence. Ghosts in a cast of characters offer extrasensory views of the physical, cultural, historical, and philosophical landscapes that influence individual and collective identities. In so doing, they enable indigenous playwrights to shape how plays are understood as indigenous and how they contribute, collectively, to critical theories of drama and its role in our lives.

Recent collections have drawn attention to indigenous drama's power to address the global instability of humanity[1] and serve as healing praxis[2] while prior works have called attention to the history and development of indigenous performance traditions.[3] In the long tradition of ghosts in indigenous plays, the three plays examined here, written by women of different nations in the early part of twenty-first century, illustrate how the intersection of theatrical traditions makes indigenous ontologies visible on stage. In *If Jesus Met Nanabush*, Anishinaabe author Alanis King uses Kwewag, a blend of many women moving through time, to mediate the narrative of two classic, semi-ghostly figures who compare their roles in society as they debate the benefactions and limitations of humanity. In *Savage Conversations* Choctaw author LeAnne Howe explores the relationship between Mary Todd Lincoln and a Dakhòta ghost who appears to her each night as she is being consumed by her insanity. Lastly, Beth Piatote's lead character in *Antikoni* becomes, literally, the haunting voice of reason as events within the Nez-Perce nation unfold according to a Greek format that perfectly compares the legal and spiritual implications of the Native American Graves Protection and Repatriation Act (NAGPRA). Writing across locations, languages, traditions, and political histories, these playwrights juxtapose specific North American tribal narratives with some of the world's most iconic narratives, from the Bible, from the American mythology surrounding Manifest Destiny, and from Greek mythology. In the blending and divergence of these stories, ghosts revitalize languages, lives, and lessons to rewrite history.

In each play several ghosts call attention to how place and time intersect. Because these plays are written by women of tribal nations, each play carries the imagination to a time and place shaped by, but not fully contained or controlled by, colonial instincts, settler sentiment, and federal laws. The setting, the costumes, the props, present not ethnographic estimates, but informed, intentional messages.

Indigenous Spirits

If Jesus Met Nanabush begins in the northeastern Atlantic region at the Champion of Champions Pow Wow on Six Nations Reserve and then follows the pow wow trail across Turtle Island. Jesus (the Judean holy son of God) and Nanabush (the Anishinaabe trickster son of the West Wind) travel the metaphorical "pow wow trail" and find themselves dreaming of Albuquerque, New Mexico, eating in small town bars in Georgia, stopping at unnamed reservation campsites, waiting in Greyhound bus stations, and eventually ending their journey at a gravesite in the Wikwemikong Unceded First Nation, where the two half-human characters discuss whether their spirits are remembered. Although the year is not specific, conversation indicates this meeting takes place in a time gap before the crucifixion of Christ but after the American Indian Movement Civil Rights Movement in the 1970s.

The true ghost of the story is Kwewag (which means "women"), "a Native female deity" with the ability to transform her physical form. In her many incarnations Kwewag is the balance to the worries of the men. The minimal costumes and props serve primarily as semiotic gestures marking various cultures. Nanabush is recognized as an Anishinaabe Fancy Dancer because he wears bells, angora leggings, and a bustle he can rattle like a butterfly, while Jesus is clearly the biblical messiah who appears wearing his traditional white robe. In this story, Christianity is out of place and out of time in indigenous North America. Although the time has passed when missionaries are supported by the state, Jesus and the stories connected to him still have relevance as cultural phenomena sustained by social systems of belief. King shows how Jesus, albeit less influential, is still present in later centuries, and then dares to suggest how indigenous and Christian traditions may be reconciled, as two very different spirits share their need to be remembered.

Howe's *Savage Conversations* is framed by nightly discussions taking place in Bellevue Place Sanitarium, Batvia, Illinois, and in the home of Elizabeth Todd Edwards (sister of Mary Todd Lincoln), in nearby Springfield. The slip of time in this play is the gap between 10:00 a.m., December 26, 1863, when thirty-eight Dakhóta warriors were executed in Mankato, Minnesota, and the moment when a character named Savage Indian, the ghost of one of the warriors, appears to Mary, the widow of Abraham Lincoln, the President who ordered what is still the largest mass execution in United States history. Savage is accompanied by The Rope, who is "both a man and the image of a hangman's noose."[4] Arguably, they are both ghosts associated with the hanging.

The scenes all take place indoors, in the confined spaces where Mary was kept by others at the end of her life, first the Sanitorium and then her sister's home, where she is surrounded by the remnants of her former life, including "footstools, silk curtains, jewelry, kit gloves, and a few hidden vessels of laudanum."[5] Mary and Savage Indian occasionally call attention to their blood-stained clothing, marking the way traumatic moments are imprinted in memory, and to the things taken from each of them: the buttons removed from his coat by the hangman's wife after his death, Mary's pearl necklace or her fancy gown, which at one point Savage Indian puts on . . . because in the afterlife he can. The most ominous artifact is the ethereal Rope with a voice who says very little and frequently seethes. Howe uses the scene, costuming, and props to remind the audience which part of America's past they are being asked to re-examine.

Antikoni also bridges multiple times and places while setting the scene for a story from an indigenous perspective. The play is modeled on Greek mythology, already considered ancient by Sophocles when he wrote *Antigone* in 441 BCE. Piatote's adaptation, set after 1990, refers to two earlier periods: the time of the Blue Coats and the time of the White Coats. The ghosts at the beginning of the story are two Nez Perce-Cayuse brothers who died during the war of 1877 between the Nez Perce and the US Army "Blue Coats." A number of tribal nations, including the Crow, who were former allies of the Nez Perce, fought on the side of the Blue Coats. Antikoni's ancestral relatives were separated when one was captured by the Crow in his youth. They were reunited on the battlefield when the brother raised by the Crow killed his own Nez Perce sibling. When they died "the Blue Coats stripped the brothers of their clothes, shields, medicine bundles, and war shirts adorned with beads, shells, and strands of their sisters' hair."[6] The bones were left in a common grave until the time of the White Coats, when they were unearthed "measured, indexed, catalogued, and arranged" before being sealed in museum vaults. The play centers on Antikoni's decision to rescue their bones and funerary objects from anthropological captivity before a contemporary Nez Perce tribal leader, Kreon, can complete a large display. Most of the play takes place in the museum where first Antikoni plans the act with her younger sister Ismene and then in the chambers of tribal court where she is put on trial for her decision. The physical spaces and objects referenced throughout the play are granted animacy and agency in a way that history did not previously allow. Piatote moves beyond the simplistic binary of Army Soldiers and Indians or ancestors and descendants to explore the nuances of shifting inter-tribal alliances and the varying views of bodily remains and the ownership of artifacts.

Translingual Identities

Although they write in English, for the modern stage, these indigenous authors effect a paradigm shift. As the ghosts connect audiences to multiple time periods and locations, they rely on a cyclical, permeable chronology that is unlike the linear back and forth found in most modern plays. These ghosts hold moments open, allowing characters to shift coordinates and revisit or previsit disparate points in time and place, in effect disrupting time as it informs dominant narratives. On these stages, costumes and artifacts mark stories and identities to be reclaimed. Jesus and Nanabush discuss the power of fancy regalia or a pure white robe. Savage Indian and Mary are trapped in a cycle of dressing and undressing old wounds and their own bodies. Antikoni has a genetic connection to strands of hair on shirts and bones in boxes. In each case costumes and artifacts are part of a construct that supports shifting agency and identities. In a world where feathers are animate and a rope is a character, these objects have voices and rights. The ghosts of these plays serve as active guides to overlapping times and places. Through them, the audience sees new truths; for example, how traces of personhood remain in bells, bones, and bandages. Voices that have always been heard across time by traditional means are now verified through modern science and given voice through revitalized cultural connections.

Another paradigm shift in these plays is a move to complicate the English script with Indigenous languages, songs, and ceremonies. Although the dominant metaphor for language loss is extinction and death, the use of these languages challenges the definition of linguistic vitality and indigenous identity. These are not the zombie-linguistics Bernard Perley warns against; instead, they are living branches, deep roots, roiling cumulonimbi of communication that connect the earth and sky and keep cultures alive. As ghosts use the words and lyrics of their ancestors, reactivate powerful transitional practices, and mediate modernity, they assert their cultural continuity and shifting shared identities.

In *If Jesus Met Nanabush*, the primary ghost does not use the Anishinaabe language, but she controls the space between worlds where Nanabush and Jesus are remembered or forgotten. Kwewag appears to Nanabush and Jesus in four forms: a Pow Wow Dance Judge, Winter Woman, a Biker Chick, and a shifting combination of Cleaning Lady, Hot Babe, and Doll. In these roles, she cycles through the play providing balance and creating physical and temporal space for reflection. Her mostly silent ghostly identities can be examined using an Anishinaabe-centric rubric, summarized in Table 13.1. The language she uses is one of signs and seasons, such that each incarnation can be associated with one of the cardinal directions, seasons, ages, cognitive domains, strengths or unusual abilities, or teachings. Reading Kwewag through this Anishinaabe lens reinforces the notion that, to understand the way they mediate the liminal space between forms of life, indigenous ghosts should be viewed through the social system of their origin.

Kwewag has only a few lines, spoken in English, the lingua franca of the play, but Nanabush, the character striving to avoid becoming a ghost, uses Anishinaabemowin in several instances, which range from the sacred to the profane. In keeping with the theme of his journey to keep old ways alive in the present, his words are spoken as he would have heard them used in his youth. He uses Anishinaabemowin to express ideas that do not easily translate

Table 13.1 Circle of Kwewag

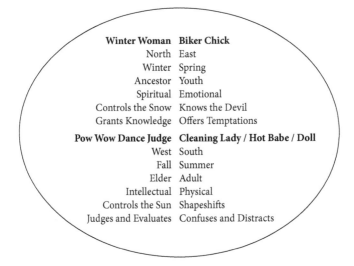

Winter Woman	**Biker Chick**
North	East
Winter	Spring
Ancestor	Youth
Spiritual	Emotional
Controls the Snow	Knows the Devil
Grants Knowledge	Offers Temptations
Pow Wow Dance Judge	**Cleaning Lady / Hot Babe / Doll**
West	South
Fall	Summer
Elder	Adult
Intellectual	Physical
Controls the Sun	Shapeshifts
Judges and Evaluates	Confuses and Distracts

into English, and he doesn't seem to mind that Jesus is not always able to interpret his comments. He teases Jesus and calls him *Gitchekendawss*,[7] which literally means "very knowledgeable" but is a bit like calling someone Smarty Pants in English. Later, as they compare stories of absent fathers and virgin mothers Nanabush exclaims, "*G'debwe naa?*" an idiomatic phrase meaning "are you correct" used to express surprise, akin to the English phrase, "you don't say."[8] This colloquial language is evidence of Anishinaabemowin developing a modern vernacular that is not always ceremonial.

Anishinaabemowin is also used for the most poignant and powerful moments in the play. In the final scene, Nanabush, standing in the graveyard trying to understand how he died, begins a soliloquy by saying: "*Gichi-miigwech g'shemnido mondah giizhigut. Maaba semaa.* (Thank you Great Spirit for this day. I offer tobacco.)"[9] He struggles to understand whether or not he will experience a resurrection similar to the one Jesus experienced, which ironically led to Christianity's global expansion and, often in the name of conversion, many negative consequences for indigenous people. However, in the time gap the play creates, Jesus has become a genuine friend, and Nanabush concludes we can only be ourselves eternally saying: "*Anishinaabe ndaaw.* (I am Anishinaabe). I'm no other race . . . I come from the heartbeat of my nation."[10] The play's concluding final line is in Anishinaabemowin: "*Kitchie miigwech g'shemnidoh name giizhigut.* (Thank you, Great Spirit, for this beautiful day)."[11] By speaking directly to the Great Spirit in Anishinaabemowin, Nanabush does what he knows many modern Anishinaabeg are not able to do because the language has been suppressed, children were punished for using it, and new generations have grown up feeling the ache of not knowing it. By keeping his first language alive, he offers hope for those working to remember Nanabush and Anishinaabemowin.

As Nanabush strives to show how both he and Anishinaabemowin can still be relevant in the modern world, he also shows the same can be true of Anishinaabe music. The play has numerous interludes and background tracks, carefully placed for maximum double entendre, such as "The Devil Went Down to Georgia" by The Charlie Daniels Band, Billy Idol's "Rebel Yell," K.D. Lang's "Diet of Strange Places," and "House of the Rising Sun" by the Animals. But it opens with Kwewag singing an Anishinaabe shake-dance song that refers to the shaking tent ceremony used to converse with the dead. King knows the oldest traditions and makes a point of creating characters who mix them with contemporary culture in a way that does not dilute or romanticize them but instead allows them to stand as equals. Just as Nanabush and Kwewag might understand the lyrical irony of certain rock-n-roll songs, they also know and protect traditional music. In Scene3, Nanabush tries to teach Jesus to sing the American Indian Movement Song, saying, "It's sung in honor of our Nations. Like 'O Canada.' Except we know all the words."[12] He tells Jesus the story of evolving musical traditions which blend pentatonic scales and handmade drums with songs of peaceful protest, adapted for the ongoing work toward civil rights. When Jesus initially struggles to learn the vocables, which he says do not sound like words, Nanabush replies, "It's its own song. You'll come to recognize its difference from our other songs if you listen."[13]

To write *Savage Conversations*, Howe, who is Choctaw, researched the language and traditions of a nation north of her own. The Savage Indian who haunts Mary Todd Lincoln is Dakhóta, and he occasionally uses his first language as he speaks of his homeland. He tells Mary, "When I was a human being, / I would sing the air thick with Dakhóta songs."[14] He blends song and ceremony and explains how words hold power and medicine. One evening he tells her about his friend who died with him on the gallows:

A death song, he sang it, then we sang together.
On the platform in Mankato, we tried to grasp hands,
shouting to the winds,
Mni Sòta Maķoce, land where the waters reflect the skies,
the land where we die.
Words caught in our throats. Choked by a muscular rope.[15]

Because Savage Indian uses the correct Dakhóta names for the land where the terrible event took place, his words remind the audience many place names hold memories of a time when land was part of a sustained relationship, not a system of reservations, allotments, and federally controlled access to resources.

Like Nanabush, Savage Indian speaks from a liminal space directly to the Great Spirit. Watching a moonrise, and remembering the shape, sound, and texture of the vast prairie, he asks, "Wakan Tanka, when will I wake?"[16] "Wakan Tanka" is also the first word of the hymn he sang as thirty-eight nooses hung from the rafters. There is a horrible irony to the song's being forced into the form of Gregorian chants and published by Stephen Return Riggs, a translator at the trials where the thirty-eight were convicted. In her script Howe more accurately represents the meaning of the lyrics. She provides more information than the version printed by the American Board of Commissioners for Foreign Missions, who were focused only on assimilation and conversion, not comparative analysis of equal religious traditions. Howe provides a literal translation of the song based on the actual meaning of Dakhóta word which reveals a syncretic song of praise to a deity known by many names. The beauty and rhythm in the original language is obvious to careful readers, and with the spare and eloquent literal meanings below each line, the song represents an unfiltered view of the way Dakhòta speak to the Great Spirit about the earth who also sings:

Wakantanka taku nitawa
(Great Spirit – what – you make)
Tankaya qa ota;
(Is large – and many/much)
Malipiya kin eyahnake ca,
(Sky – the – named)
Maka kin he duowanca,
(Earth – the – that is singing)
Mniowanca sbeya wanke cin,
(Water all over [ocean] make wet / moisten)
Hena oyakihi.
(These all around.)

Xitawacin wasaka, wakan,
(Mind/thoughts – strong – powerful/holy)
On wawicaliyaye;
(For/on account of – you have created)
Woyute qa wokoyake kin,
(Food – and clothing – the)
Woyatke ko iyacinyan,
(Drinks too/also – somewhat like)
Anpetu kin otoiyohi
(Day – the – each/every one)
Wawiyohiyaye.
(Causing to, reaching to, arrive at.)"[17]

Only two of the five verses known to be part of the song appear in *Savage Conversations*, but they render Dakhòta language, spirituality, and identity visible.

Like King and Howe, Piatote takes care to signal that *Antikoni* is not only an example of American and Indigenous theatre; it is a play about the Nimiipuu history and identity of the federally recognized nation, legally known as the Nez Perce Tribe. Although all characters have some familiarity with the language, only Antikoni and her maternal uncle, Kreon, use the language to strengthen their arguments and connect themselves to ancestral legitimacy. Early in the play Kreon introduces the terms *Titó·qan* (Indian people) and *So·yá·po* (white man) to center the play in a Nimiipuu perspective.

Antikoni uses the Nimipuutímt term *tamá·lwit* (law) to show that she prefers a Nez Perce form of justice, and she names one of the artifacts she wants to liberate, the bloody *k'áplac* (war club) of the warrior Atakolas, which she insists should not be "stored in a gleaming vitrine, while his selfsame body disarticulates beneath the floor."[18]

The majority of the Nimipuutímt words in "Antikoni" trace the network of relationships that bind the community together. They underline the importance of bloodlines and a genealogical system of proximity and allegiance between people. The story focuses on the bones and funerary items of two warriors whose spirits Antikoni believes are not able to rest until they are equally honored and united in the Shadowland. She says an *himíyu* (ancestor) should be acknowledged and allowed to rest with their belongings, not held captive to the present as part of a display. She emphasizes the importance of respecting *nú·nim titílu* (our ancestors) of the past in order to live well in the present and, eventually, be welcomed by them to the afterlife. Knowing how each relative, living and dead, fits into the web of one's personal history is a right and responsibility. These terms for relations are verification of indigenous identity that is not based in the analysis or measurement of blood or bones.

Through the Nimipuutímt language, the play teaches the importance of gender and birthplace identity. As Antikoni moves through the story, the names others use for her explain her connections to various characters: to Ismene she is *né·ne'* (a woman's older sister); to the Chorus of Aunties she is *nu·nim páplaq* (a granddaughter through her maternal side); to Haimon she is *sí·kstiwa* (a chosen darling or literally a nestmate). The rules of marriage are clarified when Haimon addresses Kreon as *tó·ta* (father) while Antikoni addresses him as *nonʔtáq* (an uncle through a woman's mother's brother). And the tradition of careful naming is confirmed by the Chorus of Aunties who tell stories within the play. A summary of the relationships the Aunties trace is in Table 13.2.

The significance of all these names is that every person is connected to many others and individual and collective identity is formed and maintained as these connections extend from life into death, preserved by habit, memory, and, sometimes, communication between humans and ghosts.

In the course of their debate over the removal of the warriors' remains, Antikoni and Kreon discuss language maintenance as a means of preserving cultural identity and understanding traditional forms of justice. For Nimipuutímt speakers the concept of truth is enmeshed with the concept of speech itself. Kreon commands Antikoni to "*ʔikú·ytimx* (speak in the language of truth.)"[19] In response, she uses an older form of the language and speaks of herself in the third person, which offers a prelude to her departure

Table 13.2 Names Used in Stories by the Chorus of Aunties

qáni	man's little sister
ʔácqa	man's younger brother
peqíˑyex	man's brother's male child / nephew
máma	man's sister's male child / nephew
qaláca	father's father
piláqa	mother's father
cikíˑwn	brother in law (in story)
laymíwt	littlest sibling (in story)

to another plane of existence. When a guard does not fully understand her older dialect, Kreon comments: "Our languages do not die, though sometimes they sleep."[20] The play thus reminds audiences that languages, like ancestors, can be remembered.

Lessons of Love

All of the ghosts address the question of whether the connection love forges can last for eternity. Mary and Savage Indian, with their nightly bedroom rituals, address it most explicitly. Savage Indian reads aloud the inscription "Love is eternal" on her wedding ring,[21] she speaks to her long-dead husband: "Oh what a great heart-smasher you are, Mr. Lincoln. Adieu, my confessor, my all-in-all, lover, protector, ghost husband."[22] Together they question whether the love and pain experienced in life extends beyond death. As she invites Savage Indian to take her husband's place and he willingly comes to her they prove that dreams do not recreate or compensate for a life as it was lived.

Both Jesus and Nanabush agree that "humans are of the earth and the spirit world is the only place else that humans can go,"[23] which means the gap between these two places is the distance love must encompass. For both, being loved across time equates with existence. As with the ghostly Kwewag, their consciousness depends on the memory of others. King's play applies this to identity broadly, showing that one must listen to oneself and know that one's soul is loved long after leaving.

Antikoni addresses this question of whether love can withstand physical separation when Antikoni's sister accuses her of "choosing the dead over the living"[24] because Antikoni wishes to show her love for her ancestors by asserting her connection with them across time. She is concerned that their physical remains must be handled properly to remain connected to her and to the entire community. By contrast, their uncle, Kreon, says:

> I bring their story to life, I redeem what remains—
> What remains of being human.
> Love, betrayal, tragedy: by these grand themes
> I return to the departed their flesh, their humanity.
> It is the story, not the body, that matters, that endures.
> . . .
> I have chosen the living over the dead.[25]

Showing how Antikoni and Kreon disagree about topics as important as love and the law is an important decolonial act. While many writers call for postcolonial changes, few represent a blend of individual principals, tribal national identity, and nuanced multi-national engagement in one piece. The call and response nature of *Antikoni* from Greek mythology to Nez Perce history illustrates the importance of world theatre's continuing to address the evolving human condition.

Truth and Reconciliation

By moving through and beyond their own physical lives, ghosts thus become teachers with the ability to answer questions and evaluate history. The ghosts in these three plays showcase the diversity of indigenous nations while also highlighting historical truths that need to be reconsidered and reconciled.

Kwewag, in her many forms, represents the variety of ways to be an Anishinaabe woman—across seasons, times and temperaments. Too often American Indians and Canadian Aboriginal people are represented as stoic and sad stereotypes, much like ghosts, defined by their past and only barely visible in the present. King works to dismantle these expectations. Kwewag is not just one woman. Nanabush is fixed in only one location or culture. Together they are fully aware of many nations. Nanabush refers to friends in Oklahoma who are Kiowas and Foxes and, when Jesus arrives, they are introduced to a Jew from Nazareth.

The specific history the play works against is the confusion surrounding the lost years of Jesus and, by inference, the idea that a person with no connections and true community can serve as a role model for building a peaceful community. In the play, Jesus explains to Nanabush his life between his youth and final days.[26] However, he accepts as inevitable that he has been destined to die in order to join his heavenly father and that violence and sacrifice are necessary. Both Nanabush and Jesus attempt to bring peace and knowledge to humanity, as storytellers and examples of infinite love.

The less obvious topic addressed by the play is the fact that many of the Christians who came to North America believed they had the authority to punish and demand sacrifice of even the smallest children in order to save their souls. For the numerous boarding school survivors punished physically, mentally, and emotionally in the name of Jesus, a conversation between Jesus and Nanabush is long overdue and can be considered a part of ongoing truth and reconciliation efforts. Over time some Anishinaabeg have chosen to become Christians. Their journey to understanding both traditional and Christian spirituality may have included the questions raised within the play: can humans accept their limitations? Can people learn to love, forgive, and support one another? Theological comparisons between world religions are at the heart of decolonial thinking because they allow individuals to confront oppression and allow the oppressor to find a way forward.

A similar situation exists in *Savage Conversations*. Savage Indian offers a first-hand account of history that is rarely included in textbooks. As a ghost he can cite facts from several centuries: "Ten million Natives in the New World in 1492. Nine million Natives dead by 1869 ... Five million Natives alive in the New World in 2010. Of the Dakhóta "Our Council fires burn undaunted. We live."[27] Continuity is important to him. Although United States federal representatives, immigrants, and settlers were encroaching on Dakhóta territory throughout the 1850s, what some might see as a response to human rights abuse and ethnic cleansing became known as the Dakhóta Uprising of 1862. In battles to protect their land and families, Dakhóta warriors who killed US citizens were viewed as terrorists, even though they were fighting to save their homeland. As has often been the case in large-scale military actions, events impacting many escalated from the behavior of a few. One young Dakhóta's killing of five settlers while out hunting resulted in the Dakhóta War. In the end, the Dakhóta were outnumbered, and the Mdewakanton Dakhóta leaders were forced to surrender. The US Army captured over one thousand prisoners, including women, children, and elders, of whom four hundred ninety-eight were put on trial. Of the three hundred, Lincoln commuted the sentences of all but thirty-eight, including Savage Indian, who was executed publicly. He recounts the event: "In that moment in Mankato, I was misplaced. / Maybe the Nightjars carried my spirit to safety, / Back to the beginning even before Mother Earth existed."[28] His auto-narration affirms his identity as a Dakhóta who belongs to the earth from which he was separated. His words reinforce the bond between the people and the land at the heart of the struggle between the US and the Oceti Sakowin confederacy.

Just as Savage Indian presents a different side of history, he also sees a different side of Mary. He calls her Gar[29] Woman and accuses her of not being who she claims to be. By this he means the victim. He says to her, "you bring a child into the world and intensely regret it."[30] Howe's play suggests Mary may have suffered from the syndrome known as "factitious disorder imposed on another" because she hastened the deaths of her own children.

> I have seen the ghosts of Abraham, Eddie, Willie even Tad,
> Shrink when you enter a room,
> Shadows escaping your burning sun.[31]

The desire to hurt others is a social dysfunction familiar to Savage Indian. After federal attempts to exterminate indigenous people failed, it could be said the US itself suffered from a mass case of "factitious disorder imposed on another," as it legally maintained a paternal relationship with tribal nations but steadily worked to reduce their populations. Both Mary and the ghost she conjures have hidden histories worthy of re-examination. Toward the end of the play Mary says to Savage Indian: "In the future I see your feathered headdresses, / Boxes of your people's bones made ready for study. / We are a pair, you and I, / Relics to be studied."[32] If Mary was wrong about some things in her life, *Savage Conversations* imagines her being right about the need for a reckoning in America.

The study of relics is also raised as a topic in *Antikoni* when a modern young woman confronts the commodification of her ancestors. Her actions stem from rights afforded by the Native American Graves Protection and Repatriation Act (NAGPRA) as a lineal descendant. Because the funerary items contain traces of DNA, she has a legal right to an opinion on their fate. However, the debate with her uncle moves beyond the question of possession to include burial versus display, which each represent different responses to the colonial history of the region. Whether descendants should remember but bury the past or memorialize it through public display is not a choice made easily.

The ghosts at the beginning of the play are the two Cayuse brothers who killed one another in battle because one had been taken captive as a youth. Both men's remains were held for many years in a museum, a place Antikoni believes is not healthy for the spirits of the dead or the living. She says: "No drum or song or sweetgrass smoke, no prayer may be given Our Ancestors here. And what is denied the dead is denied the living ten times again. We remain captives with them."[33] It is not only lamentable that their spirits are not properly laid to rest along with their personal belongings, but it is also a sign that ceremony and social systems have been disrupted and disrespected.

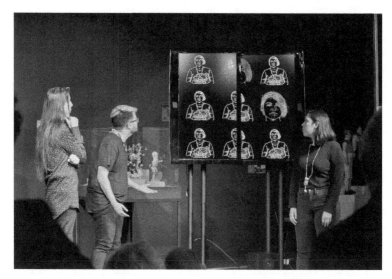

Figure 13.1 In the play's final scene, Kreon (Phillip Cash Cash), Haimon (Thomas Tallerico), and Ismene (Skye Chayame Fierro) call out to Antikoni's image (Fantasia Painter) as she continues to morph before them. Courtesy of Irene Yi (photograph) and Michael St. Clair (video design).

As Antikoni and her uncle Kreon debate how to best venerate the warriors, Piatote weaves reminders of many captives whose narratives have either been forgotten or twisted into different stories by dominant myths of the American West. Ishi, Geronimo, Sitting Bull, Captain Jack, and Chief Joseph are all mentioned such that their biographies haunt the collective psyche of the nation.

Blending the themes of NAGPRA and biographical truth, Antikoni confronts the problem of controlling the narrative. As a direct descendant of the warriors, she has the right to reclaim their remains and their histories. Her final act of giving up her life to set the truth free, explaining that "it is better to die a noble death than to live as a captive,"[34] echoes the acts of many of the warriors who did the same before her.

Artifacts of Hope

The characters in these three plays, in post-human form, address common symptoms of the human condition from perspectives that are indigenous and based in specific tribal nations. By placing these ghosts on stage, inviting their indigenous languages into the script, and making space for them to revise their own and their ancestors' narratives, King, Howe, and Piatote lead audiences to new philosophical landscapes.

The grand themes of humanity span many cultures, but the ghosts of these plays offer views rooted in different histories, connected to different places and expressed in words that create meaning in different ways. When Savage Indian appears to Mary he says, "When I am myself tonight, every word is a weapon."[35] This is a profound lesson. Words can be weapons, but belief in one's articulations is perhaps the more powerful tool for navigating life and what may lie beyond it. Ghosts offer an opportunity to have the last word and watching them on stage is a reminder to be aware of the roles we each play.

As Alanis King, LeAnne Howe, and Beth Piatote create ghosts who follow the narrative trails of the Bible, the mythology of American Manifest Destiny, and NAGPRA, they look honestly into the mirror of society. In a play written decades after Emancipation, the Civil Rights movement of the 1960s, and at the dawn of the Black Lives Matter movement, Mary Todd Lincoln says in *Savage Conversations*: "My husband's spirit tells me that in the future, / Metropolitan police of the district / Will shoot black men / And black children on / The streets of Washington like moving targets."[36] Howe suggests it will take more than one community to protect the children of the future from gar-like social systems intent on devouring youth, hope, and sustainable peace. Despite the difficult histories they address, the language loss they resist, and the fact that we cannot know if love is eternal, these plays become artifacts of hope. *Savage Conversations* ends with one word, "yes," spoken by the seething Rope. *If Jesus Met Nanabush* ends with Nanabush opening the spark of a common lighter. *Antikoni* ends with overlapping voices and a trail of ceremonial smoke, followed by one final honor beat. They all call us to see the ghosts among us and to plan carefully for the day we are among them.

Notes

1   Michelle Raheja, et al., *In the Balance: Indigeneity, Performance, Globalization* (Liverpool: Liverpool University Press, 2017).

2   Yvette Nolan, *Medicine Shows: Indigenous Performance Culture* (Toronto: Playwrights Canada Press, 2015).

3   See Rob Appleford, *Aboriginal Drama and Theatre* (Toronto: Playwrights Canada Press, 2005). See also Mimi D'Aponte, *Seventh Generation: An*

Anthology of Native American Plays (New York: Theatre Communications Group, 1998); Hanay Geiogamah and Jaye T. Darby, *American Indian Performing Arts: Critical Directions* (Los Angeles: UCLA American Indian Studies Center Press, 2010); Monique Mojica and Ric Knowles, *Staging Coyote's Dream: An Anthology of First Nations Drama in English* (Toronto: Playwrights Canada Press, 2003); Christy Stanlake, *Native American Drama: A Critical Perspective* (Cambridge: Cambridge University Press, 2009).

4 LeAnne Howe, *Savage Conversations* (Minneapolis: Coffee House Press, 2019), 3.

5 Ibid., 87.

6 Beth Piatote, *The Beadworkers: Stories* (Berkeley, CA: Counterpoint Press, 2019), 138.

7 Alanis King, *Three Plays: If Jesus Met Nanabush, The Tommy Prince Story, and Born Buffalo* (Markham, Ontario: Red Deer Press, 2015), 21. The orthography used in *If Jesus Met Nanabush* is a lovely example of 1970s Odawa dialect and appears here exactly as it was published in the book.

8 Ibid., 24.

9 Ibid. 47.

10 Ibid., 54.

11 Ibid.

12 Ibid., 33.

13 Ibid.

14 Howe, 28.

15 Ibid., 29.

16 Ibid., 37.

17 Ibid., 80.

18 Piatote, 140.

19 Ibid., 165.

20 Ibid., 168.

21 Howe, 9.

22 Ibid., 11

23 King, 28.

24 Piatote, 145.

25 Ibid., 170.

26 King, 26.

27 Howe, 48.

28 Ibid., 29.

29 Gar is a kind of a fish.

30 Ibid., 30.

31 Ibid., 31.

32 Ibid., 101.

33 Piatote, 139.

34 Ibid., 144.

35 Howe, 30.

36 Ibid., 56.

Works Cited

Appleford, Rob. *Aboriginal Drama and Theatre*. Toronto: Playwrights Canada Press, 2005.

D'Aponte, Mimi. *Seventh Generation: An Anthology of Native American Plays*. New York: Theatre Communications Group, 1998.

Geiogamah, Hanay and Jaye T. Darby. *American Indian Performing Arts: Critical Directions*. Los Angeles: UCLA American Indian Studies Center Press, 2010.

Gibbons, Reginald., and Segal, Charles. *Antigone*. Oxford: Oxford University Press, 2003.

Howe, Leanne. *Savage Conversations*. Minneapolis: Coffee House Press, 2019.

King, Alanis. *Three Plays: If Jesus Met Nanabush, The Tommy Prince Story, and Born Buffalo*. Markham, Ontario: Red Deer Press, 2015.

Mojica, Monique and Ric Knowles. *Staging Coyote's Dream: An Anthology of First Nations Drama in English*. Toronto: Playwrights Canada Press, 2003.

Nolan, Yvette. *Medicine Shows: Indigenous Performance Culture*. Toronto: Playwrights Canada Press, 2015.

Perley, Bernard C. "Zombie Linguistics: Experts, Endangered Languages and the Curse of Undead Voices." *Anthropological Forum* 22.2 (2012): 133–149.

Piatote, Beth. *The Beadworkers: Stories*. Berkeley, CA: Counterpoint Press, 2019.

Raheja, Michelle H., Phillipson, D.J., Gilbert, Helen. eds. *In the Balance: Indigeneity, Performance, Globalization*. Liverpool: Liverpool University Press, 2017.

Riggs, Stephen Return, ed. "Wakantanka taku Nitawa," in *Dakhóta Odowan: Hymns in the Dakhóta Language*. New York: American Tract Society, 1868: 29.

Stanlake, Christy. *Native American Drama: A Critical Perspective*. Cambridge: Cambridge University Press, 2009.

Index

Within page references, *n* indicates additional information within a note, the number of which follows; *ill* refers to an illustration